MARQUIS de PORTAGO

The Legend

For Robert Daley

Bob – many many thanks for your help with this project .. you brought the 'ghost' of Fon as alive as anyone – and helped me get my head around the legend.

Best wishes –

Ed McDonough

28/10/06

Ed McDonough

Foreword by Sir Stirling Moss

This book is published by:

Mercian Manuals Ltd
353 Kenilworth Road
Balsall Common
Coventry
West Midlands
CV7 7DL
01676 533304
www.mercianmanuals.co.uk

Distribution worldwide by the same.

ISBN 1 903088 27 5

Printed in Italy.

CONTENTS

Dedication

Dedication-This book is dedicated to Harry Miller Jr., my cousin, not the Indy car builder, and Joe DeVito…they were the reality of my 1950s.

Acknowledgements

Not only did many people contribute material, information, recollections and photographs to this story, but they also became part of the story itself, sharing views and opinions and entering into the quest to find the 'real' Portago.

The invitation to meet and talk to Mrs. Carroll Petrie, Portago's first and only wife, was an amazing event, as was a visit to the ancient family home of Sir Michael Leighton, the cousin of Portago, and related to the Spaniard on the marquis' maternal side of the family. Sir Michael was of great assistance in providing information about family background, as was his friend and advisor Martyn Freeth, a Shropshire genealogist. Invaluable help with this project came from several sources. Henk Kruidner, a Dutch lifelong Portago follower/fan, approached publisher, Peter Shimmell of Mercian Publications, and convinced him that the long neglected Spaniard was worth a searching biography. Henk backed the project to get it off the ground and funded many of the photos and the travel. Searching out photographs was as interesting as the research, trying to find the unpublished and the unknown. In spite of the great visual impact of Portago, his short time in the limelight meant there were relatively few photos. Help with photos also came from many people, especially Ted (Ferret Fotographics) Walker, Graeme Simpson who made the connection with Sir Michael Leighton, Jorg Thomas Fodisch, Alan R. Smith and Walter Baumer and several others. Every effort has been made to correctly credit all photos, and the author apologises for any omissions.

Mrs. Carroll Petrie in her New York home in November 2005 when the author visited her. ***(Credit - Ed McDonough)***

I have as always to thank close friends and colleagues Peter Collins and Mike Jiggle who fortunately never tire of searching through journals and papers in search of relevant 'deep' and not so deep background, race reports, news items, the address of an obscure bobsleigh organisation, etc. Loredano Harley translated innumerable pages of Italian text for me so I could read Italian accounts of the Mille Miglia accident. A variety of assistance came from many other sources: Marcye M. Gough of Lawrenceville School, Romina Power, daughter of Tyrone Power and Linda Christian, motor racing historian David MacKinney, one of few people with knowledge of the Panhard Monomilles, and Terry O'Neill for his research on the Bahamas Speed Weeks. Jennifer Santo of the Locust Valley Library in Locust Valley, New York found accounts of Dorian Leigh attending social events as the Marquise de Portago! Herman De Wael was very generous in supplying bobsleigh results and information from his own extensive archives. Stephen Payne continued to dig out material late into the project. Help in researching the horse racing career of Portago came from the British Horse Racing Board, the National Horse Racing Museum, the Federation Internationale des Gentlemen-Riders et des Cavalieres, and the Jockey Club. John Randall, the statistician for the Racing Post in London, provided the most detailed and authoritative information on Portago's equestrian career. Lord John Oaksey dipped into his memoirs for stories of Fon and his sister Soledad. The Bruguera Tennis Academy in Barcelona searched Spanish tennis records for any mention of Portago as a Davis Cup player. Adrian Hamilton turned up memoirs of his father, who co-drove with Portago on a couple of memorable occasions. Keith Schellenberg, a British Olympic bobsled team member, provided accounts of events and Charles Harbord turned up even more bobsleigh information. Max Keith trawled Australian motoring journals in search of Portago information, and George Perfect helped track down Maserati information. Peter Marshall was able to confirm details about an Alfa Romeo owned by Portago in the late 1940s. Drivers who shared their experiences from the 1950s included Roberto Mieres, the Uruguay-based Argentinean always keen to talk about the 'old days', Australian Tony Gaze, Sir Stirling Moss, the late Cliff Allison, Roy Salvadori, Robin Widdows and the American World Champion Phil Hill. Journalist Bernard Cahier sat down with the author at Monaco to recount his memories of Portago.

I want to thank Nancy McDonough for the last proof-read. Finally, it has been a pleasure to work closely with Peter and Richard Shimmell at Mercian Publications, as they allowed me a hands-on role in the production of this book, and Peter even pursued me to the south of France to make sure I was still writing!

Foreword

I remember when Fon Portago came on the scene in racing in the early 1950s. It was a very different time then, and motor racing itself was very different. I wasn't particularly close to Portago, but he was one of those people who was very easy to like. It was an era when we were all much friendlier with each other, and spent more time together. In the 1956 Tour de France, which came just after the Italian Grand Prix that year, I was driving a Mercedes Benz 300SL with George Houel. Fon and his friend Ed Nelson were our closest rivals in that event, and as a result I paid a lot of attention to him and we were together at the beginning and end of the special stages and races. Now, George was a good crumpet chaser, but Portago really had that department all sorted out. He was good-looking and of course he was an aristocrat so he was very attractive to women.

That was a period when racing drivers behaved much differently than they do now. Everything was much more relaxed and I am certain we enjoyed ourselves much more than drivers do today. Racing had a lot of characters then. Fon Portago was a great character and and he attracted others. He and Harry Schell were great friends and they got up to all sorts of things together. They would often be found in a local casino wherever we were racing, losing the money they had just won! People like Porfirio Rubirosa were racing then, a classic playboy of the period, and he would show up with an entourage of fantastic women.

In spite of the enjoyment, the racing was very serious. I remember when Fon first came on the scene. I thought he was quite competent and he was the sort of person race organisers really liked. He would bring in the crowds to a race. I know he was serious about his racing, though I don't think he was as professional as I was. He was more of a serious amateur who happened to be very able and quick, especially in sports cars. I remember when the Cubans held their first big race in Havana in 1957, I was driving the Maserati 200S which was much quicker than everything else in practice. In the race, Fon was having a battle with Fangio, and then my engine blew up. Fon led Fangio in what must have been his best race until his throttle cable broke, and Fangio won. It was clear then just how good he was. He made a lasting impression on me, because of his driving and the kind of person he was.

INTRODUCTION

Marquis Alfonso de Portago has been a background shadow dancing across the pages of post-war motor racing for over fifty years. The biographies have nearly always been the same: a portrait of a swashbuckler, the pouring out of the long, full family name, reference to the many and varied sporting achievements and finally death in the Mille Miglia after kissing Hollywood actress Linda Christian at the Rome checkpoint. It was, and is, the stuff of legends, fired by portraits of the unshaven but handsome aristocrat with cigarette dangling from his lips.

The many articles about the Spaniard rarely had details or dates of his various achievements and failures, they often contained many clear errors and contradictions, and in the end, told us relatively little about the man who may have been a truly brave soldier of sporting fortune totally without fear, or a dilettante, a self-promoting fool…it was never clear in much of what was written about him. Brock Yates asked the question as to whether Portago was a “gentleman racer or aristocratic clown”. (Yates, Car and Driver, May 1986) Portago's existence gave free rein to many writers, but the reality of the man remained distant and vague. The creation of the legend of Portago started early, before he even went near a racing car. It started in the achievements of a compulsively competitive boy and young man, but it was rooted even deeper in generations of an adventurous family. By the time he was a well recognised sports car and Grand Prix driver, the legend was well established. His title and his seeming brashness made him an ideal male of 1950s fantasy. Machismo made him a man's man as well as a sought after target for women. In the 1950s, not only was this possible, but it was an ideal. The ephemeral nature of the man, his underlying shyness, isolation, mistrust all made him a great candidate for legend status. Much of what was written was inaccurate and just plain untrue. That, however, is the nature of a legend, and the Fifties were a ripe period for fantasy. Portago was an ideal type for that decade. The truth was that he did manage to live up to the fantasy.

The author's own personal spark of interest in motor racing ignited in those same early days of the 1950s and diverged from American hot rods and Bonneville to Europe, pushed mainly in that direction by Juan Fangio's heroic drive in the 1953 Mille Miglia, Portago's legendary shadow appeared just as early for the author. While I was certainly not aware of his first appearance in the 1953 Carrera Panamericana, I did retrospectively discover his 1954 drive in that event, but that was just after he had begun to get some attention in the motor racing press for his successes in the 1954 Nassau Speed Week. I was 13 and beginning to go car-mad and the big motor racing events were the Indy 500, the Le Mans 24 Hours, Bonneville, the Mille Miglia, the Carrera Panamericana, and then racing in the Bahamas at Nassau came on the scene, just after the 12 Hours of Sebring had been inaugurated in central Florida. To a 13-year-old in 1954, all the reporting was about big, big tough and heroic men…and it was real. Then a Spanish marquis was part of the scene, pursued in Life magazine by Hollywood actresses. As Woody Allen said, ‘I was a dumb kid’, and I believed it. This was my real world and legends just needed to be legends. The ‘truth’ could come later. Predictably I went on to have a similar rose-coloured glasses view of Wolfgang von Trips.

The truth is that motor racing people aren't like that now, and they weren't like that then. The portrayal was, well, 1950s. But the Portago kind of character struck a deep chord. They resonated, as they say now, for many people and their lives became the stuff of legend. It was never clear to me why Portago's life never did get the Hollywood treatment. Perhaps in the 1950s the heroes still never died. Then the '60s came along and we were all going to a different place, the anti-hero had arrived and he was a different sort of guy. Ironically, one of the first true anti-hero types had arrived and died two years before Portago did…in a racecar. That was James Dean, though in truth his symbolic meaning to the culture wasn't recognised until the next decade, my memory tells me.

When the post-Portago stories appeared as they have ever since his death, the story remained essentially the same, the quotes the same, the description of the international sports star the same, the vagueness the same. Virtually every story starts the same…the “17th Marquis de Portago had his first motor racing experience in the sensational 1953 Carrera Panamericana sitting alongside Luigi Chinetti”. Not so. He wasn't the 17th Marquis and his first motor racing was in Paris. But we will come to that in time.

The author's 13-year old persona accepted Portago in the way that he had been portrayed, the machismo and recklessness to be revered and held up as a fantasy role model. As the years went, and political correctness came, that model was overtly scorned, though still secretly admired by many. Now perhaps it's time to find something of the 'real person' if that is possible. The search has been fascinating, turning up many connections to the man and the period, not only in motor racing but in personal terms as well.

James Dean, perhaps the most famous 1950s icon, and also a racing driver...with a dangling cigarette.

Perhaps the real turning point in the search for 'Portago the man' came when I met the person whom, as writer Brock Yates said in 1986, "discovered Portago". That was American author/journalist and one-time deputy commissioner of police, Robert Daley. Daley, as we will see later on, as a 25 year old journalist paying his own way to the 1956 Olympics in Cortina, Italy was to get $50 a story from the New York Times. He was smitten by the noise and sensuality of the bobsled event and hauled himself out of bed early in the morning to see and hear the crash of blades against ice. He looked for English speakers to talk to and ended up talking to an erudite and polite English-speaking member of the Spanish bob team…Alfonso de Portago. Daley was the first to write about him, to publicise him, to grasp the significance of the legend. I am indebted to Bob for sharing the story with me. Though Portago is not here, it was like going back in time to take hold of the '50s, to wander through the 'life-is-cheap' era and meet one of its legends. Daley said his own life had been changed by his meetings with Portago, and it all started in Cortina with just a number of *'conversations in the snow.'* Daley, of course, went on to write the well-known motor racing book, The Cruel Sport and the novel The Fast One, and many more. This novel based its two main characters on Portago and American Phil Hill. "Principe Cavelli", the Portago, character draws heavily on Daley's experience of meeting the Spaniard, and reflects the perceived nature of motor racing in the 1950s.

If meeting with Daley was a turning point, sitting in the tenth floor apartment of Carroll Petrie, overlooking Central Park in New York, was the occasion of coming closer to the reality of Portago than I had been, or imagined I would get. There was an added odd poignancy to this meeting with the woman to whom Portago had been married from 1949 until his death in 1957, as the meeting occurred on November 22, the 42nd anniversary of the assassination of John F. Kennedy. As with everything, life moves on, and '9/11' replaced JFK's shooting as the horror event in American memory. There was little mention of the occasion anywhere. It was just an odd feeling to be sitting in New York as close to Portago's ghost as I could get on this particular day…another real time warp in the Portago saga and another wander amongst legends.

The Heritage

Motor racing, equestrian sports, bobsleigh and some other sporting arenas have seen their share of royals and aristocrats, though given the class-related nature of some of those activities the overall total who were particularly successful is relatively small. Prince Bira…Birabongse Bhanuban of Thailand, formerly Siam, is perhaps the outstanding example of successful pre-war participation by a member of a royal family, while Prince Jorge de Bagration of Mouhrani, heir to the throne of Georgia, was a busy sports car racer through the 1960s. Italians Prince Gaetano Starrabba of the house of Giardinelli and Count Carlo Trossi were among many Italian nobles who spent many serious years in motor sport. Other Italians included Marquis Antonio Brivio and Counts Giulio Masetti, Giovanni 'Johnny' Lurani and Baron Bruno Sterzi. Poland produced Count Stanislas Czaykowski who raced Mercedes and was killed at Monza on the same day as Borzacchini and Campari in 1933. Sir Henry 'Tim' Birkin was an enormously successful pre-war British racing aristocrat, while J.T.C. Moore-Brabazon…Lord Brabazon of Tara…was less so. Also from Britain were Sir Gawaine Baillie, Lord Selsdon, Earl Howe, the Earl of Dumfries and 1965 European Touring Car Champion Sir John Whitmore.

The list of racing nobles from the rest of Europe is fairly long, though the number who are remembered even by keen fans is equally small. The Swiss Baron Emanuel de Graffenried was a professional pre and post-war driver who did very well in Formula 2 and made occasional Grand Prix appearances, notably with the Alfa Romeo team in 1951. At the time of writing, he was living with other aristocrats in a luxury home for older people in Lausanne, where he described himself to the author as 'only a baron amongst a few princesses and an ex-king'! Carel Godin de Beaufort of the Netherlands was often referred to as a count but was in fact a *jonkheer*, the lowest Dutch title, which was also held by Gijis van Lennep. There were also Prince Nicholas of Romania, Prince Leopold von Bayern, Count Louis Zborowski and Prince von Hohenlohe.

And, there was *Graf* Wolfgang von Trips. Trips was without question the most successful titled person to take part in motor racing, and would have won the World Championship in 1961 as a Ferrari driver but for his death at Monza towards the end of the season. Trips was a top-line driver and was known more for his ability as a driver than his family title, though like Portago, the title was part of the charm and the legend. It is another quirk of history that Portago picked von Trips as a likely future world champion in 1957, and Trips similarly saw Portago as one of the drivers who would surely rise to the top in racing. This pair, especially in that their careers overlapped for a short period, epitomized the glamour and romance that still surrounded nobility and motor racing in the 1950s. Arguably they, with Sir John Whitmore, Baronet, were the most successful of all racing nobility and aristocrats. This list, of course, includes only drivers who brought their titles with them to motor racing, and omits the drivers who gained their titles after and because of motor racing: Sirs Stirling Moss, Henry Segrave, Jack Brabham, and Jackie Stewart.

What was clearer to outsiders in that era, when some aristocrats still had appeal to the public, was that certain members of noble families seemed destined by their heritage to become racing drivers, an occupation that in the 1950s still had parallels with knights errant, crusaders and heroes on horseback. Indeed, Portago was often described as a 'crusader several centuries too late' or 'modern-day dragon-slayer'. Nigel Roebuck's 1976 retrospective article referred to him as 'Conquistador'.(Roebuck in Autosport May 4, 1976) Brock Yates brought this romanticizing down to earth somewhat decrying the tendency of some writers to consider Portago as a "combination of D'Artagnan, Leonardo and Doc Savage". (Yates, Car and Driver, May 1986) If becoming a top sportsman at the Olympic bobsleigh or at Le Mans or in a Grand Prix car was a modern equivalent of jousting, then hardly any driver could have been better prepared by his forebears and his genes than Alfonso de Portago. Portago said himself in interviews that had he been 400 years earlier he would have been an adventurous knight.

Ken Purdy summarised Portago's background emphasising the adventurer ancestors: "Spanish history is studded with the (family) name. In the sixteenth century one of Portago's forebears, Cabeza de Vaca, was shipwrecked on the Florida coast. He *walked* to Mexico City, recruiting an army as he went. Another conquered the Canary Islands, another was a leader in the fight to drive the Moors out of Spain. Portago's grandfather was a governor of Madrid". (Purdy, 1972, p.66)

Portago's full name has often been the subject of discussion and contention, as it includes both family names *and* titles and those appear differently according to what is being emphasised. Thus the name is Alfonso Antonio Vicente Blas Angel Francisco Borjia Cabeza de Vaca y Leighton. Cabeza de Vaca and Leighton refer to the paternal and maternal lineage, while all the others are forenames. After the death of his father in 1941, Alfonso inherited his father's family titles: he became the 11th Marquis de Portago, 13th Conde (Count) de Mejorada, the Duke of Alagon. These titles are encompassed in the further title of Grandee of Spain. The Marquis de Portago title had descended from his father's paternal ancestor's while the Mejorada title came down through his father's maternal relatives. On his father's side, Alfonso's immediate predecessors were a confluence of the Spanish Cabeza de Vaca and Carvajal families. While the name Cabeza de Vaca sounds grand indeed, the origins are somewhat more humble. The name translates as 'head of the cow' and indeed a shepherd Martin Alhaja is reputed to have served his King Sancho and the Christian army by marking a difficult pass through the Serena Mountains north of Seville with the skull of a cow in the 13th century. This assistance allowed the army to surprise the Moors and defeat them at the battle of Las Navas de Tolosa. Alhaja's reward, as was the custom, was a title. Cabeza de Vaca later became the family name. (Nye, Classic and Sports Car,May,1985)
The thread of this story appears briefly in many Portago biographical articles. Hans Tanner seems to be the first person to have looked into the adventurous side of the family in any depth, and is probably the source of much of what was written later. It isn't entirely clear where Tanner got his information, but it may well have been Portago himself:

Family tree: left to right - A painting of Cabeza de Vaca after his walk across the USA; Portago's grandfather, the 15th Marquis; Alfonso's father; Portago with his Godfather, King Alfonso XIII in 1929.
(Credit - Petrie Collection)

"The rise of Portago's family began with an adventure which raised a humble shepherd named Martin Alhaja to sudden nobility back in 1212. In July that year King Sancho of Navarre, marching against the Moors, found his army halted north of Seville by the mountains of the Sierra Morena, then believed unpassable. He was about to abandon his plan of attack when Alhaja, a local shepherd, told him of a pass he had found while searching for new pastures, and the entrance to which he had marked with a cow's skull. King Sancho and his army set out next morning, found the skull and the pass, fell on the unsuspecting Moors, and routed them in the Battle of Las Navas de Tolosa. Alhaja was rewarded with a deed of nobility and the title of Cabeza de Vaca-'Skull of the Cow'."

"The shepherd's descendants also had a knack for distinguishing themselves in battles and adventures, both on land and sea. One of them, Pedro de Vera Mendoza, set sail from Seville under the flag of Ferdinand and Isabella to fight the wild tribes of Teneriffe and brought the Canary Islands under Spanish rule. Pedro's grandson, Alvar Nunez Cabeza de Vaca, fought brilliantly in the Italian wars, and was appointed royal treasurer with an expedition searching for the elusive El Dorado, the legendary land of gold in recently discovered America. The date was 1527, and young Alvar was not to see Spain again for 12 years. The expedition landed in Florida and was beset by a series of disasters in which everyone perished, or so it was thought. Years later, however, other Spanish explorers heard of a white god of the Indians, and on investigation found him to be Alvar Cabeza de Vaca. The lone Spaniard had made his way painfully across the vast land which was to be the southern United States, finally reaching that part of Mexico now known as Lower California. In his travels he had discovered the land that was to be Texas, and traversed the wilderness which is now New Mexico. As soon as he returned to Spain the King, greedy for gold, sent him out again, this time to

South America. Eventually he became the first governor and chief justice of Paraguay." (Tanner in Modern Motor September 1957, p.54)

Some 228 families claim descent from the Solferino family, the head of which was the 1st Duke of Solferino in the early 17th century. Amongst the 228 are several interesting families and a few related to this story. Some of these married into the Solferinos or were direct descendants of the 1st Duke. The Cabeza de Vacas married into this line in 1868, the Carvajals in 1739, the Sartorius family in 1903, and the Munoz family in 1940. Alfonso Portago was descended from Cabeza de Vacas and Carvajals and was related to Munoz and Sartorius, and from the Sartorius and Munoz families came his cousins who were on his bobsleigh teams in 1956 and 1957. The Solferino 'clan' has other interesting descendants: the Gonzagas and the Olazabals, one famed for military and religious endeavour, and the latter for more modern sporting prowess.
Alfonso de Portago's connection to the Solferinos through the Cabeza de Vacas is interesting for other reasons. The Solferino family tree consists of thousands and thousands of aristocrats and demonstrates the way in which almost every noble family of Europe is related to every other. There is another very interesting historical connection.

Jean Henry Dunant was a Swiss born in 1828, and was a man with deep moral and religious convictions. From a wealthy and socially responsible family, he worked with a number of charitable movements, and when the Young Men's Christian Association was formed, he was the person largely behind it becoming a worldwide organisation in 1855. It was while he was on a business venture in Italy in 1859 that he stopped at the town of Castiglione Della Piave. His arrival was on the very same day as the nearby Battle of Solferino, ten kilometers south of Lake Garda in Northern Italy. This battle was the final engagement of the 2nd War of Italian Independence, a fierce struggle between an allied Sardinian and French Army commanded by Napoleon III and the Austrian Army. Days before the battle King Victor Emmanuel arrived in Brescia, to be joined by Napoleon and the King of Sardinia. The Italians had been oppressed by the Austrian occupiers for some ten years and their liberation seemed near at hand. The Austrian Emperor himself led his troops and on the 24th of June 300,000 men faced each other in the battle area which covered several small towns. One of these where much of the crucial fighting would take place was Guidizzolo.

The battle lasted nine hours and was immensely bloody. Over 3000 Austrian troops were killed and over 10,000 wounded, and the Allied armies had 2400 dead and 12,000 wounded, and a further 11,000 men from both sides were missing. There were reports of wounded and dying soldiers on both sides being shot or bayoneted. The Austrians had to yield but it was a costly and horrendous battle.

Jean Henry Dunant felt compelled to offer assistance, and from his own experience, was able to organise medical relief, working from a base at Castiglione and Guidizzolo. After returning home, he wrote his memoirs of the event, and they were sufficiently rousing to assist him in establishing the International Red Cross. While it was only a coincidence, it was at Guidizzolo nearly 100 years later that Portago should have his fatal accident in the Mille Miglia, where his body and that of the other victims of the crash were removed by the Red Cross.

King Alfonso XIII of Spain, and Queen Victoria Eugenia, granddaughter of Britain's Queen Victoria. ***(Credit - Petrie Collection)***

On Alfonso's paternal side, the Cabeza de Vacas and the Carvajals united in 1891. Dona Angela de Carvajal y Jiminez de Molina was the daughter of Don Angel Maria Jose de Carvajal y Tellez-Giron and Dona Josefa Ximenez de Molina de Molina y Jiminez. The Molina title had been granted to the family by King Alfonso XII. Dona Angela was born in Madrid on March 8, 1868, was baptized in the Church of San Salvador and San Nicolas. She married Don Vicente Cabeza de Vaca y Fernandez de Cordova-Alagon in Madrid on September 19, 1891. Vicente had been born in Madrid on February 17, 1865. His father was Don Mariano Cabeza de Vaca y Morales, Gomez de Teran y

Carvajal, Marques de Portago, Conde de Catres. He was already a Carvajal so in fact Angela was marrying Cabeza de Vacas and more Carvajals. Vicente's mother was Dona Maria Francisca de Borja Fernandez de Cordova-Alagon Vera de la Cerda Cernisio y Bernardo de Quiros, Manuel de Villena y Colon, des Conde de Sastago. Angela's title was 11th Condesa de Mejorada. Dona Angela and Don Vicente had four children:

Don Antonio Cabeza de Vaca y Carvajal who was born on September 24, 1892.
Dona Maria del Carmen Cabeza de Vaca y Carvajal was born on September 7, 1893, and married Don Salvador de Vilallonga y de Carcer.
Don Angel Cabeza de Vaca y Carvajal. He died at the age of 62 in 1959, and in 1916 had become the IV Marques de Moratalla.
Dona Maria de Lourdes Cabeza de Vaca y Carvajal was born March 13, 1903, and married Don Carlos Sartorius y Diaz de Mendoza.

Dona Angela, the paternal grandmother of Alfonso de Portago died on June 4, 1924 in Madrid at the age of 56. Her husband, Fon's paternal grandfather Vicente died at age 56, on November 15, 1921, also in Madrid so Alfonso never met his paternal grandparents.

A map of the Solferino area in Italy, scene of the Battle of the Solferino.

Alfonso's father, Don Antonio, became the tenth Marquis de Portago, a Grandee of Spain in 1924 and the XII Conde Mejorada in 1915, a title passed to him from his mother. He was married twice, first to Dona Maria de los Dolores Castillo Gascon in Paris. They had no children and Don Antonio married for a second time on November 20, 1927. He married Olga Beatrix Forestier Leighton-Eyre (or Ayre), and they had two children, Don Alfonso Cabeza de Vaca y Leighton who was born on October 11, 1928, and Dona Maria de la Soledad Cabeza de Vaca y Leighton, who was two years younger.

On his maternal side, Portago was descended from two well-known and well-recognised families, the Leightons and the Eyres. The Leighton lineage passes down from Tihel de Lathune living around 1155 and who had:

Richard Fitz Tihel who held the Manor of Leighton, Salop as a fee in the feudal barony of FitzAlan; he had Sir Richard (1200) who was father to Richard (1241) who had William (1256). His son was Richard de

Leighton, Constable of Oswestry and between 1284 and 1300 he asserted his right to establish a park at Leighton; he had Sir Richard Leighton who had Richard de Leighton (1312); he had John de Leighton. (Some early dates are approximate.) Some 12 generations later, Captain Baldwin Leighton, who was born in 1717, had six daughters and Edward (Rev.) Rector of Pontesbury and Cardiston, Sir Baldwin Leighton, the 6th Baronet, and Thomas, born in 1751. Thomas and his wife Mary Louisa had Reverend Francis, Rector of Cardiston, who with his wife Catherine had a son Edward William Forestier in 1839. Forestier married Beatrice Jane Eyre in 1886 who was the daughter of John Eyre of Eyrecourt Castle, County Galway, Ireland.

Col. The Right Hon. John Eyre was an Englishman who went to Ireland with General Ludlow and acquired large estates in several counties in the 1660s. Eyre descendants included numerous High Sheriffs, MPs, military leaders, Governors of Galway, and many who colonized America, Australia and New Zealand, as well as many adventurers. Beatrice Jane Eyre, one of seven daughters and three sons of John Eyre, herself had two children, a son Charlton Dudley Forestier and a daughter Olga Beatrice, who was later to become the mother of Alfonso. It is from this connection that Portago's mother is often described as Irish, though the Eyres were English living in Ireland.

Loton Park, home of Sir Michael Leighton.
(Credit - Ed McDonough)

The Baronetcy of Leighton passed from Sir Baldwin Leighton, the 6th Bt. who was the great uncle of Edward William Forestier to Sir Baldwin the 7th Bt. to Sir Baldwyn the 8th Bt. to Sir Bryan Baldwin Mawddwy Leighton, the 9th Bt. to Sir Richard Tihel Leighton the 10th Bt. His son, Sir Michael John Bryan Leighton is the 11th and present Bt. who resides in the family seat at Loton Park, a 17th century house near Shrewsbury. It was the second baronet who moved to Loton from Wattlesborough Castle, the original ancient family seat. Sir Michael founded the hillclimb circuit at Loton Park in 1960 out of his own interest and experience in motor racing. Sir Michael told the author that several other relatives including the former sports car driver Andrew Fletcher had been involved in motor racing to some extent. Whether by coincidence, fate or design, it is of more than passing interest that Portago's living English relative maintained an interest in his career and accomplishments, though they never met. Sir Michael told the author that he was sitting listening to the radio with his father in 1957 when it was announced that Portago had been killed in the Mille Miglia. His father was so shocked "he fell off the chair"!

Sir Michael Leighton.
(Credit - Ed McDonough)

The Leighton family coat of arms at Loton Park.
(Credit - Ed McDonough)

The Early Years

Portago's wife Carroll McDaniel Petrie maintained contact with Alfonso's mother until the mother's death in February1980 in Lausanne, Switzerland, and with his sister Soledad, the Marquesa de Moratalla. She had met Portago in 1948 at a time when he was attempting to establish himself as a successful sportsman, and she learned most of what she knew about his family sometime later:

"His mother was English and his father was Spanish, and speaking from what I learned subsequently but didn't know then, his mother had been a nurse to a very wealthy and prominent American, Frank Mackey, who she married on December 14, 1920. On his death on February 24, 1927, she inherited his fortune. I believe he came from Chicago and he had founded the Household Finance Company which was a very big company, and that was where the family fortune came from. This was the money that kept the family going for so many years, and it was the source of Fon's money, as he never earned any himself. Then on Mackey's death, his mother, Olga, married Fon's father the Marquis de Portago, a Grandee of Spain. She had not any children with Frank Mackey but with Portago she had Fon and his younger sister Soledad. Fon was born in London 1928, and at that time they had a residence in London and also one in Biarritz. Fon's early schooling was in London, and then when he was a little older it was here in New York and the USA when the war was on. After Fon's father died in May 1941, the mother married a younger Spaniard, Don Isidro Martin-Montis on April 17, 1943 in Madrid. Martin-Montis was the son of the Marques de Linares, and he was quite a lot younger than she was, and he was gracious and charming and made her very happy. They came to New York and lived for quite a while in the Plaza Hotel. I think the mother, Olga, went to Newport in the summer and they may have had a residence there. The children loved and respected Martin-Montis. He seemed to have become the 'father' they knew. The things that were said about Fon's actual father were hearsay for me because he was already deceased by the time I met Fon, as was my own father. He had a reputation as an athlete and was involved in many sports, but I didn't have first hand knowledge of any of this. I only met the stepfather Isidro Martin-Montis. It turned out to be an extremely happy marriage. After they left the Plaza Hotel, I believe they stayed at Newport and possibly in Palm Beach."

Alfonso de Portago, 2nd left, at his 3rd birthday party in 1931, his sister Sol to the left in the photo. This was in Biarritz. *(Credit - Petrie Collection)*

Portago's father, rather like himself, has been described as multi-talented and an expert in many sports. The truth may be slightly more modest, but indeed he was a man of some accomplishments, and like many Spanish nobles, was able to mix with important personalities and political figures. His occupation is listed in genealogies as the X Marques de Portago, a Grandee and XII Conde de Mejorada. After his marriage to Olga Mackey, there was a substantial amount of family wealth, though his own family home is described by Carroll Petrie as "not lavish…before his marriage he had a title but not much money".

The 16th Marquis de Portago in 1931. ***(Credit - Petrie Collection)***

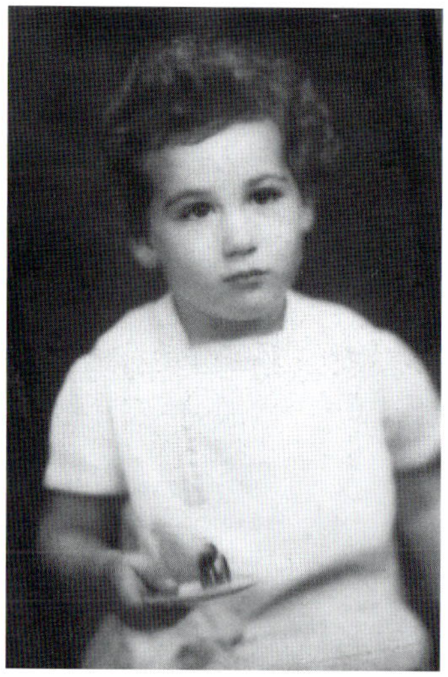

A portrait of the young Alfonso in 1931. ***(Credit - Petrie Collection)***

A photo of Alfonso with his father in 1932 from a Spanish magazine, showing the family interest in large dogs. ***(Credit - Petrie Collection)***

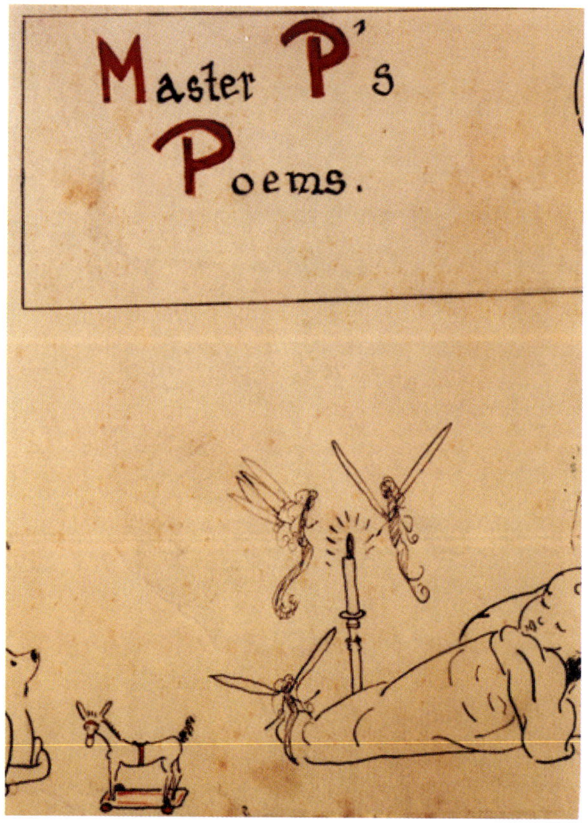

A book of poems in a book dedicated to 'Master P' in 1931. ***(Credit - Petrie Collection)***

The 16th Marquis reads to Alfonso and his sister Soledad in 1933. *(Credit - Petrie Collection)*

Carroll Petrie said Alfonso always loved and protected dogs, large or small. This was taken in 1933. *(Credit - Petrie Collection)*

Alfonso and 'Sol' with their mother, Olga in 1933. *(Credit - Petrie Collection)*

Don Antonio is described by Brock Yates as following in the family's adventurous footsteps and as "an ardent supporter of Franco, a noted polo player, yachtsman and as a profligate gambler; he once won $2 million at Monte Carlo. He died in 1941 while playing polo in defiance of his doctor". (Yates, Car and Driver, May 1986). He died in 1941, and he may have been a polo player though some photos which appeared in European papers and magazines purporting to be the 'playboy marques at polo' in fact were photos of Fon's stepfather Martin-Montis. Don Antonio did enjoy big and expensive cars, and also fancied himself as a possible export to Hollywood. There was at least one story that he had raced a Bugatti at least once. Other articles about Portago's family claim that his father had 'fought fiercely in the Spanish Civil War against Franco'!

An interest in cars was sparked at an early age. This is the family Rolls Royce in 1933. *(Credit - Petrie Collection)*

Alfonso and 'Sol' use the Rolls Royce as a playground, 1933. *(Credit - Petrie Collection)*

This 1910 Spanish sled poster may have helped to spark Portago's interest in the sport. *(Credit - Petrie Collection)*

Alfonso, 2nd left, and Soledad, right with two friends at St.Moritz on a winter holiday in 1933. *(Credit - Petrie Collection)*

Don Antonio used his contacts to get a minor role in the 1935 film *Sanders of the River*, which was based on a bibliography of eleven stories written between 1911 and 1928. The film was released in Britain in April 1935 and was the first in a series of colonialist epics from Alexander Korda's London Films, and it was the first film to have all three Korda brothers involved: Alexander was the producer, Zoltan the director and Vincent was the art director. Zoltan wanted the film to be a sensitive examination of African culture and society, but it emerged as 'an unwavering celebration of British colonial rule', a real piece of propaganda, and maintaining author Wallace's racist view of Africans as deceitful, child-like and violent. The film nevertheless attracted American Paul Robeson to the role of Bosambo, in spite of his serious involvement in political activism in the 1930s. Robeson later 'disowned' the film though his singing and acting earned it a large audience.

A portrait of Alfonso aged six in 1934.
(Credit - Petrie Collection)

The interest in equestrianism started early; this is Alfonso with his pony watched by his mother Olga.
(Credit - Petrie Collection)

A poster advertising the 1935 film Bosambo, in which Portago's father had a small part.

Leslie Banks played British Commissioner Sanders who ruled the West African territories in the manner of a strict father. When Sanders goes on leave, his 'kingdom' falls into disarray and is restored with the help of Bosambo, the loyal chief played by Robeson. Don Antonio had the minor role of Farini, but also in the film as an extra was one Jomo Kenyatta, later the president of Kenya, who was apparently pleased with the film. It was remade in 1963 by Big Ben Films, an offshoot of the Korda London Films as *Death Drums Along the River*.

The young Portago was at school in London during the period the film was being made, and there was no record of whether he had seen it. The family moved between London and Biarritz and Madrid during Portago's early life. He had few close friends, though there seemed to be regular attendance at birthday parties of other well-off and titled children, especially when the family was in Spain or Biarritz. Fon and his sister had ponies when they were quite young, family photos showing Fon with his own pony in 1934 when he was five and a half, and by 1937 Fon and Soledad were riding regularly with adults both in Spain and France. Both Fon and his sister were tutored at their European homes, and occasionally when they spent time at St. Moritz in Switzerland which became an annual event except during the war. After Don Antonio died in 1941, his mother remained in Madrid most of the time until she married Martin-Montis the following year and the family moved to New York.

The sporting Marquis, Alfonso playing football in 1934. *(Credit - Petrie Collection)*

Alfonso as cowboy in 1934.
(Credit - Petrie Collection)

Alfonso in serious mood at the beach at Biarritz in 1934.
(Credit - Petrie Collection)

This Bugatti was the first of a series of pedal and motorised cars in the family, shared with 'Sol' and one of the dogs.
(Credit - Petrie Collection)

A family riding expedition in 1935, with from left, Soledad, mother, father and Alfonso. *(Credit - Petrie Collection)*

The photos portray a close relationship between Alfonso and Soledad.
(Credit - Petrie Collection)

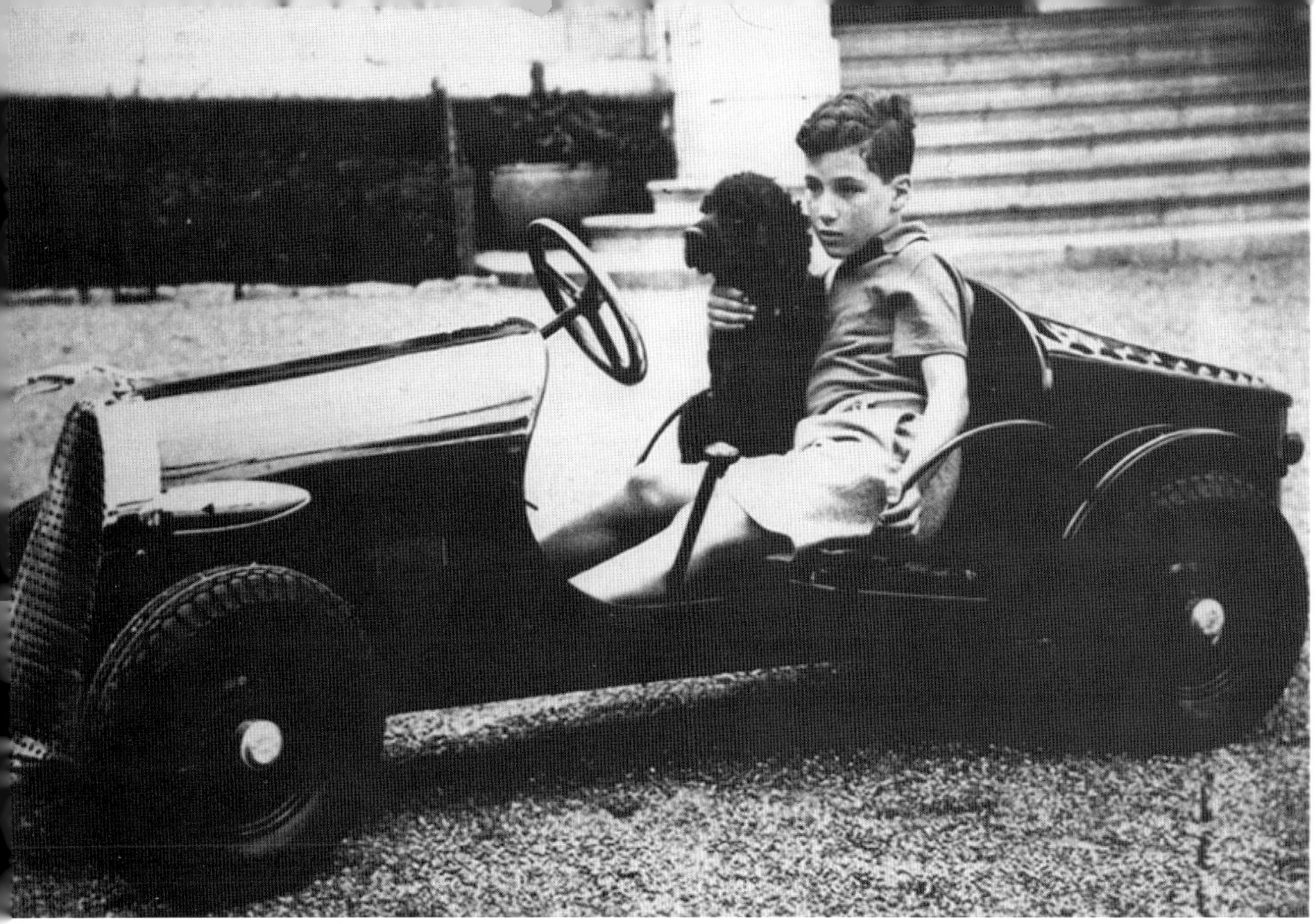

By 1936, the size of the cars had gotten bigger, and this one had a motor. ***(Credit - Petrie Collection)***

Perhaps this photo taken in 1936 would belie the later tale that Portago couldn't change gear!
(Credit - Petrie Collection)

The car is shared with one of the many Portago family canines.
(Credit - Petrie Collection)

Carroll Petrie, who now lives very close to the famous New York landmark, the Plaza Hotel, was aware that the family had lived there for sometime after fleeing Europe for the United States, and at some point in their residence there Fon was sent to Lawrenceville Preparatory School in New Jersey. The school responded to the author's enquiries by acknowledging that he had been a student there: "Unfortunately, Mr. Portago's time here was rather short, and our records for him are incomplete. He enrolled as a II Former (9th grader) in September 1944 and it appears as though he left after two years." There were reports that he was expelled from the school after a month, but that is another part of the legend. Nevertheless his academic career, in any formal sense, was short, and he again had a number of private tutors. It was also while living at the Plaza Hotel that Alfonso de Portago met and became a close and lifelong friend with a young hotel employee, Edmund Gurner Nelson. As a teenager, Portago became much more interested in spending his time in adventures with Nelson than in any academic pursuits.

Alfonso in 1937 in a suit, something he would have a disdain for as a young man! *(Credit - Petrie Collection)*

By 1939, Alfonso was beginning to enter equestrian competition, and is shown practising his jumping.
(Credit - Petrie Collection)

Both Alfonso and 'Sol' took regular training and instruction to improve their riding, this in 1939. *(Credit - Petrie Collection)*

One of these pursuits was women. Dorian Leigh recounts a story told to her by Portago's mother that at the age of 16 he was managing to spend a lot of his money in the Copacabana nightclub in New York where he had met a chorus girl named Mara. He bought her a mink coat, charged to his mother, and gave it to her, even though they had never been alone together! (Leigh, 1980)

This portrait was done in 1944, when the older looking 16-year old was chasing a dancer who worked in a New York club. ***(Credit - Petrie Collection)***

Sporting Success

Some years after the death of Portago, his widow Carroll McDaniel Portago had met and married Milton Petrie. They had become very central figures in the New York and wider American social and charitable scene and Carroll Petrie played, and still plays, a large and active role in social and charitable events. She was willing to agree to an interview with the author. The author confesses to having been very uncertain as to how this would work, as the issues were sensitive and difficult, and the events took place 57 years ago. However, Mrs. Petrie was open and direct and was able to provide, for the first time, a context in which to understand Portago's nature, activities and ambitions. She was able to put to rest some myths, and more importantly willing to share her thoughts and feelings about her life in the rather tempestuous 1950s. We discussed the starting point and agreed to begin when she and Portago met:

"That is a good place to start because, believe me, what I am going to say is what Fon was like. I was sitting in a restaurant in France. It was the old Maxim's in Paris. He was at a different table and he had to pass our table on his way out. I was with some Argentine friends and he looked at me and he said 'I am going to marry you', and he kept walking. I was overwhelmed and laughed in amazement and said 'who is that?' The reason I tell you this is that it is so indicative of his determination to do what he thought was right with his life. It was stunning. I never saw this man before, and I was with someone else, which didn't disturb him (Fon) in the least. But it was a much smaller world, and you could place people easily. It was the kind of thing that could have happened at the time in the late 1940s and in the 1950s but wouldn't happen now. He never explained why he did that. He had come from a family of means and they were titled and that made him *entitled*. That was just his decision and very much the way he was."

"That was in 1948, so the next stage didn't happen all that quickly. He was 20 years old at the time and he had a stable of horses. When I met him, Fon was a sportsman with a stable of horses in France. Fon had grown up with horses and I believe they had horses in several of the places they lived. When I met him, he was still very young, as was I though I was four years older than he was. He was very active with steeplechase racing at that time. But when I met him, I didn't know about those activities, and I didn't even know who he was. This young kid…I was 23 or 24 and ought to have known better…who was this kid saying something like that to me? He wasn't as he later looked and was portrayed. The scruffy look came later! That came after the horse period. He wouldn't have gotten into a restaurant in 1948 if he dressed as he did later! He was very much involved with the horses, and I eventually was involved as well. We went to the Grand National and I eventually was there helping to take care of the horses. Fon and his sister were more involved in equestrian activities from their early days than ever became known amongst the motor racing people, but that was their big passion. For his sister Soledad, it still is."

"In retrospect, it was like he planned his own life and he stuck to his own plan, almost like there was a list of things for him to do. Like so many 'Englishmen' he was always very interested in sports. I didn't view him as an Englishman but he was very English in many of his ways. However, he had his own sense of nationality, a very strong sense that he was a Spaniard and a Grandee of Spain and that was foremost in his mind. That is interesting because his own father didn't live that long. In those days, in families like that who came from tremendous wealth, the men were sportsmen. The father's occupation was listed as 'the 10th Marquis de Portago'. I used to go see them when Fon played polo in 1950 and 1951 amongst all those families like his own. It was very exciting when the polo teams from Argentina would come to America to play and then to Europe and the Europeans would come here to America."

"Fon's family, his father, had standing but not a vast amount of wealth themselves. They were Grandees but they didn't have the kind of wealth like Fon's mother brought to the family. He didn't inherit wealth from his father. His mother, Olga, had the money and she always controlled the purse strings. I know there were many stories about how wealthy he was, and that is not surprising. By the time I met him, he already had his own stable of horses. She didn't just go buy them, but the money would have come from her. Fon never worked, but they didn't in those days, and it wasn't just him. Great wealth would have been made by a grandfather and it came down through the family. It hadn't been made on the Spanish side, but by Olga's first husband Frank Mackey. Fon was never the sort of person who had great amounts of money that he 'splashed out'…he never had it. He had already bought the next horse or the next car, but that would have come from his mother. A lot of what has been written about Fon just isn't true, especially about money and vast wealth. He never had great amounts of money with him or even in a bank account, but the people who wrote about him didn't understand the way the family worked, and that Fon always had to go to his mother for money."

"I don't know a great deal of detail about his activities and accomplishments in sports before I knew him. I knew he was a tremendous athlete but I don't know the detail of those things. I know and have read stories about what he did, like the swimming championships but I didn't have any first hand experience of that. If he played Jai Alai or tennis, I believe it must have been things he did as a boy. He didn't play tennis after I married him so I don't know about the stories that he was a French tennis champion. If he played tennis then it was when he was a boy, and he may have won something because he was so competitive. But he never won a big championship later when he was an adult. If he played Jai Alai, I think it was as a 'minor' activity, and I am certain he never was serious about it. Jai Alai was not a sport that people like Fon played seriously or professionally, as far as I was aware. I know from the time I met him, it was only horses and then cars until he took up other things like the bobsled. His focus was horses, which started when he was quite young if you look in the family photo album. When I married him, he rode in the Grand National. I know he did have a flying license…I remember his mother talked about that but that was before I knew him. I also heard the story about him flying under a bridge. I don't know if that is true, but like others I wouldn't be surprised if it was. I suspect he had convinced his mother to let him have flying lessons when he was quite young, perhaps 17 or 18 in the USA, but he never took it seriously. He was probably riding horses when he was at school, though he didn't stay at school very long. I think he probably stopped horse racing and jumping about 1952 or 1953. I knew him for about a year before we got married on December 1, 1949. After that we would spend the winters in St. Moritz. I think he started dabbling with the cresta and bobsleds perhaps the first winter we were in St. Moritz, so that would have been in 1949 or 1950, and again in 1951."

"It may have been true that he started with the cresta because he saw it at St. Moritz, but I don't think he started doing it as an accident. He was just very competitive and I think that was in him. So if he saw something that interested him and he liked it, he wanted it more, and that meant that he would do it seriously. If it was something competitive, then he would be very competitive. Ed Nelson was partly involved with the cresta but that was mainly because he was hanging around and traveling with Fon at that time and I think probably encouraged him to try it. Ed…Edmund Gurner Nelson…had been selling in the kiosk at the Plaza Hotel. He was selling newspapers and magazines. When Fon went there as a young boy with his mother, they didn't know a lot of people. Fon got to know Ed Nelson who was just working there. He was a bit older, and they became lifelong friends. They both liked women…a lot…as apparently had Fon's father. I think it was something about being Spanish and it was being Spanish at that time when it was more permissible for Spanish men to behave towards women in a different way than other men. It was seen as very flattering to women, and I guess in some ways it still is. It was after the war, when there was a more permissive attitude, and because the war was over and we had won the war, certain behaviour was acceptable. The 1950s was a whole period of 'anything goes'. It was just the right time for a 'Fon' to be around."

"Ed Nelson was a very good looking fellow, but I don't think many people knew much about him. He was very 'nice' but I mean that in the sense of nice because he did everything that Fon wanted him to. Fon was calling the shots. They were friends and Nelson was available for whatever Fon wanted to do. I think they were both very competitive and focussed on winning. I never thought that it was anything but a real friendship. Fon's father had died when Fon was very young, as my father did when I was very young, I think that gave us a major point in common. Neither of us had a major male figure in our lives, in our families, to emulate, so Nelson was the significant male connection. I think they knew each other for quite a long period and they did a lot together, so it was boys growing into men together. After the war was over, and my future mother-in-law moved back to Europe, I think Nelson went with them. Later I knew that my mother-in-law could never understand and accept Nelson. I could because I was the same vintage, and I could see that Fon had no role model, and Nelson was older than Fon and available to him. It was very much Fon saying 'today we are racing' and Nelson would get in the car. He didn't think about it, he did what he was told to do. Nelson would never have even been in St. Moritz if it hadn't been for Fon, so I think the stories about Nelson taking a lead in activities and getting Fon involved just weren't true. Nelson had been a poor kid who had no one. His father was deceased and he didn't have an easy time. He had a stepfather who was young and he wasn't interested in Nelson, so Ed was on his own."

While there is no evidence that Nelson was ever 'employed' by Portago or by the family, there is also no record of him having any source of income, and he was therefore dependant on Portago, and as he accompanied Fon and the family, his expenses were met by the family, who also had others travelling with them. Carroll Petrie believes Nelson was with Portago on that day at Maxim's when she first met her future husband, though she had no recollection of where he had been living, or where he lived after she and Portago were married. Nelson's connections with Portago were sufficient to ensure him access to all the elite sporting and social venues, unusual for someone from very modest origins. Nelson would take part in the winter sports at St. Moritz, play polo in France and often appear in the winner's enclosure at horse racing tracks. Some reports have described Nelson as having been well-known in European winter sports and around motor racing, and that it was Nelson who encouraged Portago into racing, two facts denied by Carroll Petrie. Brock Yates said that Nelson, who was 14 years older than Portago, was born in Estelline, South Dakota, was an Air Force veteran and had lived in Paris since 1949, and was allegedly married to a Hawaiian girl, a person of whom there is no further record, nor does there appear to be any comment from anyone who ever met her. (Yates in Car and Driver May 1986)

The author had asked Mrs. Petrie, among other things, whether Portago had owned exotic cars either before they had met or after they were married. She said she didn't recall anything particularly interesting, and he generally saw most cars as simply a means of transport. However, an article in the French motoring paper La Vie de Auto December 17, 1998 carried the story of a very rare Alfa Romeo 6C 2500 with Ghia cabriolet bodywork. This car, with chassis 915 592 and engine 923 702, had been with one owner from 1957 to the late 1990s. It was thought there was probably only one such car ever built until a second Ghia-bodied machine was also found. The first car was completed on September 30, 1947 and delivered to its new owner at Turin on June 11, 1948. The new owner was listed as Marquis Alfonso de Portago. The second car, chassis 915 593 with engine 923 330, was also completed on September 30, 1947 and was delivered to an Alfa Romeo concessionaire in Lugano, Switzerland on July 8, 1948. So far, no other record of Portago's association with this car has been found. Despite the paucity of information about Portago's ownership of this car, Alfa Romeo 2500 Register Secretary Peter Marshall, the world authority on the 6C-2500 and 1900 models, did indeed confirm that there was documentation to confirm Portago's purchase of the car. Marshall had discussed the car and its history with its French owner, Serge Charpentier.

This is the Alfa Romeo 6C 2500 Pinifarina Cabriolet which Portago owned in 1948, and is now in France.
(Credit - La Vie d'Auto)

This horse show took place in Paris in 1949, at a time when Portago was almost a full-time equestrian. ***(Credit - Petrie Collection)***

Portago won a number of competitions at French shows in 1949, and this was at Tramontane. ***(Credit - Petrie Collection)***

Carroll Petrie was aware that Portago's involvement in equestrianism was quite serious, virtually full-time, when they first met, though it wasn't as a professional but as a wealthy amateur sportsman. The difference for Fon was that he was then, and had been for sometime, immensely competitive. Fon and his sister had a growing stable of horses outside of Paris near Chantilly, and both rode and competed regularly as amateurs. During 1949, before his marriage to Carroll MacDaniel, Portago had nine wins in various races, one in a flat race and the other nine over jumps at a number of meetings, all in France.

Portago married Carroll McDaniel in Biarritz on December 1, 1949. ***(Credit - Petrie Collection)***

"When we got married, we lived in Paris. We had a two-bedroom apartment on Rue Pergolese, which is a little street off Avenue Foch. I think we moved into Avenue Foch about a year later, after I had had my daughter Andrea. Andrea was born back in the USA, so she was 100% American. I was…and am…a Carolina girl. I grew up knowing that my great uncle was the governor of Georgia in the 1860s. Can you get more southern than that? I went to college in Spartanburg, at Converse College, but I wanted to have my children in the USA. Although I lived abroad I hung onto being American. Then we moved into 40 Avenue Foch in Paris. That was our permanent residence for the entire time we were married. That was where we spent a great deal of time. I still maintained a contact with people in the USA, especially in the south, as I was always a real Carolinian. I don't think it was an accident that South Carolina was the first state to secede from the Union in the Civil War! I think I have a close affinity with that part of the world, but we were also very much at home in Paris. The fact that Fon should somehow have picked me out in Maxim's, as the independent kind of person I was, seems really like fate…more than coincidence."

The Portago/McDaniel marriage was a major social event in Biarritz in 1949. ***(Credit - Petrie Collection)***

The young Portago looks serious in this wedding photo. ***(Credit - Petrie Collection)***

The author is indebted to the historian and statistician John Randall of the Racing Post in London, the well-known daily horse racing newspaper. Randall corrected the long-standing error that Portago had been a three-time French horse racing champion. In fact he was the champion amateur rider in France on two occasions. In addition to his 10 wins in 1949, Portago was victorious in 1950 on twelve occasions, seven in flat races and five times over jumps. He was joint third in 1950 in the amateur riders' combined table. 1950 would also be remembered for one of two of a very limited number of events in Britain. In March, Portago entered Garde Toi for the Cheltenham Gold Cup in Gloucestershire. Lord John Oaksey recounted for the author his recollections of both Alfonso and his more recent memories of his sister Soledad, who continues to enter horses in major races to this day. In 1994, Soledad, the Marquesa de Moratalla, owned a very successful horse, First Gold, which had won the King George VI Chase. She didn't attend many of the races but was represented by her trainer and jockey, father and son team Francois and Thierry Douman, and by her old friend, Sir Peter O'Sullevan, the respected commentator and the "Voice of Racing". Sir Peter had been introduced to the Marquesa in 1950 when Fon was racing at Cheltenham, and they became lifelong friends and colleagues. Her horse, The Fellow, won the Cheltenham Gold Cup in 1994 at its fourth attempt. Lord Oaksey also recalled that the competitive Marquesa represented Spain in Grand Master bridge tournaments. In 1982, she gained an international reputation at the Bridge World Championships at Biarritz. In the Rosenblum Cup, in which most of the world-ranked players battled for six days, a relatively little known Spanish quartet reached the semi-final from 129 teams. The toughest player from this quartet was Soledad, Marquesa de Moratalla. Each Spanish player played 64 deals per day, and the Spaniards just lost to the French in the semi-final, and the French went on to win.

Portago's performance at Cheltenham in 1950 was remarkable, as he finished third on the nine-year old Garde Toi behind F.L.Vickerman's Cottage Rake, one of only four three-time Gold Cup winners, and Lord Bicester's Finnure.

1950 saw Portago work seriously on winning the French amateur steeplechase championship. ***(Credit - Petrie Collection)***

Portago then entered Garde Toi in the Grand National in April. The race is remembered for the victory by Freebooter, ridden by Seamie Power, an Irish jockey and was the 10 to 1 favourite. It was a Waterford horse with a Waterford jockey in Waterford colours so there was a great Irish celebration. Her Majesty Queen Elizabeth had her first entry at the Grand National with Monaveen which finished 6th. Portago's Grand National debut was interesting but not as glorious as his 3rd place at the Gold Cup, as he and his mount fell early in the race.

Not all the Portago competition was that serious.
(Credit - Petrie Collection)

1951 was Portago's most successful season, with thirty wins, sixteen in flat races and fourteen over jumps. This helped him become 1951 French Amateur Champion overall, second in the Flat race table, and second in the jumps table. His title was due in large part to his versatility, riding regularly in both types of events, winning an impressive number of times and generally finishing well.

The Portagos at a Paris nightclub.
(Credit - Petrie Collection)

Portago always said that jumping was an extremely exhilarating sport.
(Credit - Petrie Collection)

These photos show not only how serious Portago was but also how fit he was in 1950.
(Credit - Petrie Collection)

Polo became yet another sport that Portago was highly skilled at, and he played often through 1950-51.
(Credit - Petrie Collection)

1952 was an equally successful equestrian year, with seventeen victories, eight on the flat and nine over jumps. This gave him his second overall French amateur championship, this time third in the Flat table and third over the jumps. He had also run at the Grand National for a second time, this time on Icy Calm, which had to be pulled up before the finish. The 1952 race was won by Teal.

Carroll Petrie remembered that Portago had been considering a change from horse racing around 1952, though he didn't stop racing horses until the end of 1953:

"I guess, after Andrea was born in 1952, this became the start of the change towards Fon's interest in racing cars, but it wasn't something that seemed part of his plan then. He had the stable of horses and had been very active with polo as well in the early 1950s and with racing the horses. But he was filling out. He was four years younger than me but he was growing and getting heavier. This was a something to do with living the way we did after Andrea was born and having a regular life and it was part of him being 24 instead of 20 when we first met. There was then a period when he was constantly dieting, dieting, dieting, and then suddenly one day he said he was going to be in a motor car race."

In an interview in 1957, Portago himself characterized the change of direction in a very light-hearted way by saying that after a few weeks away from home, and eating in too many restaurants, he had put on some ten kilos, and he knew that he was unlikely to be able to keep his weight down sufficiently to ride.
He didn't manage to retain his French Championship in 1953, in spite of gaining another sixteen race wins, nine in flat races and seven over jumps. He was, however, joint second in the amateur riders' joint table, with a joint third in the Flat table and joint seventh in the jumps table.

This 1950 match was near Paris, though Portago played at several venues in France and Spain. ***(Credit - Petrie Collection)***

Portago thus rode the winners of 85 races in France in a five-year period, forty-one flat race winners and forty-four over jumps. John Randall dismisses the oft reported "several hundred" winners as exaggeration typical of both winners and their families. In Portago's case, while he might have tended to exaggerate his accomplishments, it's just as likely that the exaggeration was down to enthusiastic journalistic license. Some of the same reports had Portago as a fencing and Spanish swimming champion and a member of the Spanish Davis Cup tennis team, though there isn't evidence for these claims. Nye picked up some of Portago's exaggerations from a recording made in Cuba in 1957. (Nye, Classic and Sports Car, May 1985) He has Portago claiming that he reported the drugging of his horses to Scotland Yard in 1952, that he rode 150 races a year, that in one week at Pau he rode 32 winners in 36 races. Not true! Hans Tanner had Portago as a champion swimmer and boxer, and had elevated his equestrian titles to "world champion for gentlemen riders" for three consecutive years. (Tanner, 1958)

Portago at full gallop in 1951. ***(Credit - Petrie Collection)***

Winning another polo match in 1951.
(Credit - Petrie Collection)

A royal award ceremony. The man to the left of Portago in the photo is his stepfather Isidro Martin-Montis.
(Credit - Petrie Collection)

The end of horse racing overlapped the beginning of motor racing in 1953. Carroll Petrie recalled the social side of the start of Portago's motor racing:

"He started doing some races with Harry Schell. Harry and his brother Phillip Schell were good friends of ours, and Harry remained a friend of mine. They were around when we were in New York and we spent time together in France. There were some Argentine drivers, and some of them including Fon were well known, Fon for his horse racing as well as being a marquis, so they did some racing where they were invited along to join other French drivers. That happened before the big car events. I remember Carlos Menditeguy being here for some of those races. Some of those people were really sportsmen and driving was just one of their sports. There was another Argentine driver who raced one of Fon's cars later on and I think he was in Paris as well. That was Roberto Mieres who became a well-known yacht racer as well as Grand Prix driver. "

"I went with him to some races but not many. He didn't really want me there. Part of that was because of the way he saw the racing and the people involved. He felt many drivers were not sportsmen, but people who became sportsmen because they saw it as a career. But that was Fon and his way of seeing things. Racing for him wasn't a career. That wasn't his point in life. His point in life was to prove himself...to himself, and I guess to the rest of the world. It is hard to say exactly how it came about. My perception was that he was so competitive that it was almost bound to happen. Don't forget his mother was in her forties when he was born. She had that English obsession with sports and gentlemen, where sport was neutral ground where people could prove themselves. Fon had this love of sports, and of people or the contact with people through what he did in sports. He was shy, and shy about people, but he liked them and he wanted to surround himself with people. That was what I was doing in his life at that time. There was no accident that he got into the English upper class sports, the sports of gentlemen. He fit into that scene very well. It was what he knew best from the English side of him and his early background in England. He was Spanish but he knew the English way of life much better than the Spanish. He was Spanish in so far as he didn't consult me about racing or his other activities, but he was quite English in his approach to those activities. I went to some motor races but he wasn't exactly overjoyed that I was there. I think my presence there would have made him nervous. Other wives were there, but not many. That was partly because not many of the men were married. That was what I assume. The other part was that there were other men like him who didn't want wives around because it was *their* sport...their activity. And of course, my children were young...they were only six and three when he was killed, so I was with them and not at the races. I knew some of the motor racing people very well. There was Harry Schell who was a friend and had a house, which he had bought in Paris. His brother wasn't involved in racing though I recall that his parents were. Harry had a lot of charm, he was well educated, and he was good value as a friend, nice to have around, and erudite. I met Fangio a bit later. I didn't know him as well as Harry but I liked him, he was a very nice man. I know from what I have learned since that Fangio thought highly of Fon, and I believe that was quite genuine. It was partly because Fon started at the 'deep end', and I also think Fon's determination must have been evident to some people. I know Fon respected Fangio like most drivers did, and I think it was a mutual respect."

"I don't know how much many of the people Fon knew and spent time with knew about him. There are things I think some did but many missed and there are things I can say about him that don't quite match the way he was often portrayed. He was very sensitive, and very sensitive to others. I have to work to think of some examples because it is now fifty years. But I have this picture and knowledge of him as an extremely sensitive human being. It wasn't sensitivity just about himself, but it was about others. He was always a very kind person. All of his life he loved and cared for animals as well. It wasn't entirely that Avenue Foch was full of strays, but he did find animals in the street and brought them home. I certainly saw him do that, and I think he always did that. Wounded cats and dogs always got brought home, different sizes and shapes. He wasn't what I would call a 'doting' parent. When the children were young, that was the time when he was most involved in racing so he was not there a lot of the time. I would also say that he wanted a family, but he also wanted his freedom, and that was something that was not always easy to balance. I could never say anything negative about him as a human being. He was an absolutely fine human being and he cared about other peoples' feelings. I guess what I am saying is that he was a highly sensitive human being. There was the playboy image that he created or was created about him, but you should not forget that both of his parents were not young. They were not people in their twenties when he was born. Out of the life he had, he had a tremendous sensitivity. He did funny things sometime. Once he told me that he had taken our daughter Andrea out to lunch. I asked where he had taken her and he said to the Plaza. Well, she was a few years old and couldn't have had any idea of where she had been taken or what it was all about. But it was okay because it was time spent with her, just the two of them. They were only six and three when he died so there was really only very little time for them together. I knew that he was a 'naughty boy', but I could never condemn him for it because I knew what was in his heart. There were many times when there were problems. My mother would say 'Carroll, he's your husband, not theirs'! "

Carroll Petrie acknowledged the 'controversial' nature of some of Fon's behaviour but took exception to the distortions that were created by journalists. She said that she didn't want to be portrayed as a person who didn't know what was going on, or that she just accepted it, because some of it wasn't true and what was true happened in a context:

"Many, many things were said about Fon and me and our life. I knew much of what was going on and being said. There were the reports that we were going to get a divorce, and that was written about by Ken Purdy, I think it was. But that was not true. I wasn't always happy with what was written then or later by some so-called 'experts'. In those days, almost 50 years ago, religion and beliefs still played a very strong part in what you did. I had been asked to convert to Catholicism but I was born and had been brought up in the Baptist Church and there was no such thing as divorce. I am from a Southern Baptist family and it was solidly against divorce, and with my great uncle having been the Georgia governor, it just wasn't a possibility, and neither was conversion a possibility. You don't turn your back and walk away. You might turn your head, and you might be halfway out the door, but you don't go. You don't do it, so that is why what was written about divorce was never true. It is very different today, but that was the 1940s and 1950s. Those days were an eye-opener for me, because I don't think Americans were that free with marriages. There were other things about him that didn't fit the image that was created. He didn't drink. He really didn't like it. I think I saw him once have a glass of champagne too many and he didn't like it. I drank because it was from growing up in the south, from growing up in a country club atmosphere and something being put in my hand at the age of 18. I don't think I was ever drunk in my life! So, in spite of the so-called social whirl around motor racing, Fon never drank. If we were alone, we would have dinner at home when the children were young, and we would go to the cinema in the Champs Elysee. We would walk there. We both liked walking a lot, and I still do. We were very active. He was a sportsman and kept himself fit and active. When people like Harry were around, they didn't drink a great deal. I never saw Harry drunk and that is not the picture people have of him either as far as I know."

Carroll Portago had also spoken openly to Ken Purdy in interviews in the 1950s. The subject of divorce was raised in one of these interviews, and Carroll responded in her typical forthright way: "Another thing: there was very little that was sneaky about Fon. He moved quite beyond commonplace deception. I knew him, I think, better than anyone else, and there was very little indeed in his life that I did not know about. We could talk about anything, and we did. I can assure you that some of the explanations, excuses, that he gave me at one time or another when we talked about something that he had done were strange and wonderful, often hilarious, even, but you could not laugh at him because he was absolutely sincere. All one can say about it, really, is that he was unable to resist a beautiful woman, any more than he was unable to resist any other kind of challenge. He could not be changed. It was a facet of his nature, and not by any means the most important, either. Most of his attachments were completely casual. One was not, but even that had ended before his death. After all, the essence of Fon's whole personality was his maleness. He was totally a man, and he was almost ferocious in his determination to live by his own rules." (Purdy 1972, p.71)

Motor Racing 1953 - 1954

The motor racing era of the Portago story has been the subject of innumerable articles, many by some of the better-known writers in the sport. Nevertheless, the details of the Spaniard's period in racing evaded even some of the best. Most of these writers were impressed by Portago's initiation at perhaps the most dangerous road race ever, the Carrera Panamericana.

The reality is that his introduction came at a somewhat more mundane level. Hans Tanner was one of the few people who seemed to be aware that Portago's longtime friend and occasional bobsled partner Edmund Gurner Nelson had allegedly introduced him to what Tanner referred to as "midget car racing on dirt tracks" in France, and Portago dabbled in this type of racing off and on in1953 and according to some reports later as well. Carroll Petrie says that it wasn't Nelson who brought this about, though he was always in attendance at Fon's sporting events. According to Tanner (1957) he won his first race in Paris "without any trouble". He spun at a later race at Strasbourg and according to Tanner coined his oft-used phrase 'if you want to win, don't spin'. Whether that was really a Portago original is of course open to question. He went on to further wins at Metz and Paris. The later reports of his first big races all had accounts of just what a poor and totally inexperienced driver he was, though most of the reports seem to have been written without any knowledge of these earlier dirt track events.

The author was somewhat mystified by what appeared to be assertions about these early races which were contradicted by some existing substantial evidence. The mystery was resolved when the pages of the family photo album, put together by Portago himself, and seen by hardly anyone outside the family, were turned and there were several photos dated in the early months of 1953, accompanied by French newspaper clippings. There indeed, was Fon awaiting the start of a race on a dirt track in something closely resembling an American quarter midget. Ed Nelson did take part in some of these races with Portago. The race recorded in the Portago family album took place in July 1953 at Reims, but not on the road circuit. The event was held at the Cynodrome Courbevoie in front of a large crowd. The local papers described the cars as 'brashly coloured Midgets, 2.2 meters in length and 1.1 meter high, using an American Indian motorcycle engine of 1200 cc. producing some 50 horsepower'. They weighed 160 kilograms and required considerable exertion on the part of the driver to get through the corners at speed. The drivers included a mix of so-called celebrities and regular drivers. Guy Bachelart, a race car builder, was present with Maurice Paoli, an ex-Indochina paratrooper with 200 jumps to his credit, as well as being a motocross rider. Other drivers included Jules Devoos (Belgium), Franco Traiter (Switzerland), and Frenchmen Rene Pari, Jean Deligny, Jean-Julien and Jean-Michel Le Huede.

This is one of the several midget races Portago took part in; this is July 1953 at Reims, and this photo shows the driver line-up before the main race. Portago is second in the line. *(Credit - Petrie Collection)*

Portago works hard against a German rival in a practice heat.
(Credit - Petrie Collection)

Learning the art of drifting in 1953.
(Credit - Petrie Collection)

Nelson had problems in one of the heats but the final saw a grand battle between the German Strechdorf and Portago, and this feature race was won by Portago, one of his earliest if not the first victory of his motor racing career. Around the same time, the Paris domiciled Brazilian, Nano da Silva Ramos, who became one of Portago's close friends, had met Gurner Nelson and suggested that Nelson bring Portago along to watch the Sable-Solesmes Rally, and this is one of the events which served to spark Portago's early interest in road racing.

Though these were small cars, they were capable of 80 mph.
(Credit - Petrie Collection)

Portago leads on the inside. ***(Credit - Petrie Collection)***

A young and trim Portago after winning one of the first races of his career. ***(Credit - Petrie Collection)***

What appeared to have confused those few historians who were digging around in the Spaniard's early race career, was that he was not only taking part in these midget races on dirt tracks, but was also involved in another French series, with equally small single-seaters. These early races turn out to be part of the Panhard Monomille series which was established in the early 1950s as a kind of celebrity one-make championship. Panhard had built many types of racing cars but these were 850 cc. single-seaters. There were races all over France and the series was contested by regular drivers Bayol, Armagnac, Storez, the up and coming Jo Schlesser, Cornet, and Vidille, and the 'celebrities' who joined in occasionally were Harry Schell, Roberto Mieres, Jean Lucas and Alfonso de Portago. While it is certain that Portago took part in some of these races in 1954 and even possibly as late as 1955, he also seems to have been a Monomille racer very occasionally in 1953. The participation of celebrities seemed to have served the purpose of drawing big crowds to watch the more serious antics of the regular French racers. The significance for Portago, however, in both Monomille and Midget races was that he was getting race experience. As we will see shortly, this creates contradictions, as many reports have his first motor racing after these lesser events. In this series, run by DB's Rene Bonnet, Portago would always manage to set a practice time in the top three, but then almost always draw a slower car for the races.

This poster uses a Panhard Monomille to advertise the 1953 film Race Against Death! ***(Credit - Paul Vesey)***

A 1953 Panhard Monomille.
(Credit - Author's Collection)

Front view of a Panhard Monomille. *(Credit - Author's Collection)*

This limited form of racing was interesting but not much more. In mid-1953, Portago was in the USA and on his way through New York, and he met with Luigi Chinetti at the New York Motor Show, having previously met him in Paris. Chinetti was just starting up the business of selling Ferraris to Americans. He had won at Le Mans, most recently in 1949. According to Tanner, Chinetti offered Portago the chance to be his co-driver in the 1953 Carrera Panamericana. What the Spaniard probably didn't grasp at the time was that what he was being given was the job of navigator, sitting beside the Italian American for several arduous days…and he was probably paying for the privilege, as Chinetti was one of the first of the motor racing entrepreneurs post-war to encourage wealthy men to pay for the chance to go racing without all the fuss of owning a car.

Portago with his wife, on the left, at lunch with friends shortly before departing for the Carrera Panamericana.
(Credit - Petrie Collection)

IV CARRERA PANAMERICANA
MEXICO
Rueda
ORGANIZADA POR LA
ANA
DEL 19 AL 23 DE NOV. DE 1953

Portago himself described the transition from horses to cars in an interview with Bill Grauer and Barratt Clark done in 1957: "I used to ride horses all the time, it was a full-time occupation. I raced a lot and I was a leading amateur rider in France for three years. I went away for a couple of weeks and when I came back I found that I had put on 14 kilos. There are many ways of losing weight. I think Rubirosa and Aly Khan have the best way, but I'm married. I tried practically everything, couldn't lose any weight, and that was the end of my riding career. At that time, a friend of mine had been doing a little automobile racing and he got me interested in it and I think I went to the automobile show with him and met Chinetti, who asked me to come and drive in the Pan American. What it really involved was sitting next to him while he drove, and I was naturally very frightened, but I suppose it had a charm all of its very own, and that's when I decided to take it up as a career." (Riverside Records, 1957) His weight gain, which prompted his move from horses to cars, seems to vary in several reports from eight to ten to fourteen kilograms!

Variously known as the 'Carrera' or 'Mexican Road Race', the event had a not surprisingly short life span. Just short of two-thousand miles, it started in Tuxtla Gutierrez in Mexico in the state of Chiapas, just north of the border with Guatemala and ran for five days northward over mountains and plateaus, through Puebla, Mexico City, Leon, Durango and Chihuahua to finish at Ciudad Juarez, almost in sight of El Paso in Texas. The 1953 race started on November 19 and finished on November 23. The 1953 race was the 4th running, and in that year it would be the final and deciding round of the World Sports Car Championship, giving it greater importance and news coverage. While it was expected to be a straight-forward fight between Lancia and Ferrari, the Americans took it seriously as winning the production classes sold big sedans in the USA in the age of galloping power.

Luigi Chinetti with the Ferrari 340MM at scrutineering before the Carrera Panamericana. ***(Credit - Savory)***

A surly looking Portago with Chinetti before the start.
(Credit - Arzamendia)

The race comprised eight stages, and Juan Fangio won in a Lancia D24 in relatively easy style, his rhythm and pace keeping him out of trouble. He was one of the drivers running alone, saving weight and doing his own navigation. The 177 car field set off at 6.00am on a Thursday morning, with thousands of spectators on hand, and the police beating the locals with little restraint to keep them away from the cars…a sign of the times in Latin America. Jean Behra soon took the lead on the first 329-mile stage in a 3-litre Gordini, from Phil Hill's Ferrari and Louis Rosier's heavy Talbot. Lancia's veteran driver Felice Bonetto was soon ahead on time and finished the first stage in the lead from the other works Lancias of Piero Taruffi, Juan Fangio and Eugenio Castellotti. Umberto Maglioli's 4.5-litre Ferrari followed ahead of Behra and Giovanni Bracco, another road racing veteran in a Lancia.

Rodger Ward with his Lincoln before the race started. ***(Credit - TK Automobilia)***

The Ferrari 345 can be seen as the cars go to the start at Oaxaca. ***(Credit - Savory)***

Piero Taruffi kisses his wife as he approaches the start in his Lancia. ***(Credit - Arzamendia)***

After a night stop, the cars set off for the 256-mile run to Puebla, over very difficult roads. Soon a Lincoln crashed into a crowd killing six people. The experienced Antonio Stagnoli crashed his Ferrari and he and co-driver Scotuzzi were dead. Taruffi went past Bonetto at some 150 mph near the Popacatapetl volcano. Taruffi won the stage but Bonetto still led overall on time and big Lincoln Capris dominated the production car classes. Taruffi again won the next short stage to Mexico City while Phil Hill crashed without any serious injury. Then the 4th stage claimed the life of Bonetto who was still leading but coming under pressure from Taruffi and Maglioli. Bonetto's Lancia spun in the village of Silao, striking a light pole. He was thrown out and suffered a broken neck. Taruffi slowed and Bracco retired. Though Maglioli won the stage, Fangio took the lead. One of the great Italian heroes had been killed. It was hours before competitors knew about Bonetto's death, but in 1953 there was no consideration given to halting the event. It was part of what the Carrera and road racing was in the 1950s...until 1957 in fact. The Carrera was '50s motor racing, and in some ways it was the '50s.

Chinetti and Portago at one of the early controls. *(Credit - Savory)*

Portago has got himself down low in the car as the car leaves a stage start. (Credit - Savory)

Maglioli lost a wheel on his Ferrari on stage five but took over Mario Ricci's car and was back winning stage seven. The relaxed Fangio was still in front overall. Over 35 cars were timed at over 150 mph on the 7th Parral to Chihuahua 186-mile stage! The final run to the finish was 230 miles and Maglioli in the 4.5-litre Ferrari averaged 138.3 mph! However, he was only 6th overall behind Fangio, Taruffi and Castellotti in Lancias, Mancini's Ferrari and Rosier. 57 cars made it to the finish.

Bonetto between stages in his Lancia; he would die when his car crashed into a pole. ***(Credit - Arzamendia)***

Chinetti and Portago on the open road at speed. They retired shortly after this was taken. ***(Credit - Arzamendia)***

This is Di Poli's Ford having problems, an example of the larger American stock class. ***(Credit - Arzamendia)***

Fangio in his Lancia. Here he is seen in a practice session.
(Credit - Arzamendia)

And where were Chinetti and Portago? The pair, especially with Chinetti behind the wheel, had set off with realistic hopes of doing well. Their Ferrari 340 MM (chassis 0286) had a 375 engine and would be quick on the long open roads. American Autosport correspondent Walter von Schonfeld had been given a ride in the car before the race and had reported it as “the fastest this writer ever had the pleasure and thrill of being in” (Autosport, Dec.4, 1953,p.724).

The car was indeed very quick, but it suffered from an intermittent misfire on the first stage after the start. Some work was done on the engine, but on only the second stage, a fuel line broke and could not be repaired. The implication in the few reports of the time indicated that in fact the engine problems were serious and the car was not going to make the distance. As Alfonso de Portago had virtually no reputation in motor racing, he was barely mentioned in any reports. However, it was later reported that he was less than impressed by being a passenger. One of his virtues was that he wasn’t afraid to say when he was afraid, and he was indeed very frightened, hanging on as Chinetti drove the 340 MM at full tilt over the Mexican roads. He was quoted as saying he would never again be a passenger in a race car. That fear, however, only extended so far, as he wasn’t beyond frightening other people who he took for a ride. Actress Linda Christian was one of those, but we will get to that story a bit later. While the Carrera Panamericana would linger on for a few more years, even the pervasive though unacknowledged view that ‘life is cheap’ wouldn’t sustain events such as this for very much longer. Portago later recalled that every driver was given a booklet at the start of the race. He was handed the booklet and was trying to find a place to put it so it wouldn’t fly out of the car. On a long straight, Chinetti hit a bump and Portago bounced into the air, and that’s when the booklet disappeared.

A photo of Fangio on one of the stages in the Lancia.
(Credit - Arzamendia)

When Portago was interviewed by Ken Purdy, he reflected on this early race experience: “All he (Chinetti) wanted me for was ballast. I didn’t drive a foot, not even from the garage to the starting line. I just sat there, white with fear, holding onto anything I thought looked sturdy enough. I knew that Chinetti was a was a very good driver, a specialist in long-distance races who was known to be conservative and careful, but the first time you’re in a racing car you can’t tell if the driver is conservative or a wild man, and I didn’t see how Chinetti could get away with half what he was doing. We broke down the second day of the race, but I had decided by then that this was what I wanted to do more than anything else. I used to think that flying was exciting, and for a long time riding seemed very rewarding. I rode, mostly steeplechases, twice a week at least for two years. But those things can’t be compared with driving. It’s a different world. So I bought a 3-litre Ferrari.” (Purdy, 1972,p.68)

Hans Herrmann was a leading driver in one of the smaller Porsche 1500s. ***(Credit - Arzamendia)***

By the time Portago would come back for the 1954 Carrera, a number of drivers and other people would have gotten used to the Spaniard being accompanied by a variety of strikingly beautiful women. One of these would be Dorian Leigh. She was an internationally known model, the sister of the equally renowned Suzy Parker, also a well-established model. Dorian had gained even wider fame as the model photographed by Richard Avedon for the Revlon 'Fire and Ice' cosmetic advertising campaign. She was a regular in the current international social set, and wrote her memoirs in 1980, including a detailed account of her long-standing relationship with Portago. This affair would appear to have begun in much the same way as his impulsive first encounter with Carroll McDaniel, and his later liaison with Linda Christian. In fact, he met both Dorian Leigh and Linda Christian in exactly the same place, L'Elephant Blanc nightclub in Paris. This was in the spring of 1952. Leigh was with a friend, Robert Balkany, and Portago was there with another model/socialite Eliza Hunt.

In her autobiography, written in 1980, Dorian Leigh recalled that she was annoyed by the way Portago continued to stare at her, but admitted she was struck by how handsome he was. Balkany claimed that he would have already found out who she was, and his somewhat 'predatory' approach to women had become apparent. (Leigh, 1980). Robert Daley would pick this up in his characterisation of Cavelli, based on Portago, in The Fast One. (Daley, 1978) When they met, he told her he had seen her photo in Lisbon, where he had been travelling with yet another model, Veronica Compton. Leigh was swept off her feet by this forward and flattering man with a cigarette dangling from his lip, wearing a black leather jacket. He had already established himself as not an ordinary member of the social set. "The night I met him at L'Elephant Blanc was the last time I saw him in a suit for a long time…he hated protocol." (Leigh, 1980, p.93) She was aware that his style was not a copy of the then popular 'motorcycle gang' look, as she said his jacket was handmade for him at the Paris shop Dorian Guy.

Though Dorian Leigh was still married and had young children herself, she managed to learn a great deal about Portago in these early days of what would become a fairly lengthy though tumultuous relationship. At the time Portago first stayed with Leigh in the Berkley Hotel in Paris, his wife was in Biarritz with their three-year-old daughter Andrea. It was clear that Portago had recounted tales of his childhood to her, especially accounts of his father who he portrayed as an internationally known womanizer, and of his grandfather who outraged society by marrying a beautiful gypsy girl. This would have come as some surprise to his paternal grandmother, Dona Angela de la Carvajal, a titled woman who hardly would have seen herself as a 'gypsy girl'. This repeating pattern of exaggeration tends to render some of the accounts of the Portago family as told to friends as somewhat suspect, and much of this suspect information is what has filtered into the public image over the years.

There is a rich vein of tales that Portago told Dorian, some revealing accurate pictures of the way in which Portago's mother endeavoured to protect the family finances through the development of a trust which Portago could call upon. There were also wilder tales of his schemes to raise money, everything from smuggling gold coins to allegedly splitting the fee his mother was paying a detective who she had following him. This is supposed to have involved Portago making a deal with the detective to share $150 a day, and the detective would stay in work as Portago wouldn't tell his mother that he knew about this particular scheme to keep an eye on him. Whatever the vagaries of the Leigh account are, she confirms the notion that Portago rarely had much money in his possession or at his disposition and had to go to the Trust for any substantial sums. She also had insights about the family not seen elsewhere. She says that Portago's mother Olga's first husband, Frank Mackey, when he was quite ill, shot himself in the bathroom of the house they were living in, and that Olga climbed on an outside ledge to get into the bathroom as the old man died. Apparently, she had at first been seen as a fortune hunter, but then was recognised for the good care she provided for this much older man. Several years later, it was Portago's father who was the fortune hunter when he met and married Olga, allegedly getting her to sign a prenuptial agreement giving him a large allowance before they married.

Leigh claims the credit…or the blame…for Portago's failure to maintain the weight he required to continue as a competitive rider in horse races. He had apparently been very self-disciplined when it came to weight and fitness, living on lean meat, milk, coffee and cigarettes! Leigh's interest in fancy eating in the best Paris restaurants seems to have coincided with more or less the end of Portago's riding career. She also claims a role in suggesting that he turn his interest in cars to good use in taking up motor racing. While she was certainly a significant part of his life at the time, it is unlikely that a woman would have had such influence, and that, as Carroll Petrie said, he always seemed to be working out what his next challenging activity would be and that agenda was his own, not someone else's.

When Dorian Leigh returned briefly to the USA in early summer 1952, she says that she talked about the future with Portago, who she claimed was saying he wanted to get a divorce. She also stated emphatically that she learned that it was quite routine for Portago to lie regularly about his relationship with his wife, and with other women. This becomes a regular pattern in the Portago story, repeated in the later relationship with Linda Christian. Nevertheless, she admits being smitten by Portago, and was not herself trying to divorce her husband Roger at the time anyway, hoping that Roger might take the initiative for this himself at some stage. During July 1952, Dorian accompanied Portago on a holiday to Crete in company with Ed Nelson, whom she called Gurner, and his then 'girl friend' Patsy Morgan-Dibbyn. She described Nelson as a person who had established himself as an 'unofficial valet secretary', though he was inclined to refer to himself as Portago's "homme d'affaires". (Leigh, 1980, p.102) She described Nelson as a thoroughly evil and amoral man who had a terrible influence on Portago, encouraging him to gamble what money he had, and his schemes to make money. The trip to Crete was apparently a cover for one of these schemes as somehow the pair had heard of hidden war booty on Crete in an old well. The scheme evaporated when they discovered that the supposed well had disappeared when a naval base had been built over it sometime after the war had ended.

Though Dorian Leigh was still married to Roger Mehle, she and Portago were together in New York and Paris late in 1952, and at one point he seems to have brought her to Biarritz while both his mother and wife were there. Carroll was now pregnant with their son. Portago and Dorian Leigh met again in the spring of 1953 and then she had become pregnant. She had had at least one abortion previously and decided that she must do this again, and had the pregnancy aborted at a clinic in Lausanne, Switzerland. She claims that Portago promised that a year from that time, they would both be divorced and they would have another child together. Leigh says both that she believed these promises and also suspected that he was lying, and continually making excuses to see his wife. She said she had assumed they were estranged, when clearly they weren't. Nevertheless, Leigh would remain closely involved with Portago through the remainder of 1953 and through 1954, and the relationship would get even more complex, and occasionally bizarre.

The Ferrari 340 MM as driven in the 1953 and 1954 Carrera races, as it is today.
(Credit - Birner)

Ferrari 340 MM Chassis 0286AM

Chassis 0286Am was built in early 1953 and made its debut at the Spa 24 Hours as a practice car for Villoresi, Carini, Ascari and Maglioli. Villoresi drove it at the Senigallia race in early August and was quickest but retired with an engine problem. Ascari and Farina then won the ADAC 1000 Kilometers at the Nurburgring with it. It was sold to Franco Cornacchia and then to Luigi Chinetti, who entered it for the Carrera Panamericana, with a full width windscreen added. When the fuel line broke on the second stage, Chinetti and de Portago ran out of allowed time. The car was repaired and Chinetti drove it to Mexico City where it was sold to Carlos Braniff. Conflicting reports argue that the car was always a 375 MM Spyder and always had a 375 engine, while others clearly labeled the car as a 340 MM with a bigger engine added at a later date. It was indeed a 340 MM.

Braniff raced the car briefly and it was sold to Alan Guiberson and was rebuilt for the 1954 Carrera. Phil Hill was second with it at March Air Force base race in early November and it then went to Mexico, where Hill and co-driver Richie Ginther won three of the eight stages and finished second overall. It was raced in 1955 by Carroll Shelby and Ken Miles, and sold in October to Lou Brero Sr. who raced it Nassau. When he died in April 1956, his son dissembled the car and it was stored until 1994. Bruce McCaw bought it in 1994, had it restored and Phil Hill won its first post-restoration race at the 1997 Monterey Historic races.

Though Portago apparently didn't like the notion of being a passenger in the Carrera, he was reported, again in several accounts, as going straight out and buying a 3-litre Ferrari which he would drive himself. This was more poetic or journalistic license as he had already ordered a car many months before in May 1953. This 250 MM was then sold to Franco-American race driver Harry Schell, who had become friendly with Portago while the Spaniard had started trying out the Panhard Monomille 850 cc. race cars, and was one of the participants. Schell lived in Paris, not far from Portago's Avenue Foch apartment. The car changed hands between the pair in December, after the Carrera Panamericana and it was Schell who entered it for them at Buenos Aires 1000 Kilometers on January 24, 1954.

While entries for this race were organised through the usual channels in Europe and Britain, the Argentinean organizers approached the SCCA, the Sports Car Club of America, for four entries, and when the SCCA put it 'out to tender' they were overwhelmed with 47 applications. The American drivers were still unknown beyond their own shores, but Phil Hill, Carroll Shelby, Bob Said and Masten Gregory were selected as the 'best of the Americans' at the time. Schell's Ferrari was listed in the pre-event publicity as being shared by " a Spaniard, de Portago".

The Buenos Aires race provides another good Portago 'myth', as the author views it in retrospect. As an indication of just what an inexperienced driver the marquis was, many subsequent biographies report the race as a serious problem for Schell who allegedly handed the car over to Portago while it was in second place and the 'newcomer' promptly dropped several spots. The reality was different, as the 36-car field had some very quick competitors in it. Maurice Trintignant and Louis Rosier were the early leaders as they pushed their fast 4.5-litre Ferrari to the front on the long stretches of the 9.6-kilometer circuit. Ian Stewart's Jaguar, Bonomi's Ferrari and Schell had all made good starts, but Schell was driving close to his practice time to keep up with the others. Phil Hill's 4.1 Ferrari was out early with gearbox trouble and Ian Stewart's Jaguar crashed, allowing Schell up a place. The Farina/Maglioli 4.5 Ferrari had sailed past Schell early on, and the Parnell/Salvadori Aston Martin DB3S also got past, but they retired just before the pit stops. Schell came in and needed to change tyres, but Trintignant had also lost time. So the Schell/Portago car was elevated briefly in the changeover but dropped to where it was before the stops began. The Autosport correspondent, Dr. Vincente Alvarez, made no mention of a so-called incident in which an angry Schell was supposed to have called Portago back in because he didn't know how to change gear. The Spaniard was reported as going 5 seconds a lap slower as he took over his stint, which is indeed a small margin on a long and dangerous circuit. The story goes on that Schell got back in the car, which is likely only when they made a second or third driver change. The smaller Ferrari finished three laps behind the big 4.5 of Farina and Maglioli, a very impressive result.

Ken Purdy (1957) attributed the information to Portago himself, having interviewed him at length at Sebring in 1957. He quoted Portago as confirming the story:

"Harry was so frightened that I would break the car he wouldn't teach me how to change gears, so when after 70laps (the race was 101 laps), he was tired and it was my turn to drive and after three laps, I saw Harry out in the middle of the track frantically waving a flag to make me come into the pits so that he could drive again. We eventually finished second overall and first in our class. I didn't learn to change gears properly until the chief mechanic of Maserati took me out and spent an afternoon teaching me." Purdy (1957) Portago himself said he didn't learn to change gear until he had bought his Maserati A6GCS.

Portago in his first major long distance race as a driver, the Buenos Aires 1000 Kilometers in 1954.
(Credit - V.Alverez/Whitefly)

The French magazine Automobile Historique seemingly quotes Nano Da Silva Ramos, a driver close to Schell as recounting the incident as having happened in practice, where Portago was some 30 seconds off Schell's pace, though less so in the race. The story in that account is that Portago was taken the day after the race to the parking lot of a large supermarket and taught to change gears, including finding reverse! (Automobile Historique, May 2004, p.35) Nigel Roebuck said that the incident had occurred in practice at Sebring, a few months after Buenos Aires in an article in Competition Car and elaborated on it in a later piece in Autosport, adding that the reason for this had been Portago's lack of interest in things mechanical and the fact that he had only driven American cars with automatic transmissions. Nigel Roebuck recently said to the author that he probably had drawn on the Ken Purdy material for that story, and was now more likely to accept that such tales could well have been inspired by Portago's own wish to impress an interviewer. Doug Nye (1985) seemed to draw on the Purdy quotes when he wrote about Portago, placing the event at Buenos Aires, but adding a "red flag" to Schell's appearance on the track to call the Spaniard in. The story appears in several other accounts, largely similar to Purdy's interview, with elaboration. Brock Yates (1986) acknowledges Purdy as his source, adding that it was Guerrino Bertocchi, who was indeed Maserati's chief racing mechanic, who became the tutor of gearshifting. One of the issues raised here is not only the accuracy of reports written after the fact, but something in Portago's own character which could not resist dramatizing many of the events in his life. Robert Daley will later describe Portago's love of having an audience for outrageous stories, and even Carroll Petrie confirmed that it would not surprise her at all to know that many of the stories had been seriously 'elaborated' for dramatic effect. "That's the way he was" was her view. Robert Daley seemed able to recognise when Portago was just telling "outrageous tales", and Ken Purdy on the other hand accepted the stories on face value.

Portago told the story of Buenos Aires to Bill Grauer and Barratt Walker: "I had met Harry Schell and we decided to go to Buenos Aires for the 1000 Kilometers race. Harry had been driving for about seven years and he seemed pretty much like god to me, but he wouldn't show me how to change gear, he wouldn't show me how to drive his car, he was terrified I'd break it in practice. The race was a 1000 kilometers and after about 700 kilometers, Harry was naturally a little tired and came into the pits, and said 'ok, now you drive it', and I got into the car, drove one lap, which was ten kilometers, and saw Harry out on the track with a red flag trying to make me stop because I was going slowly, so I stopped the next time and Harry got back into his car and finished the race in second position. That was my first race-two laps." (Riverside Records, 1957)

The author's view is that this is one of the 'outrageous stories' which Robert Daley would say Portago was so fond of telling. Portago had driven in practice with some degree of competence, and his race laps were slower than Schell's but competent. How could Schell have decided to step out onto the track before one lap had been completed? And Portago's distance in the race had been reduced from three laps in one account to one lap in this account.

Roy Salvadori recounted for the author an anecdote which also appeared in his own autobiography: " I was on my way out to the Buenos Aires race with the Aston Martin team, and I think we had just come back from Casablanca. I was on an Aerolineas Argentinas flight which had to make a stop at Lisbon because there was no radio operator. This didn't make John Wyer too happy, as you can imagine, and John got into a terrible row with the captain as no announcement had been made. I wanted to stay out of the way so I went and sat with what I thought was an Italian mechanic. He was rather scruffy but then he started to speak to me in three or four languages. I was very surprised he was going to Buenos Aires to drive a Ferrari. I then found out he was the Marquis de Portago...and very famous! Then to add to it, when our Aston retired in the race...I was driving with Reg Parnell...it was Schell and de Portago who took our second place."

When the Sebring 12 Hour previews started to appear in February, Portago was mentioned as Schell's upcoming co-driver at Sebring, as they had done so well at Buenos Aires, and there was no mention of the so-called gear-change incident. While one report in Autosport had the pair in the Ferrari they shared in South America, a slightly later one put them in the 2-litre class in a Maserati. While this was inaccurate, it is an indication that Portago had either decided to buy an A6GCS Maserati or had already done so. This would undermine accounts that Portago bought the smaller 2-litre Maserati after Sebring as he had been so overwhelmed by the speed of the bigger Ferrari as was reported in numerous later stories. In fact, Autosport of March 19 ran a news story in which it was revealed that Portago had ordered the very first of the new 1954 2-litre Maseratis and it was on its way to him. The 1954 car had improved brakes and suspension and was seen as a potential rival to Ferrari's 2-litre Mondial.

The Sebring race took place on a cool Sunday in Florida on March 7. The race, as in Mexico in November, was expected to be a Lancia walkover, and the Lancia team was there in full strength, with cars for Taruffi/Manzon, Fangio/ Castellotti , Ascari/Villoresi and Italian privateers Porfirio Rubirosa/Luigi Valenzano. Briggs Cunningham had a new 4.5 Ferrari for himself and John Fitch, and Bill Spear shared his similar car with Phil Hill. There were numerous

American-powered Allards and several Jaguars and Aston Martins, and a little OSCA for Stirling Moss and Bill Lloyd, reported as the first non-English car to have been driven by Moss.

The great Albert Ascari in practice at Sebring in 1954. *(Credit - Eveleth)*

Portago with Harry Schell before practice at Sebring in 1954, with the same car they raced to second in Buenos Aires. ***(Credit - Eveleth)***

At the 10.00am start, some of the 'American iron' got the jump on the fancied runners, but the Lancias and Ferraris scythed their way through to the front, Schell up amongst them in the early laps. By the end of the first hour, there had been dropouts, and a woman spectator had run across in front of one of the Briggs Cunningham cars and nearly became a tragic statistic, and the Lancias were in front. Taruffi/Manzon were first from Ascari/Villoresi, and Fangio/Castellotti, with Spear/Hill 4th and Schell/Portago 5th. After an hour and a half of racing Schell was in the pits, but not for a driver change. The Ferrari's rear axle had failed and the car was out before Portago could get a drive.

Another 'mythical' tale arose from the Sebring race, which again was repeated and repeated afterwards. Portago had told Bill Grauer and Barratt Walker that at Sebring they had trouble with the clutch and Harry thought they should take the clutch to pieces, and Portago agreed with him because he knew Schell had mechanical knowledge. Then when it was apart, Schell told Portago that he didn't know anything about mechanics. So they put it back together again and at the end of this process, they had 53 extra nuts and bolts. Portago said that the clutch didn't break, but the rear axle broke. The number of nuts and bolts tended to change as the story got retold, and it doesn't take a great deal of mechanical knowledge to know that, if there were 53 nuts and bolts in a clutch, and they weren't put back in, that the clutch would not work...but it was good meat for the legend!

Portago at Sebring with Dorian Leigh.
(Credit - Leigh)

As the race went on, the Italian tide began to turn, and one by one the Lancias ran into trouble. With the Fangio and Ascari cars gone, however, Taruffi held the lead by nine laps with an hour to go. The Moss/Lloyd OSCA had crept up to second on reliability and persistence but was a long way behind. Then the Lancia failed to show up, and eventually Taruffi appeared pushing it for over two miles. That gave a dramatic win to the OSCA and Moss, but the carefully driven Rubirosa/Valenzano Lancia was next. Taruffi was given 3rd but then protested for not having a working starter motor and the Macklin/Huntoon Austin Healey was 3rd. The winning OSCA had won overall and on the Index of Performance, causing serious embarrassment to the much larger and quicker works cars from Ferrari, Lancia and Aston Martin.

Rob Walker, long-time privateer entrant, later to become best known for the giant-slaying victories of Moss and Maurice Trintignant in little Coopers over an array of front-engine Grand Prix cars, was also working as a journalist. In his report to Motor Sport in June and July 1954, Walker gave an account of the social side of the Sebring race and a list of those staying at the 'fashionable' Harder Hall Hotel on the edge of the town of Sebring in central Florida. These included Wacky Arnolt, Tommy Wisdom, Morris Goodall, Harry Schell and Schell's driving partner, the Marquis de Portago, whom Walker referred to as "thrice European Steeplechase Champion". The Lancia team was based there as well and that included Fangio, Ascari, Taruffi, and Manzon, along with Porfirio Rubirosa.

Rob Walker admitted his surprise at the number of reporters present attempting to keep track of the romantic antics of Rubirosa and his own entourage. He also told of Lancia's dismay at receiving a massive two thousand pound hotel bill for the week, part of which was attributed to Piero Taruffi leaving his bath running every morning until it poured through the tiles onto the guests in the dining room below. Rob Walker didn't mention that Portago seemed to have a redhead in tow and that would have been Dorian Leigh.

After Sebring, Portago was back at home for the birth of his son Antonio on March 24, 1954. He would be known as Don Antonio Cabeza de Vaca y McDaniel. He would eventually assume the title Marquis de Portago on January 27, 1959. He would sadly die at an early age of 35 on March 6, 1990 in New York.

Motor Sport (June 1954) also carried an account of the Monthlery race meeting on April 25, which featured the Coupe de Paris. Portago wasn't at this meeting but the report carried details of the race for Panhard Monomille cars with 850 cc. engines. These cars were now popular and 30 French drivers were present to provide a thrilling show as the cars were flung about "with more enthusiasm than flare". This would appear to be the first reporting of the Monomille race series outside a French publication, not surprising as both British and American motoring journals tended to stick to largely national events when it came to the lesser categories.

Chassis 0390, the car Portago and Schell raced twice is still being raced in historic events today.

The Ferrari 250 MM, chassis 0390, as it is today. ***(Credit - Bernardi)***

Ferrari 250 MM Vignale Spider Series 2 Chassis 0390
Numerous reports have the Buenos Aires/Sebring car as chassis 0332, a similar car belonging to Oliviera and then sold to Pinto in Portugal. More detailed investigation indicates this is inaccurate and that the car was chassis 0390. Further confusion surrounds the original owner, which is listed as both Portago and Harry Schell. An American company, which owned the car at one time, argued that they had seen papers of origin which had Schell buying the car in November 1953 as a used, ex-works race car. The stronger evidence seems to support the view that in fact Schell bought it from Portago. After Sebring it was sold to Roger Bear in Florida and then raced spasmodically in the USA in 1954/55. The engine was swapped in 1971 after it had changed hands six times in the USA and had been left outdoors where the block cracked. It passed amongst several more owners and after full restoration, appeared in the retro Mille Miglia three times as well as other events, and is now in Japan.

By May 21, Autosport had stopped calling Portago the "Marquess de Portago" and the reference shifted to "Marquis", the occasion being the advance news that he would be returning to racing at Aintree on May 29, recalling that "several years back, he competed successfully on horseback; this time his mounts would be two Maseratis". (May 21, 1954, p.11) A week later the magazine announced that both Portago and Roy Salvadori would be in 2-litre Maseratis in the 30 mile sports car race, and they were also listed for the Aintree 200, the feature race for Formula Libre cars. Presumably this meant the same A6GCS models would be driven in both races. The issue was academic as for unspecified reasons, Portago and his new Maserati never turned up.

The Maserati's debut was then rescheduled for the Le Mans 24 Hours in mid-June. If there had been any truth in the stories that Portago had 'down-sized' to the Maserati to give himself a chance to get used to proper racing cars, then choosing Le Mans to start seems a bizarre choice, and it is much more likely that he fancied the new Maserati and bought it. Hans Tanner agreed with the view that choosing Le Mans as a place to learn a new car was somewhat strange. Tanner also reported that Portago had gone to Modena to pick up the new car and drove it through the Alps in bad weather just to get acquainted with it. He drove it to Paris, and then took it to Le Mans himself. He would drive it at Le Mans with the young Argentinean driver Carlos Tomasi, not Alessandro de Tomaso as some articles had it.

Lancia and Mercedez Benz decided not to enter at the French circuit, as did Alfa Romeo, though that was less surprising. Then the transporter carrying the works Maseratis had an accident on the way to France and was late, and the factory team was excluded by the organisers. This left Portago with the lone Maserati, something which would 'help to bring him' to the attention of the Maserati team. The race then looked certain to be a battle between Ferraris and Jaguars, with the Cunninghams considered to be an outside possibility. Rubirosa, fresh from his good second place at Sebring brought his Ferrari instead of a Lancia to be shared with Italian driver Baggio, though much more attention was being paid to Zsa Zsa Gabor, Rubirosa's then girl friend who was 'prominent' in the pits. Portago had decided to give himself a little extra night practice and was caught out when he lost concentration and spun, causing a fair bit of body damage. This left a great deal of work to be done before the start, and the car only just made it to the line.

Much to the French crowd's delight, first car away after the 57 drivers sprinted across the pit straight to their cars was the Talbot of Blanc, but he was swamped by Ferraris and the Cunningham before they even reached the Dunlop Bridge. At the end of lap one, the three wailing 4.9 Ferraris of Marzotto, Gonzales and Manzon sped past in a red blur with a short gap to another blur, this time green as Moss, Rolt and Wharton went by in Jaguars. Wharton already had a dent, and then came the white and blue Cunningham-entered Ferrari, Aston Martin, Talbot, Cunningham and all the rest. The lead pack was rushing down the long Mulsanne Straight at 180 mph.

The Maserati A6GCS in practice at Le Mans.
(Credit - Petrie Collection)

A trio of Bristols held British hopes high in the 2-litre class but in the first hour they were being led comfortably by the Maserati of Portago. Rain had started shortly after the flag had dropped and the Spaniard was going quickly and competently in what was his first race in the wet, certainly his first important one. After the first fuel stops, one of the Bristols moved into the class lead, and then at four hours it was a Gordini which was in front in this group, though the black and yellow Maserati of Portago sounded and looked very strong. Portago had adapted the Spanish national colours for his own use, emphasizing the black which seemed to favour in his own attire. Three Ferraris led the race overall but Stirling Moss was right with, and occasionally, amongst them. At quarter distance the rain eased and darkness fell. A Bristol was back at the head of the 2-litre group, though Portago grabbed that spot back around the 8th hour. Then shortly before half distance, the Bristols were 1-2-3 in the class as the Portago/Tomasi Maserati ground to a permanent halt with no oil pressure. That was the end of a promising Le Mans debut. If the Maserati was indeed purchased as an easy car to become accustomed to racing with, then it either had worked or the whole notion of playing himself into racing had been abandoned by Portago. Even in the early days of his motor racing, he went as quickly as he could. There really wasn't ever a question of taking it easy. Portago/Tomasi had moved up from 27th at the end of the first hour to 26th at the end of the second, and then were 23rd, 21st, 19th, 16th, 18th, 16th, 14th and 14th at the end of the tenth hour until their retirement just before the halfway point. Another interesting point is that Ed Nelson was listed as a third driver for the Maserati, but there is no evidence that he actually drove it. (Wimpffen, 1999)

Carlo Tomassi in Portago's Ferrari at Le Mans 1954.
(Credit - Petrie Collection)

The Ferrari of Trintignant/Gonzales went on to record a fine win from the Jaguar C-Type of 1953 winners Rolt and Hamilton, with the amazing Spear/Johnston 5.5-litre Cunningham in 3rd. The difference between the first two cars was less than two minutes, and most spectators and motor racing people present felt they had seen the best ever Le Mans race as the Jaguar pursued the Ferrari in the pouring rain.

On June 26, with most of the significant sports car drivers in Italy for the Supercortemaggiore Grand Prix, won by Mike Hawthorn's Ferrari Monza 750S, Portago was at Metz for the Metz Sports Car Grand Prix. He took the Maserati, repaired after the Le Mans engine trouble, and won the event on the tight circuit at 82.697 kph from the Maserati of George Monneret. It is rather unfortunate that Portago's first reasonably significant race victory seemed to elude almost every motoring journal, and virtually no details were ever reported. The field was not particularly competitive, but a victory was evidence of a level of skill that was far in excess of what had been reported only a few short months before. Hans Tanner said that the car had been taken to Modena to be repaired after the problems at Le Mans, and Tomasi had the job of driving the car from Modena across the Alps to Metz. He encountered a big snowstorm in the mountains, rain coming through France and arrived at Metz an hour before the race was due to start. Portago had packed and was ready to leave for Paris by train, thinking the car wasn't coming. He had not practiced, nor even seen the circuit before the race started. He was in the lead after only five laps. Tanner says Portago drank some champagne at the victory celebration, the last time he would do so.

A week later, on July 4, Portago brought the Maserati to Reims for the 12 Hours, having contacted veteran Louis Chiron to partner him in this grueling sports car event. The race started at midnight, and this year rain had set in just before the start and continued on and off for the entire 12 Hours. Whereas Le Mans was dangerous mainly for the great difference in speed between the cars, at least the drivers had a chance to get used to driving before night fell. Not at Reims. It started well after dark, and the weather conditions made it a fraught contest throughout. Oddly, though there were many incidents, none were serious. Stirling Moss in the Jaguar had caught up the rear of the field in only fifteen minutes of racing.

A poster advertising the Reims 12 Hours race in July 1954.

Portago and Chiron were well down the field at the start, and sensibly both decided to stick to a conservative pace. They had managed to work themselves up to 9th spot behind the Loyer and Rinen Gordini at the halfway point. Progress continued as Picard's Ferrari moved into the lead of the 2-litre class, ahead of the three Bristol coupes, which were running as consistently as they had at Le Mans. With less than an hour to go, the Maserati engine faltered and Portago/Chiron became the very last car to drop out before the finish. They had gotten up to third in the two-litre class, a significant achievement as Portago and Chiron were running the car with almost no assistance from mechanics. Ed Nelson and some friends were on hand to do the refueling and tyre changes. All were greatly disappointed when the car arrived in the pits with an hour to go, in a cloud of smoke, and the Maserati was retired without the bonnet being opened.

Maserati A6GCS-Chassis 2076

The Portago Maserati has always been something of a mystery car. It was completed on May 29, 1954 and delivered to Portago for Le Mans, with engine number 2057. The car only did the few races in the Spaniard's hands and its subsequent history is unclear. One car emerged recently in Jersey claiming to be 2076 but there is no confirmation of this.

This series of the A6GCS saw 52 cars built between 1953 and 1955, with the inline six cylinder engine and a displacement of 1985 cc, producing 170 bhp. At 830 kg. the cars were quick, had a top speed of 146 mph and very popular amongst especially Italian privateers.

The German Grand Prix was run at the famed Nurburgring on August 1, and though Portago by now had Grand Prix ambitions according to interviews he gave later, he was there to take part in the supporting sports car race for cars up to 1500 cc., the Rhineland Cup. He had been discouraged by the unreliability of the Maserati after Le Mans and Reims, and pressed his mother for funds to buy another car, which in some ways was an equally illogical choice, an OSCA MT4. One report says that the OSCA was a present to Portago from his mother. The race looked to be between four twin-cam Porsches with some good Porsche drivers including Hans Hermann, von Frankenberg and von Hanstein, new Lotus cars, one of which was being driven by Colin Chapman himself, and the two OSCAs. The other OSCA was driven by Wolfgang Seidel but Portago had a brand new 8-plug head in his car.

The Portago OSCA at the Rhineland Cup at the Nurburgring in 1954, where it ended upside down. *(Credit - Archive Fodisch)*

Alfonso de Portago made a statement about just how good a driver he was by posting a stunning sixth fastest qualifying time on his very first glimpse of the 14-mile Nurburgring circuit in the Eifel Mountains of Germany. He would later recount that this experience made him fall in love with racing at the Nurburgring, the circuit he thought was the best in the world, and the one which challenged the driver more than any other. He did manage to sustain a damaged axle in practice, and this was repaired with the help of the East German EMW team in their mobile workshop. Hans Hermann went into the lead of the 100-mile race in his Porsche from von Hanstein and Portago, who sat on the German's tail as this trio left the others behind. As von Frankenberg and Polensky caught up with Portago on the fourth of seven long laps, the fighting got fraught. Portago pushed far too hard to stay ahead, went off and turned the OSCA over. He didn't actually damage the car very much or himself at all but was bitterly disappointed. Hans Tanner added to this tale in an article in Motor Racing : "In the Nurburgring race Portago was right up with the Porsches on the twisting parts of the circuit, only to lose ground on the straight. Halfway through the race he overdid things and crashed in the Schwalbenschwanz. He was taken off to hospital, but could see no reason for such action and had a fight with the ambulance driver, dumping him in the back and driving the ambulance to the Ring. He spent the rest of the day with a smirk on his face and a bare bottom showing through a large tear in his trousers." (Tanner in Motor Racing June 1957, p.151)

It was a full month before the next event, the Tour de France which would begin on September 3 and take nine days to complete on September 12. In his relatively short career, Portago had already taken part in five difficult long distance races, an unusual feat for someone new to motor racing and something that was not particularly noticed at the time nor in subsequent discussions of his career.

Portago during practice for the 1954 Tour de France. ***(Credit - Autopresse)***

The 1954 Tour was the fourth in the series and this one would begin and end at Nice and cover no less than 6000 kilometers in three stages with nine separate tests of very different types and degrees of difficulty. There was a complex though well thought out handicap formula in relation to engine size and this made it a contest where smaller cars could do very well. 124 cars started, comprising three groups of touring and special series touring cars, series or production sports cars and Gran Turismo cars, and a virtually free class for sports cars where it was thought the eventual winner would come. Two sports Gordinis, much as they had appeared at Le Mans, took the early initiative as the cars left Nice and headed west to Pau before turning up the coast. They turned inland to Le Mans and then back out to Brest before going all the way to Dunkerque. Then the surviving field, after a day's rest at Brest, turned south to Roubaix. Pollet's 2.5-litre Gordini had a long hard battle with the 3-litre Gordini of Guelfi for almost the entire first seven days of the event, holding the first two places outright, with only three penalty points between them. After the last of the special stages, the cars were on the road sections to the finish and at this point Guelfi's navigator made a mistake and they went an incredible 180 kilometers off course, and Pollet won.

And where was Portago during all of this? He was being co-driven for the first time by his friend Ed Nelson in the OSCA, which had been repaired after the Nurburgring accident. It seemed a wise choice of car as the good performance of the small engine cars could produce good results on the road and competitive sections, even though it was running in the large sports group. The pair was right up with the 1953 winner Peron and then managed to take the lead by stint of some very hard driving. When they got to the Peyresoude Hillclimb, they were changing the spark plugs and broke one in half. They were in the infuriating position of being unable to remove the lower portion of the plug, and they were out.

Edmund Gurner Nelson gets his first opportunity to co-drive with Portago at the 1954 Tour de France.
(Credit - Autopresse)

In late November, from the 19th to the 23rd, it was again time for Carrera Panamericana. Portago had obviously not been put off the race itself by his unpleasant experience as Chinetti's passenger the previous year. However, he obviously decided not to put anyone else in the same position as he had been. Whether this was a tactical choice to save weight in the car, or was prompted by some other motivation is just unknown. He had taken Ed Nelson with him on the Tour de France, though the need for a navigator was slightly more significant in the French event, given that arrival at and departure from time controls was an essential part of being competitive in that event. He also went to the Ferrari factory to purchase an ex-works 735S with body by Scaglietti. This car had in fact been the Trintignant/ Gonzales 2nd place car at the Monza Supercortemaggiore race in late June, and then Gonzales and Masten Gregory were to race it at the Tourist Trophy at Dundrod. The Northern Irish race was a disaster as they crashed it in practice and didn't start. It seems likely that Portago had already done the deal with Ferrari at Monza in June. This car was chassis 0428M. What horrified the staff at Ferrari was the sight of Portago attacking the Ferrari with a large paintbrush, used for painting houses, and a can of black paint!

Portago gets ready to be one of the early starters of the 1954 Carrera Panamericana.
(Credit - Autopresse)

V
PANAMERICAN
RACE
MEXICO
INTERNATIONAL COMPETITION
MEX. $ 1,465,000.00 IN PRIZES
NOVEMBER 19 — 23, 1954

Portago gives an interview as he drives up to the start line.
(Credit - Author's Collection)

The fifth Panamericana was again the final round in the 1954 World Sports Car Championship. As usual, the race had a number of tragedies, and this year two drivers and two service crewmembers were killed on the way to the start. There were no works Lancias, Mercedes or even works Ferraris this year, partly in recognition of the fatal accidents in 1953. However, there was a locally sponsored 4.9 for Umberto Maglioli, a 4.5 for Phil Hill...the same car Chinetti had driven with Portago in 1953, and another 4.5 for Jack McAfee. Chinetti was back in a 4.5 Ferrari. Roberto Mieres and Louis Chiron had agile 1.5-litre OSCAs, and Giovanni Bracco showed up in a 3-litre Ferrari, having said that he would not race in Mexico again after the death of Bonetto. The draw was just too much for these drivers to resist, or as Bracco said many times "some of us can not think about it."

Portago and Roberto Mieres, who he had met in Europe, teamed up to practice for the Carrera, and Portago said later that they did 12,000 kilometers to learn the route. Their respective 200 kilometers and 180 kilometers in the event itself would prove frustrating after learning the route so well.

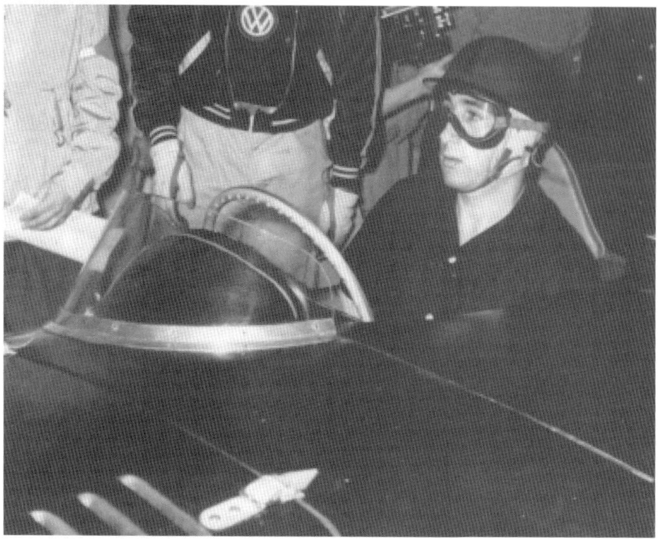

Portago shows some strain before the start.
(Credit - Arzamendia)

Chinetti talks to spectators at the 1954 Carrera.

Phil Hill and co-driver Richie Ginther won the rugged first stage to Oaxaca but McAfee rolled the Ferrari, injuring himself and killing co-driver Ford Robinson. Before this, Portago had overtaken McAfee, which was the only other car to start before him. Then a piston burned because of the poor quality of the local fuel, something which affected the other four-cylinder Ferraris. Mieres was well up overall in the little OSCA and a large number of Alfa Romeo 1900 saloon cars were managing to threaten the much larger Lincolns. The OSCA Mieres was driving was in fact the same car which Portago had used at the Nurburgring and in the Tour de France. Some reports have this car as having been purchased by the Argentine driver. When the author spoke to him, he was his usual immensely open and friendly self, fully acknowledging he just couldn't remember: "I wouldn't have paid money for that, would I?" Portago himself said he had sold the car immediately after the Tour de France.

Maglioli's winning Ferrari.
(Credit - Arzamendia)

Long-time Alfa Romeo test driver and once a member of the factory Grand Prix team, Consalvo Sanesi, was leading the class for the smaller production saloons. Rubirosa's Ferrari didn't manage the first stage. Maglioli managed to reverse positions at the front on stage two, but Hill managed to turn it round again on the next stage, with Palacio's amazing Spanish Pegaso in 3rd and achieving mind-blowing speeds on the straight sections. On the next run from Mexico City to Leon, the leading 2-litre Borgward of Bechem managed to tangle with the Pegaso and both cars were destroyed. Then on stage five, a second Borgward hit a huge vulture at full speed, and Mieres experienced mechanical problems and had off-road excursions putting him out. Some reports of the period quoted Portago as saying, on the way back to civilisation, that he was already thinking of the next Carrera. His lack of success seemed only to have the effect of encouraging him to work harder.

The amazing Pegaso crash from which the driver walked away. ***(Credit - Arzamendia)***

Palacios Pegaso after its huge crash.
(Credit - Arzamendia)

This is Phil Hill and Richie Ginther in the same car Chinetti/Portago shared in 1953.
(Credit - Arzamendia)

Cornacchia's Ferrari goes over the finish line.
(Credit - Arzamendia)

Ferraris took the first four places at the finish, with Maglioli 24 minutes ahead of Hill, and Cornacchia was 3rd in front of Chinetti. Maglioli had taken half an hour off Fangio's previous best and had averaged 107 mph for over 1900 miles…on open road. The very existence of such a race made it easy to believe that racing drivers of the time were something of a superhuman breed, a myth many of them quietly cultivated. Portago, like many other drivers of the period, would not miss a chance to talk about the 'nearness of death', especially if a journalist was around to listen.

Portago was still relatively unknown in the motor racing world at the time, though his other exploits were the subject of discussion and gossip in society columns and amongst the French social set, and he was well known of course as an accomplished amateur flat and steeplechase rider. It isn't recorded whether any of the other Carrera competitors knew or cared that Dorian Leigh had managed to be present at the beginning of the Mexican event.

Dorian's second marriage was now coming to an end and she claimed that Portago had had a number of discussions with her before the Mexican race about an impending divorce. She said he thought he should get divorced from Carroll and they would get married, though by then Dorian knew that Portago was consistently dishonest with her about his relationship with his wife. Dorian had arranged with her lawyer, Paul O Dwyer in New York, to procure a divorce in Mexico. She saw this as very convenient as the Spaniard had recently told her he was going to do the Mexican race. She encouraged him to do the event, reiterating a claim that she had been at least partly responsible for his move up to 'bigger racing cars'. She felt that her love of eating in France was partly responsible for Portago's significant weight gain and his resulting decision to give up racing horses.

Dorian had made arrangements to do modeling work in Mexico while sorting out the divorce and after the race the plan allegedly was to spend Christmas in Yardley in Bucks County, Pennsylvania where Dorian lived at least part of the time with her three children. However, Portago came to see her in Paris before departing for Mexico, and tried to talk her out to going to Mexico. His reasoning was that the race would be impossible for her to follow and that they would be unable to meet. This was largely true, though his motives may have been different. After an argument, in which she said she was committed to the Mexican visit for work and the divorce, they agreed to meet in Juarez after the race and the divorce had been settled. Dorian showed up before the start, taking Portago by surprise. She reflected that she was fairly certain that he didn't want her there, and added that his mother was also present for the start. Dorian then flew to the Oaxaca checkpoint, but discovered that Fon had retired. When they met, he encouraged her to fly to Mexico City where they could meet after he had helped to make arrangements for the transport of the car. She also discovered that Carroll was in Mexico, watching the race by helicopter as a guest of the Mexican president, Miguel Aleman. Dorian's memoirs reveal her view that Fon hadn't wanted her there because it would cause problems between him and his mother. Her argument was that Fon had to get his mother to finance the race for him, and that Carroll was there as evidence that their marriage was not in difficulty. Carroll Petrie told the author very firmly that a divorce had not been on the cards at this or any other time.

Whatever the complexities were, Portago was staying in a Mexico City hotel with Dorian when her divorce was finalised on November 24. On that day, according to Dorian, Portago took her to an elderly Mexican judge who had agreed to perform a marriage ceremony of sorts, in spite of its lack of legality. She claimed he was doing this as a means of persuading her that his long-term attentions towards her were serious. She also admits that she treated this as something of a joke, but nevertheless went through with it. She admits that she was indeed persuaded by this somewhat bizarre tactic, and shortly afterwards she claims that they traveled to Pennsylvania where they spent most of December with her children. Whatever the truth of Dorian Leigh's recollection is, it appears she did later refer to herself as the 'Marquesa de Portago Dorian Leigh', references being made to her 'title' in gossip and news items in the 1960s.

"Mrs. Cliff Robertson (Dina Merrill) and Mrs. John Hay (Betsy) Whitney have signed up as co-chairmen of next fall's City Mission Society annual ball which will commemorate the 155th anniversary of New York's oldest charity. Shown around a Harry Winston jewelry collection, an original Givenchy line will be flown from Paris complete with mannequins under the direction of Sally (Mrs. Mundy) van der Meersch and the Marquise de Portago who as Dorian Leigh was one of the top mannequins of all time herself and who, in recent years, started Paris' first model agency a la John Robert Powers (who used to live in Locust Valley)." (Locust Valley Leader, July 20, 1967, p.9) A report in the same paper on November 24, 1966 had also reported another Mission Society benefit as having been under the "Marquise de Portago Dorian Leigh".

Dorian Leigh goes to great lengths to demonstrate that Portago was now in a long-term relationship with her. She claims he even said he was tired of depending on his mother and on Dorian for money, and even considered that he might take a job as a mechanic in a garage in Yardley. This seems highly unlikely on several counts, one being Portago's legendary lack of mechanical ability. The other doubt surrounds Leigh's claims that Portago was with her in Pennsylvania for most of December, in fact until sometime in January, and makes no mention of the fact that he would have headed to Nassau in the Bahamas.

OSCA MT4 Chassis 1142

This 1500 cc.OSCA was completed on March 17, 1954 and was delivered to the Italian driver Giulio Cabianca, with engine number 1501. Cabianca took it to the Corsa Sulla Torrichelle eleven days later on March 28, winning the class and finishing third overall. On April 4, Cabianca and Roghi drove in the Giro de Sicilia but retired. In April 11 Cabianca won the 2000 cc. class at the Coppa Della Toscana, and he then drove in the Mille Miglia on May 2, finishing second in class. He retired in the Targa Florio on May 30, and again in the Imola Grand Prix on June 20. On July 11, Cabianca was 2nd overall and 2nd in class in the Coppa D'Oro Delle Dolomiti, and then was sold to Portago for the German race and the Tour de France. After Mieres drove 1142 in the Carrera Panamericana, it was returned to Giannino Parravicini in Milan. It seems to have been sold to Robert Jenny in Switzerland in 1956 and then to Peter Kaus. Its current location is uncertain.

The first Bahamas Speed Weeks was the result of a long effort by a number of Bahamians and others to bring more tourists and tourist money to the Islands. The history is recorded in Terry O'Neil's excellent book The Bahamas Speed Weeks, and the author is indebted to him for the depth and detail of his research on the Nassau races. No one has ever managed to track down the details from those heady years, either the race results or the social antics to any significant degree, and Terry O'Neil has now mastered this formidable task.

Portago at Nassau 1955.
(Credit - Terry O'Neil Collection)

Sixty invitations were sent out by the organising committee, led most actively by Sherman 'Red' Crise. Not long before the event was due to take place, very few confirmations had been received and it looked for a time that the event would have to be cancelled. This probably would have meant that we wouldn't be discussing this now, as it seems likely that failure at the first hurdle would have put an end to the ambitious plans. A number of locals and bike racers had been invited, the locals to help guarantee support for the event. As word began to get out, one hundred requests for an entry were received from uninvited racers, and the committee was in a quandary as to what to do. This interest pushed the invitees to start responding and 52 confirmations arrived for races on the 3.5-mile Windsor Field course. Windsor Field was an ex-RAF base in WWII and suited the endeavour for its first attempt at being a racecourse.

Most of the 'overseas' cars arrived from Miami on December 7 on the SS Queen of Nassau. The parties had already started on board and were going at a serious pace. Portago was aboard. He was with his wife in one cabin, and Dorian Leigh was in another, according to reports at the time, though this was never mentioned by Dorian Leigh herself. Whether either ever knew of each other's presence was something the author was unable to ascertain, if the story was indeed true. Some sources have argued that there had been another woman in attendance at Nassau who bore a resemblance to Leigh but was not her!

All drivers were given a practice day to find their way round the unfamiliar circuit. There were complaints about the abrasive surface, the location of heavy marker drums, the lack of an Index of Performance award and the fact that races would be run in different directions. As part of the committee's first attempt, these were all dealt with, and everyone was apparently pretty happy as they went off for the first of many, many Nassau parties. It had been decided that all the races would be run counter-clockwise to avoid confusion, and extra changing of gear ratios.

Half a dozen of the entries had been recently raced in Mexico at the Carrera Panamericana, including what was described as Portago's Ferrari Monza 750S, which had arrived with its engine still requiring a rebuild which was accomplished locally by two Italian mechanics. This car caused confusion for Ferrari fans then and later, because the car had started out life as a Scaglietti-bodied 735S and had been fully updated to 750 Monza specifications. There were several days of practice and high-speed time trials with the first official competitions starting on Friday, with motorcycles first, followed by a production car race for local residents, and then high-speed trials. Erwin Goldschmidt, owner of the Ferrari which Umberto Maglioli had been driving in Mexico was quickest at just over 150 mph.

Saturday afternoon saw 5-lap heats in preparation for the upcoming Nassau Trophy Race. Amongst the larger cars, the battle was purely between the Ferrari 375 MM of Masten Gregory from Kansas, and the Ferrari of Portago, and the Spaniard finished a car-length behind the American, some distance ahead of the Allard-Chrysler of Donald Rose. Goldschmidt's Ferrari had retired with a wheel bearing failure.

The first important race, the Bahamas Automobile Club race, was next on the programme with 46 starters to fight over 30 laps...and with a Le Mans start. Some reports noted that there was at least one instance of more than one driver attempting to get into the same car! Neither Portago nor Gregory made particularly fast starts but Gregory was soon in the lead, and Fon had soon got on his tail, with Goldschmidt behind having a battle royal with the much smaller Porsche of Huschke von Hanstein. Gregory was forced to stop after 15 laps with a puncture, which let Portago pick up nearly a minute's lead. Gregory got back past the other Ferrari of Goldschmidt and the Porsche, but his brakes were going and there was no way he could catch Portago. As it was December, the light was going as fast as the cars and there were some very close calls. Portago's victory instantly made him a Nassau 'regular', having won the first major race of the new event. It also gained him his first positive international publicity as a racing driver, something that was quite important to him at the time. Possibly more importantly, he gained the respect of the other professional drivers, though there were relatively few of them at the debut of racing at Nassau.

Portago races closely with Masten Gregory at Nassau 1954.
(Credit - Terry O'Neil Collection)

The main race of the new Speed Weeks was the 210-mile Nassau Trophy Race to take place on Sunday. A number of cars were in trouble after the tough Saturday 30-lapper had taken its toll on the hard and demanding surface. Goldschmidt was out with his Ferrari irreparable, but Luigi Chinetti had arranged for a quantity of spares to be on hand for the Ferraris. This didn't look like it was going to be of help to Masten Gregory whose Ferrari 375 MM needed new brake drums, and these weren't in the Chinetti spares depot. However, a very sporting Portago handed over his spare set so Gregory could race. This is the first reported example of the Marquis' sporting generosity, of which there were several later episodes, in perhaps a more generous and slightly less serious and less 'professional' era. Another characteristic example of racing in the 1950s.

Portago and Gregory shake hands after one of their very close races at Nassau 1954. *(Credit - Autosport)*

After another Le Mans start, Gregory was away first and the Spaniard was involved in a tussle with the first half dozen cars until he broke clear and set out after Gregory. The Kansas driver was setting a quick but smooth pace to save his tyres in this longer race. Portago was quicker but had worn his tyres down by the 50-lap stage and was forced in for a change. The mechanics then managed to get the jack stuck under the car and two minutes were lost in the process. Fon was able to lap some six seconds quicker than Masten Gregory but he had too much ground to make up. The 4000 spectators, however, were thrilled by the performance and the result was well appreciated, with von Hanstein again doing well to come third in the Porsche and winning on Index. Some 59 trophies were awarded during the long and elaborate post-race party and dinner, and in spite of teething troubles, the Speed Weeks looked set to continue in the future. Alfonso de Portago had done his reputation as a driver no harm at all. What was going on behind the scenes, however, remains open to speculation.

If the Dorian Leigh memoirs are to be believed, Portago may have joined her in the USA after Nassau, though it would also appear that he was visiting with his own family at this time as well. Dorian alleged during this period in December that Fon had told her that his mother had offered him $200,000 not to see Dorian for a year, and that this was what prompted his comment about being tired of living on his mother's money. This was when he allegedly said that he would get a job in a garage as a mechanic in Yardley, Pennsylvania, and that he might start his own garage because he was very good at tuning cars. This is something that most motoring writers and mechanics would be amazed at, some saying that he knew nothing about cars, and had only driven large American machines with automatic transmissions. Portago would later say, more than once, if he ever wanted to frighten the Ferrari team mechanics, he would pick up a screwdriver and walks towards the car! All part of the legend.

MOTOR RACING - 1955

In January 1955, Portago returned to Paris where, according to Dorian Leigh, he was going to sort out a divorce with his wife Carroll. Dorian was now pregnant for the second time by Portago, the first pregnancy having ended in abortion, but also with a promise from Fon that they would have a child together in the future. Clearly, Dorian Leigh was unable to learn from her previous disastrous relationships, and another disaster was seemingly on the way. She claims in her autobiography that Fon was assuring her from Paris that progress was being made, and that Carroll had retained the well-known and later somewhat infamous lawyer Roy Cohn in New York to find a way of breaking the trust set up by Portago's mother for her two grandchildren.

Sometime between Nassau in 1954 and Sebring, Portago had gone to visit Enzo Ferrari in an attempt to get a works drive. While some reports say that he brashly demanded to be in the works team, Portago's later description indicated that he felt that Enzo Ferrari simply rejected the attempt mainly on the grounds that he had not heard of Nassau and therefore gave little credit for what Portago had done there, and Portago went away to continue driving on his own.

In March, entries were announced for the Sebring 12 Hours, and this time Portago was listed with his Ferrari Monza 750S (chassis 0482M) again, to be co-driven this time by Umberto Maglioli. Autosport, in its preview, mentioned that on the same weekend as Sebring, the Grand Prix of Dakar would be taking place in Senegal, with supporting races for Panhard Monomilles, the same cars in which Portago had some of his early races.

Sebring became something of a debacle. While the race was held on March 13, the results were not confirmed until March 21, after a number of protests were filed immediately after the race finished. In incredibly hot conditions, the race looked promising. Many more Europeans had shown up for the second running of this race in central Florida, and a number of improvements had been made to the isolated ex-military airfield facilities. Stirling Moss, as was to become his custom, was first away from the Le Mans start in the Austin-Healey 100-6 he was sharing with Lance Macklin. He was soon swamped by the bigger cars, and Mike Hawthorn went into the lead in the Briggs Cunningham-entered D-Type Jaguar from Bob Said's Ferrari and the Portago Ferrari. Frenchman Jean Redele's little Renault went end over end near the pits on only the second lap, and just as Said seemed to have the measure of the Jaguar, he came upon the Renault and crashed into the arriving ambulance. This allowed Portago into second place ahead of several theoretically faster Ferraris, though he was later overtaken by Piero Taruffi while holding off Phil Hill. The Spaniard was indeed driving with noticeable skill. Several laps into the race, Taruffi moved in on Hawthorn and Portago was right on his tail.

After two hours, Portago came in to hand over to Maglioli. Only seven cars were on the lead lap, the Ferrari being one of them. Just before Maglioli was due in at the four hour mark, he had been having gear selection problems, and ended up pushing the car into the pits. Portago went out but it wasn't long before he was caught out and ended up off the road in the sand. That was the end of his race, which was eventually won by Hawthorn and Phil Walters in the D-Type Jaguar. For the second international race meeting in succession, Portago had been a front runner, competing with the Jaguar and Ferrari and this did not go unnoticed.

Luigi Chinetti is seen in the Ferrari pit with Portago at Sebring 1954. ***(Credit - D.Gaffney/RSC Archive)***

Portago's Ferrari is shown off the road, stuck in the sand bank on the outside of the corner, and Portago is about to get out of the car.
(Credit - Autosport)

Portago had been seen several times at Sebring in the company of Dorian Leigh, which did not register with most people and was taken for granted by others as they had supposedly been together at Nassau as well. Though there is little evidence other than Dorian Leigh's own comments, he rarely introduced her to people he knew, possibly because she was already very well known, or because he would not acknowledge that they were 'together'. Behind the scenes, their relationship was difficult and getting more complicated, at least as far as she later described it in her autobiography.

Ferrari 735 Sport Scaglietti Spyder Chassis 0482M
In the races in which Portago ran this car, the 1954 Carrera Panamericana, Nassau and Sebring 1955, it was consistently reported as a Monza 750S, and has been described above as such for simplicity. However, this was inaccurate, as there was far more to this car than met the eye of the observer. When Portago bought it, apparently with the involvement and aid of Luigi Chinetti, it had already had an awesome history. When it first appeared in 1953, it had a differently shaped Autodromo-built body, simpler and without a bonnet blister. It was raced at the GP dell' Autodromo at Monza on June 23, 1953 by Alberto Ascari, who had a relatively minor accident when overtaking another car. It was then rebodied by Scaglietti, and in August raced in the Senigallia GP with Maglioli driving. In June 1954, Froilan Gonzales and Maurice Trintignant shared the car at the Supercortemaggiori Grand Prix at Monza, and then in September Gonzales was back in it with Masten Gregory this time for the Dundrod Tourist Trophy, where they had a crash in practice. It was returned to the factory where it was rebuilt, the body now being very similar to the 'standard' 750 Monza body, and it was generally up-graded to 750 Monza specifications. Portago had ordered the car sometime earlier, and it was painted in his favoured black colours for the Carrera Panamericana. After Sebring, it was sold to an American, Sterling Edwards, who had it for many years, though it had a Chevrolet engine in place. He raced it twice on the old Pebble Beach road course in 1955. It passed to Bob Witmer in 1979, then to Will Haible in 1984 who ran it in the Monterey Historic races that year and in the 1989 retro Mille Miglia. It would have appeared to have been restored with its original 735S engine sometime after 1994.

While there is little detail about the way in which Alfonso de Portago made his plans to go racing in 1954-1955, it was apparent from his actions what he was doing and how serious he was. Before Sebring, he had some discussions with the Ferrari factory, mainly through the intercession of Luigi Chinetti, and made it clear that he wanted a Grand Prix car. While Enzo Ferrari was willing to sell cars to *almost* anyone, he had a very patronising and critical view of most drivers, especially those he had not nurtured himself. He was traditionally sarcastic about wealthy sportsman, though fairly happy to take their money. Against this backdrop, he agreed to sell what appeared to be a new Grand Prix 625 for use by Portago, though it was another older Ferrari, which had been upgraded, as we shall see a bit later. That didn't mean it was not potentially competitive as it was standard procedure at Ferrari to re-build, often with a new chassis, older models with up-dated features. This car was one of the F2 500 models, chassis 0208F, which had been brought up to 625 specs.

Portago entered it for the Gran Premio del Valentino in Turin's Valentine Park on March 27, 1955. It appears in the entry confusingly as chassis 625-7 and as a Type 555F1, which it certainly wasn't. The 625-7 designation would appear to have been the series of chassis numbers Ferrari itself used to tell the cars apart. Portago's car was originally 0208F, a 500 chassis number, and would later be re-stamped 0540! This is of course an issue for historians and didn't matter a damn to people at the time, and presumably didn't matter that much to the owner. One would like to know, however, what the reactions of some wealthy owners were when they later discovered they had paid 'new' money for a well-used car! Portago was there to make his Grand Prix debut, and that was what mattered to him. It wasn't a World Championship round, but for the Spaniard it would be his first significant single-seater race, and against truly tough opposition. Motor Sport described Portago's car as a new model, with a slightly longer wheelbase than the other 625s and a 4-speed rather than a 5-speed gearbox.

Valentine Park was a true circuit of the period, running through the park on the banks of the River Po in central Turin, with some of the nearby roads used as well. The crowds were close to the action and it was a major sporting event to have a Grand Prix in a city centre. A very early post-war motor race had been run here in 1946, won by Achille Varzi in an Alfa Romeo.

Other Ferraris were in the hands of 1950 World Champion Nino Farina (625), Maurice Trintignant (625), Harry Schell (625), all works team entries, whereas Portago was entered by himself. Lorenzo Girard had an old F500 in original F2 form, and Berardo Taraschi in an even older 166/F2 Ferrari. The works Maserati opposition was provided by Sergio Mantovani, Jean Behra, Cesare Perdisa, Luigi Musso and Roberto Mieres, all in new 250Fs, with Louis Rosier and Prince Bira in their own 250Fs and two older privateers. Ferrari expected the opposition to come from the Maseratis but three factory Lancia D-50s appeared for Ascari, Eugenio Castellotti and Gigi Villoresi. Only Mercedes and Gordini were missing amongst the manufacturers, and the Germans were only doing Championship races.

Sheldon and Rabagliati (1987, p.69) mention Portago among the welcome new faces but describe him as someone who "came to motor racing with a great reputation from practically every other sport it is possible to name. He was now to try his hand at motor racing." They either discounted his sports car exploits as not significant or didn't know about them, understandable in the light of their primary focus on Grand Prix and Voiturette racing history.

Farina's car was a modified 553, now known as the 555 Supersqualo, and it was expected to be quick. The untimed practice sessions, which Portago used wisely to discover what his car was like, were interrupted by a terrible accident to Mantovani's 250F. He suffered terrible leg injuries and this resulted in one leg being amputated. He had been more successful in sports cars but his driving days were over, though he remained active on the motor racing scene for many years. When the practice was timed for grid positions, Ascari let the Lancia loose and put himself on pole just ahead of the two Maseratis of Behra and Musso. There were nine cars and five seconds between Ascari on pole and Portago on the 5th row. He was a second slower than young Perdisa, but quicker than the veterans Rosier and Bira. Cesare Perdisa had taken over the Mantovani's car, as Mantovani had crashed the Maserati team's spare. Both Perdisa and Portago were seen to be making the most of their debut opportunities

As the flag dropped, Maserati blocking tactics were aggressive and Ascari got shoved back to 4th, but it wasn't long before both he and Behra caught and passed the Argentinean Mieres and set out to chase Luigi Musso. Behra had a de Dion tube break, which allowed Ascari's Lancia to catch Musso. Musso spun under pressure and Ascari went off into the lead, though the surprise was Mieres driving one of his best races to stay on the Lancia's tail. Roberto Mieres recently told the author that he had been in awe of Ascari, and being able to stay with him at Turin had been one of the highlights of his career. He later saw Ascari's plunge into the harbour at Monaco, and recalled being terribly shocked when he heard that the great Ascari had been killed in an odd testing accident at Monza. Mieres: "Ed, in those days many people acted like it was ordinary when someone got hurt or killed. It wasn't ordinary to me and I never got used to it. I don't think anyone did. It did seem part of the racing then, but it was always awful. We all knew how close it could get. I couldn't believe it when Ascari was killed. I saw it in a newspaper and I couldn't believe it." Roberto Mieres also revealed that it was customary for drivers to act with a great deal of bravado, and that only he knew how much he was occasionally very worried about his safety. He guessed that other drivers were "good actors too".

As Ascari brought Lancia its first Grand Prix victory at Turin, with Mieres 2nd, Villoresi and Castellotti 3rd and 4th in the other Lancias, the other teams got a bit worried, as this was not what had been expected. Further down the field, Portago had been driving well and sensibly and had battled with Rosier and Bira, leading them both and pulling himself from 11th up to 7th when he damaged the sump on lap 34. Bira also struggled but was listed as unclassified in 9th and Rosier got to 6th, also unclassified. Thus Portago could well have managed 6th himself, a not unreasonable sign of his rapidly growing ability.

Only two weeks went past until the next race, another non-championship race for Formula 1 cars, the Grand Prix de Pau on Easter Monday, April 11, on the tight and challenging street circuit in the southwest of France. The entry for this race was smaller than at Turin, and had some period oddities in it. Maserati sent three works cars again for Behra, Musso and Mieres, while there were no works Ferraris, only Portago in his 625, and Jean Lucas in an old F2 500. Rosier had his private 250F Maserati and Lancia sent its three Turin cars for Ascari, Villoresi and Castellotti. Three Gordini 16s showed up for Robert Manzon, Elie Bayol and Jacques Pollet. Andre Simon also had a private Maserati 250F. Then there were two cars Portago was familiar with, Panhard Monomilles for Monomille series regulars Claude Storez and Paul Armagnac. These cars were 750 cc. supercharged cars which had moved unsuccessfully into Formula 3, and they were among the very few front wheel drive cars ever to appear in a Grand Prix. They were also, with the Italian Giaur, the only supercharged cars to run in the 2.5-litre formula. Nevil Lloyd's Autosport report described the final entry as a Volpini, but it was in fact an old Maserati San Remo 4CLT chassis with a 2.5-litre Arzani engine. The driver, Mario Alborghetti, had only done a few minor rallies, yet was allowed out onto the crowded street circuit with the works cars.

Portago's Ferrari 625 ended in the hay bales at Pau.
(Credit - Autosport)

Ascari was one of few drivers who had won this race twice before, and no one had won it three times. He looked set to break this record by setting fastest time nearly a second quicker than Behra's Maserati. Portago's car was described as one of those built for the Argentine with a 4-speed gearbox. Portago was struggling to come to terms with the very tight corners at Pau, and managed to find himself in the hay bales in the Friday practice session and again in the Sunday session when he slid on some oil left by Andre Simon. The Spaniard was again some five seconds from pole position, back on row five, with only seven cars between him and Ascari, and seven behind him. However, those in front included the two Gordinis, which on previous form might struggle to get to the end.

At the start, it was all Ascari and Behra, swapping places until Ascari built up a gap after 15 laps. Pollet had managed to drag the 3rd Gordini up from the back and passed Fon who led Simon, Rosier, Lucas and the rest. As the Maseratis and Lancias pulled away, Portago was doing his best to avoid the scenery, not entirely successfully, as first the nose and then the tail of the Ferrari gathered dents and scratches. He had also bent a wheel which saw him in the pits for a replacement after nine laps, after which he drove a smoother and more focussed race. But on lap 19, after pitting with brake problems, Alborghetti was passed at the hairpin by Pollet. The Italian either had brake failure or missed the braking altogether as he went straight into the barrier, injuring nine spectators, and inflicting fatal injuries on himself.

Ascari appeared about to beat the three-win jinx when his hydraulic brake cable broke and he stopped for repairs. This allowed Behra to win to become a two-timer at Pau, with Castellotti, Mieres, Villoresi and Ascari next. Simon and Rosier were 6th and 7th and Portago 8th, several laps down but at least getting to the finish of a difficult and eventful race. None of the Gordinis made it to the end, nor did the DB Panhards.

Racing followed very quickly now, and Portago was entered for two events at Montlhery the following weekend, the Coupe d'Paris and the Bol d'Or. He had now gotten to know some of the drivers and had convinced Louis Rosier to rent him his Ferrari 375S for what was described in the Rosier biography as the "trifling sum of 400,000 francs to the richest marquis"! Rosier's car was a 4.5-litre Grand Prix car which had been converted to sports car specs for the 1954 Buenos Aires 1000 Kilometers race. It was considered over-weight and that it would be out-classed by the 3-litre cars.

This was, by design or accident, an odd race with an odd assortment of cars. The start was delayed by an enormous argument between competitors and the clerk of the course. Andre Pilette had practiced with a 3-litre Gordini sports car, but had also been out in the open practice session with one of the 2.5-litre Gordini Grand Prix cars which had been at Pau. Everyone was surprised when Pilette was quicker on the straight than Duncan Hamilton in the 3.4 Jaguar D-Type. It had been expected that the Gordini would be fast under braking, but not on top speed. When the Pilette sports car blew up, the team brought the Grand Prix car to the line. Hamilton and Portago protested the presence of this Grand Prix car in a sports car race, but to no avail. In the race, Hamilton won the sports car category, beating a 3-litre Ferrari of Picard, and Portago brought the unwieldy but fast Rosier Ferrari into a reasonable 4th place. However, Pilette's win in the Gordini was allowed to stand, much to everyone else's dismay.

Ferrari 375 Grand Prix chassis 002-51
The car which Portago hired for Montlhery from Louis Rosier, was like several others the Spaniard had been learning on, not a new machine. It had first been raced at Siracusa by Alberto Ascari, and then Ascari won the 1951 Italian Grand Prix with it on September 16, 1951. After only two races as a works car, it was fitted with a twin-plug head and sold to Frenchman Louis Rosier. Rosier had it painted in French blue racing colours and won the Albi Grand Prix in 1952 and again in 1953. For the 1954 Buenos Aires 1000 Kilometer sports car race, it was equipped with a sports car body, and Rosier and Maurice Trintignant drove it to seventh in that race. It sat quietly for awhile before Portago used it at Montlhery in 1955, and then was sold to Ron Roycroft in New Zealand. He changed the body back to an Indy-style single-seater. Roycroft raced it four times in 1957 and 1958, winning the Lady Wigram Trophy and the Ardmore 50, both in 1958. The car changed hands many times between 1961 and Gavin Bain's purchase of it in 1968. At one point, the chassis was lengthened, a Jaguar engine and fibreglass GT body fitted. Bain had it restored to the original specifications and it 1992 it went to Georgio Perfetti in Lugano.

Only a week after Montlhery, Portago and the F1 regulars were at Bordeaux for the 123-lap Bordeaux Grand Prix on April 24. Ferrari was back with the two 555 Supersqualos for Nino Farina and Maurice Trintignant. Portago, with his 625, was the only other Ferrari driver but there were no less than seven 250F Maseratis, three of them works team cars for Behra, Musso and Mieres. The regular privateer Maseratis for Rosier, Bira, and Simon were also present, along with Stirling Moss in his own car, and the two Gordinis for Manzon and Bayol.

Stirling Moss had already had his mechanic Alf Francis fit disc brakes to the 250F and the Maserati mechanics were seen examining it to see what else Alf had done, especially after Moss was quickest in the first session. Behra and Musso then went quicker but it was an all Maserati front row, with the two works Ferraris next. Portago was slowest of all seemingly troubled by some unspecified problem with the Ferrari. Moss had a grabbing brake for the early stages and fell well behind, but as the problem solved itself, Moss was soon the quickest of all as he fought back to 4th place behind the three works Maserati drivers. Portago disappeared quietly on lap 42 of 123 with a variety of ills including a persistently overheating engine, his least spectacular race so far. This is somewhat odd as Portago was having the benefit of full Ferrari factory support for the first time, both with mechanics and organisation, and it must not have been very encouraging to gain little advantage from this. The highlight of the race was the superb performance of Stirling Moss who lost three laps when a fuel tank strap broke. He stopped and then resumed, breaking the lap record again and again as he went much faster than the works Maseratis in his private 250F. Behra managed to keep the factory Maserati in front, however, to win on the tight and twisty little circuit.

A little known fact about Portago turned up in the minute detail of Janos Wimpffen's detailed 2300 page account of the World Sports Car Championship. Down the list of entries for the 1955 Mille Miglia in the 'did not appear' section are two Ford Thunderbirds. One was entered by Alfonso de Portago and one by his friend Jean Lucas. Of course, neither car ever appeared and there was no explanation ever given in the press about this. It seems quite possible that the entry might have been something of a fantasy, as there does not seem to be a record of any competition-prepared Thunderbirds passing through the hands of either driver. This would have been one fantasy well worth seeing.

There was only a two-week break until the next event, and it was to be Portago's first race in the country where he had been born. The International Trophy Race was held on the Silverstone circuit in Northamptonshire on May 7. There was a large 26-car entry, though three did not appear and Lancia and Mercedes had not entered, nor had the works Maserati team. Six Maseratis and four Ferraris still looked to be a very exciting draw, but more attention was focussed on the British cars: two new Vanwalls were there for Mike Hawthorn and Ken Wharton; no less than seven Connaughts, two Gordinis, three Coopers and an Emeryson. The entry took a knock when the two works Ferraris failed to show up, and Portago himself then took a very big knock.

Argentine Roberto Mieres at the International Trophy at Silverstone 1955.
(Credit - Author's Collection)

Portago's long-time close friend Harry Schell at Silverstone and this time breaking his leg. ***(Credit - Author's Collection)***

In the first practice session, Portago, referred to this time by Motor Sport as "Baron de Portago", lost control of the Ferrari 625 at Club Corner and hit the bank very hard, and the Spaniard suffered a fractured leg. The gearbox had jammed causing the car to lock up and fly off the road, though some reports had him missing a shift.

In qualifying, Roy Salvadori had put the Gilby Engineering Maserati 250F on pole, with Hawthorn's Vanwall looking good in second, Moss' Maserati and Jack Fairman in the Connaught. However, the race turned into a battle between Peter Collins in the Owen Organisation Maserati and Salvadori, after other front runners fell by the wayside. Hawthorn's Vanwall retired and Wharton had a fiery crash in the other one, leaving Collins to move away from Salvadori. Portago, of course, was by this time in hospital and likely to be out of racing for sometime.

With no racing, or any other sports, in prospect for sometime, Portago was forced to face up to some of the issues in his personal life. The pregnant Dorian Leigh, fully expecting to be about to move in with him, delayed her return to Europe from the USA until the end of May 1955. It seems that, discovering that Carroll had returned to New York, she thought she would possibly take up residence in Portago's apartment on Avenue Foch in Paris. However, his mother had the adjoining apartment and this was an impossibility. She says that she found a small hotel nearby and had a key to the gate of Fon's apartment which would allow her access without being seen, and that she would be there in the evenings. At this point she had no idea as to whether Portago ever told her the truth about a planned divorce and their future, and in her autobiography states on numerous occasions that he was a liar. It is interesting that at a point when it would appear that Portago was still using crutches to get around with his broken leg, Dorian Leigh makes no mention of this. Possibly he had recovered substantially by this time, but her own account indicates she was becoming increasingly agitated. She says that when they were together she was suspicious and anxious, and this created more distance between them. In spite of what he may have said about her pregnancy, there were indications that he wanted to be out of this situation. It does also seem possible that they were not together as much as her story indicates, and much of the writing was an attempt to find some meaning and value in her own difficulties. She made no mention of his fractured leg at all.

Portago had another crash, this time at Silverstone and this time breaking his leg. *(Credit - BRSCC Archive)*

Portago in Biarritz recovering from his leg fracture. Note the crutches in the corner.
(Credit - Petrie Collection)

Apparently, she again considered an abortion but ruled this out, and instead planned her own suicide. Having failed to hear from Fon for a period of some hours, she was sure he was with another woman, something that indeed was a real possibility, as she clearly never saw or accepted him as he was. She was found by a maid slumped against a bathtub, having taken a number of pills and cut her wrists. She woke up in the American Hospital in Paris with Portago in the room. She refused an offered abortion, and claims that he said he would move her to Switzerland, possibly to reduce the gossip in Paris but so "Fon could also do a little gold smuggling at the same time". There is no further reference to this activity but it appeared to be said with seriousness. (Leigh, 1980 p.126) Nevertheless, at some point in the late summer it appears that Portago did indeed move Dorian to an apartment in Lausanne. She says they had two uninterrupted months together, which seems unlikely, as he managed to return to fitness in time for the Goodwood Nine Hour race back in Britain on August 20. Dorian, meanwhile, became somewhat immersed in the family activities of Charlie and Oona Chaplin who lived nearby in Lausanne.

It has to be said that the timing and lack of certain details in Dorian Leigh's account casts doubt on the validity of much of what she has said. Photographs indicate that Portago spent much of his recovery time in the family house in Biarritz, and Carroll Petrie confirmed this. The Leigh autobiography states that she and Portago had two uninterrupted months in Lausanne prior to the birth of 'their' son on September 27, 1955. It may only be a detail,

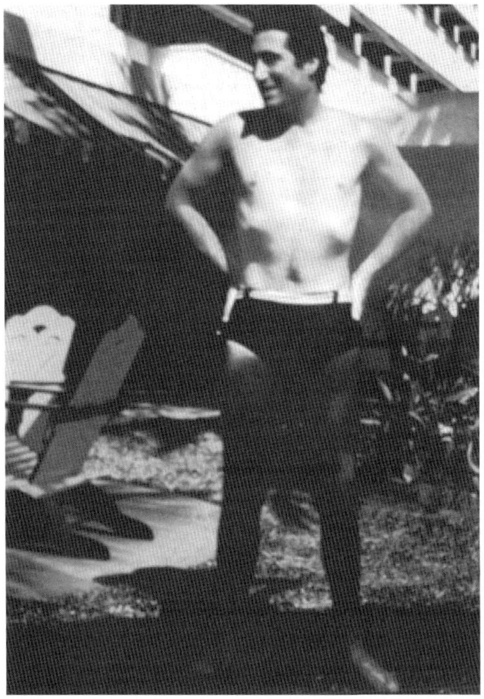

Portago did a great deal of swimming at Biarritz to get himself back in shape after the Silverstone crash.
(Credit - Petrie Collection)

but of course Portago was in Britain for part of that period at Goodwood, Aintree and Oulton Park, the latter event being three days before the birth of Kim Blas.

Whatever the reality was about Portago's whereabouts during the summer of 1955, he had recovered sufficiently to get back into racing at a serious level. On August 19, Autosport enthusiastically reported that the entry for the Goodwood Nine Hours sports car race the following day had been seriously boosted by the late entry of a factory Ferrari for Mike Hawthorn and Alfonso de Portago. Portago and Hawthorn had met up at a number of events, and had spent time together earlier in the year at Sebring. There was a similarity in style and interests, though Portago was not nearly so exuberant as the Englishman. Hawthorn was in many ways typical of a well-off young man from an upper middle class background of the time. He was very likable in social settings, though the term 'school bully' was and is also often used to describe him. At an occasion like a post-race party, he was apt to be drinking and creating some havoc, though this was generally considered 'what those boys did'. Portago was much more reserved and reticent, and saved his exuberance for sports, and to some extent his relationships with women. Nevertheless, the pair got on well, and when Ferrari decided to enter a car for Goodwood, it seems that it was Hawthorn who suggested Portago as the co-driver. Well, that is how some reports had it at the time. However, the truth was that after Portago had sold the 735S which had been modified to Monza 750S specs to Sterling Edwards, he had already indicated to Ferrari that he wanted to buy a new Monza 750S, and this (chassis 0496M) was the car, which was delivered in time for Goodwood. It was not a works car, though there were factory mechanics at Goodwood looking after it.

Portago was ready to drive again at Goodwood in August, and here he is with Mike Hawthorn, Portago acting as the team photographer.
(Credit - Ferret Fotographics)

Other late entries to spice up the long race were for another Ferrari for Ken Wharton/Jonneret, and Stirling Moss joining Huschke von Hanstein in a 1.5-litre Porsche. In the first session on Thursday, the faster cars were trying very hard to set a pace that would put them near the front, though the race would have a Le Mans start. On a small circuit, the main teams were desperate to be away from the slower cars at the start. Mike Hawthorn was fastest in the first night-time practice session in the Ferrari 750 Monza he was sharing with Portago. He was quickest before the sun went down and even further ahead of the others in the dark. He was again at the head of the pack on Friday, while Stirling Moss had the Porsche going almost as rapidly as the bigger cars. At the start on Saturday, Mike Hawthorn had been clever to turn the wheels of the Ferrari to point into the first corner.

At the 3.00 p.m. start, the field flashed away except for Stirling Moss in the Porsche and Roger's Tojiero-Bristol. There was speculation that Moss was in top gear! The Hawthorn/Portago machine was at the front of the line of 35 cars, and though Les Leston got the Connaught sports car moving first, it was Hawthorn first into Madgwick Corner. Hawthorn's huge power-slide off the line frightened several others who dodged out of the way, and there were spins and contacts during the very first lap. It was a 9-hour race, but you would never have known it. Moss got going

Mike Hawthorn in the Ferrari Monza at an early stage of the Goodwood 9 Hour Race. *(Credit - Dunn)*

late, and the Ron Flockhart/Cliff Allison Lotus 11 was hit hard by Tony Gaze's spinning Aston Martin DB3S. Tony Gaze, when asked about the incident recently at Phillip Island in Australia, closed his eyes in horror at the recollection!

Mike Hawthorn was pulling away from a pack of Astons and Jaguars and Harry Schell in another Ferrari. Within a few laps he was coming through the Goodwood chicane lifting a front wheel. At one point he lost the car at the chicane, smashed through the wattle fencing, went round the 'prohibited area' and emerged near the pit lane. But after 30 minutes, Hawthorn swept into the pits to report difficulty in changing gears. He lost twelve minutes before rejoining and then was the fastest car on the circuit as he managed to overtake everyone in an attempt to pull back the lost time. Mike Keens crashed his Cooper-Bristol, and was taken to hospital but died soon afterwards. Hawthorn made up considerable ground when he came in at the two-hour stage to hand over to Portago. The mechanics took nearly four minutes to get a wheel changed, losing all that time that Hawthorn had gained. Portago was now under immense pressure and had a spin almost immediately, but lost little time and carried on. In fact, he drove very quickly, though of course not as speedily as Hawthorn, but he certainly wasn't losing time. Before Hawthorn could take over again, the brakes needed to be adjusted and this took some five minutes. When Hawthorn got back in, he was quickly setting new lap records and after six hours, two-thirds distance, he was moving up to try and pass Ninian Sanderson for third place. He had set another sports car lap record on the 176th lap. Then at 9.33 p.m., the only surviving competitive Ferrari stopped at the pits, with a failure somewhere in the rear axle or gearbox. Portago had just gotten back into the car and was close to Hawthorn's pace but the car had been pushed very hard from the beginning. There seemed to have been little thought given at any point to sitting back and watching things develop, and in that sense, Hawthorn and Portago may not have been the best pairing for a long distance race! However, as Portago had said himself, they dropped to 42nd place and came back to 3rd, which was not a bad achievement.

According to Portago, Hawthorn's driving inspired him to drive the Monza quicker than he had done before. ***(Credit - Ferret Fotographics)***

Peter Walker and Dennis Poore in an Aston DB3S went on to win from the Titterington/Sanderson Jaguar, and Peter Collins/Tony Brooks in another Aston. Hawthorn set fastest lap for a new Goodwood record at over 91-mph. Bill Boddy, in reflecting on the fine Goodwood summer atmosphere in his report, mentioned that the bar behind the pits was doing a roaring trade and "summer frocks mingled with jeans and brief shorts". He even mentioned "that handsome Spaniard de Portago"!

The British Automobile Racing Club was organising a mixed race meeting at Aintree on September 3, which included 17-lap races for Formula 1 and for sports cars. Portago decided to enter the sports car race, which also saw Harry Schell and Herbert McKay Fraser in the entry in three-litre Ferraris. It was the Ecurie Ecosse Jaguar D-Type of Desmond Titterington, which took the lead from Roy Salvadori's Aston Martin, followed closely by the on-form Portago, Ninian Sanderson's D-Type, Fraser and Schell. On lap four, Schell came past the Aintree pits and gave a 'spinning' signal to the mechanics, an indication as to what had happened to Portago. He had spun and clipped a concrete post and then hit a second post, and during this a tyre had burst. In spite of considerable damage to the Ferrari, Portago was quickly out of the car and walking away uninjured. Sanderson won from Titterington, Salvadori and Schell. Motorsport had a slightly different take on this incident, saying that the tyre burst first and that caused Portago to go off. The journal also pointed out how well the Spaniard had been going at the time of the crash. Nevertheless, this incident helped to establish further an image of Portago as a driver likely to go off the road.

The Golden Jubilee of the Tourist Trophy was being celebrated with a well-supported sports car race on the 7.4-mile road circuit at Dundrod in Northern Ireland on September 17, and Portago was down to share his car with Frenchman Jean Lucas, but their entry was scratched and they never appeared, possibly as the Ferrari had not been repaired after the Aintree incident. It may also be that Portago took this opportunity to return briefly to Lausanne.

The International Gold Cup was next on the calendar on September 24. This was an F1 race over 54 laps of the beautiful Cheshire circuit Oulton Park, and this year the best ever entry had been promised. Portago had entered his regular Ferrari 625, but this car had now been rebuilt and re-stamped as chassis 0540 after the crash at Silverstone at the International Trophy meeting. Motorsport pointed out that this was a 4-speed, long-chassis version of the 625, a fact which had already been made clear when the car had appeared for Portago for the first time.

Portago was at Oulton Park in late September for the Gold Cup. He is seen here with Stirling Moss. ***(Credit - Neville Hay)***

After the death of Alberto Ascari earlier in the season, and in the wake of Lancia's huge financial difficulties, the Lancia team's D-50 racecars were transferred to Scuderia Ferrari for a very small sum of money. This was immensely timely for Ferrari as the Supersqualo cars were not performing well and were not much loved by the drivers. Their presence at Oulton Park was especially welcome, as the Lancias had not been seen in Britain. The D-50s were to be driven by Hawthorn and Castellotti so Portago was the only 'real' Ferrari representative there. His car was again being tended by Ferrari mechanics. There were two works Maserati 250Fs, one for Stirling Moss replacing the injured Jean Behra and the regular car for Luigi Musso. Vanwall had entered three cars for Schell, Titterington and Wharton, but Wharton had been injured at Dundrod. Tony Vandervell had attempted to get Juan Fangio or Nino Farina into the 3rd Vanwall but it didn't happen. Desmond Titterington was having his first ever taste of Formula One. The appearance of the new

BRM and several Connaughts also helped liven up British interest in the race. The organisation of the Mid-Cheshire Motor Club and the sponsorship of the Daily Dispatch had helped to produce a superb entry. Just to add to the excitement, the Ferrari and Maserati transporters had managed to bang into each other while traveling together from Paris to Calais on the way to Britain!

Portago at Oulton Park with Harry Schell, and Gurner Nelson on the left. *(Credit - Neville Hay)*

Hawthorn led the two Maseratis and teammate Castellotti to win the fight for pole position, Italian cars taking up the entire front row. The Vanwalls were on the second row with Salvadori's private 250F. Peter Collins only managed to get the BRM into 13th spot on the grid, one place and 1/10th of a second ahead of Alfonso de Portago.

The Maseratis of Musso and Moss were first away, but they were quickly passed by the two Lancias of Castellotti and Hawthorn, and it was this foursome which put on a fantastic show in the early laps. Peter Collins had managed to dodge through the traffic and had quickly got as far as fifth with the BRM. Collins then got past Castellotti and Hawthorn to frighten all the front runners thoroughly with the BRM's pace. Moss led and Collins pressed Musso but on lap 10 he was in the pits with zero oil pressure. Halfway through the race, the surface was covered in oil, which the Maseratis managed well, but it slowed the Lancias. Several cars had spun, and on lap 35 Portago joined them when he spun and hit the banking, damaging the steering enough to put him out of the race. This was after a stop to check a failed rev counter drive, which cost a minute and a half delay. It was evident that the gearbox was tightening up and this probably caused his spin. In fact, the Motor Sport report said that Portago "had spun off on Lodge corner, after which it wouldn't restart, the gearbox having seized." This was to be his last race with the 625 and he sold it immediately after the Oulton Park race. Neither Lancia was running well near the end, but Musso retired giving Hawthorn 2nd and an amazing Titterington brought the Vanwall in 3rd, with Castellotti down in 7th after several stops.

Castellotti leads Hawthorn in the Lancia D-50 at Oulton Park.
(Credit - Author's Collection)

Mike Hawthorn in his Lancia D-50. *(Credit - Ferret Fotographics)*

Mike Hawthorn at the wheel of his Ferrari 250 SWB. *(Credit - Jean Ireland)*

Ferrari 625 F1 Chassis 0208/0540

The car, which Portago bought and ran in the 1955 season, started life as one of the 1952 F2 cars, the 500 Formula 2. Chassis 0208 was raced eight times in 1952 by both Laurent and de Tornaco and appeared in the Monza, Belgian, Dutch and German Grands Prix amongst others. It appeared no less than 14 times in 1953 raced by Swaters, Laurent, de Tornaco and Cole. It had only managed a 6th place in 1952 but had some second place finishes in 1953 and Swaters won the Avus GP in 1953. Then de Tornaco was killed while testing the car at Modena in September 1953. This occasioned its rebuild as a 625 with the same chassis number and it continued in Belgian hands. Laurent and Swaters raced it nine times in 1954 with the best result a 3rd at Helsinki. It was swapped with the factory for a 750 Monza but Johnny Claes drove it to 11th in the 1954 Dutch Grand Prix. For 1955 it was rebuilt again for de Portago as an updated 625, and he raced it as 0208 until it was restamped 0540 after his International Trophy crash. After the Oulton Park Gold Cup, it was sold to the Healey Motor Company. It was restored in 1993, sold to a German, and then to Carlos Monteverde in 1998 and then to David Vine who raced it regularly in historic events. The car is now in Switzerland.

The Ferrari 625 of Portago as it is today, taking part in historic racing. (Credit - Birner)

There was now a break in the racing schedule until early November when the Venezuelan Grand Prix would take place in Caracas. Dorian Leigh's memoirs imply that Portago had been close at hand during the late stages of her pregnancy, and that by this time "Fon seemed to be looking forward to the birth of our child as much as I was." (Leigh,1980 p.128) Whatever his sentiments were, however, he had been racing immediately before the birth of a son, Kim, on September 27, just a few days after the Oulton Park race. She described the child as looking very much like his father, and later photographs seem to indicate that was so. Kim was named after a friend of Portago's, Kim Blas, though Blas was in fact one of Portago's own forenames, and this seems more than just a coincidence. Dorian Leigh goes on to say that Portago contacted his sister to sell his stable of steeplechase horses to her in order to give the money to Dorian so she wouldn't have to return to work. The money was supposedly sent immediately but when it arrived, Portago took it to the casino at Constance and lost every cent, and Dorian was back at work within ten days! She returned to New York, though she had managed to keep her suicide attempt and the birth of the child a secret. She was living in New York in hotels while taking on some modeling work and apparently attempting to find a film or television job as well. Her 15 and 16-year-old children had been in boarding schools for some time and the younger 7-year-old lived permanently with Dorian's parents. While Portago's whereabouts are overlooked at this point in the autobiography, it seems he was back in Paris and then in the USA, presumably in New York. It is more than likely that the story of the horse sale and subsequent alleged gambling was a convenient means by which Leigh could escape from the relationship. Portago owed her $15,000 by this point, and this debt was never paid.

Then it was time for the end of the year racing, with the Grand Prix of Venezuela taking place over 87 laps of the four-kilometer Caracas street circuit on November 6. Apparently the press were treated so badly by the organisers that very little in the way of results got out of the country for sometime, except that Juan Fangio had won in a three-litre Maserati. This was a sports car race in spite of the title of Grand Prix, and there was a good entry. Both Castellotti and Cornacchia were eliminated in a first-lap accident, though Eugenio Castellotti took over the 2-litre Ferrari of Harry Schell and eventually finished fifth. After the early lap confusion, Fangio and Maglioli chased Musso's Maserati and Chico Landi in a Ferrari. Not far behind was Robert Manzon in a 3-litre Gordini but Fangio finally got past Musso on lap eight, but Portago, in the Ferrari Monza, chassis 0496M, had gotten onto Fangio's tail and followed him closely. The race turned into fierce fight between Argentinean Fangio and the younger Italian Musso with Portago watching them both, and learning a great deal in the process. When Musso's car slowed near the end, Portago was past into second, but Fangio had moved much further ahead. He did later acknowledge that he saw Portago as a talented competitor, something he would confirm sometime later when they had a much closer race in Cuba. Baron de Graffenried was 3rd, also in a 750 Monza with Carini 4th in a similar car. The organisation of this first international race in Venezuela was problematic, but the spectators showed up in large numbers and loved it, and most of the drivers said they would be back. Portago would later say that the presence of the Italian motoring press and a number of racing personnel from Ferrari at the Caracas race was a turning point for him, as he got a great deal of coverage for his pursuit of Fangio. The author would see several pages of clippings from that race in the Portago family album, which Portago himself had carefully constructed.

The start of the Venezuela Grand Prix, a sports car race, in early November. ***(Credit - E.Munoz)***

Portago is on the front row in #10.
(Credit - E.Munoz)

Portago arranged for the Ferrari to be shipped to Nassau for the second running of the Speed Weeks, though it is thought it may have either gone to Chinetti's premises in New York for a rebuild or even back to the factory, as it would get well used at Nassau.

Portago himself was back in Spain, then in St. Moritz in Switzerland and then in Cortina in Italy. His early flirtations with trial bobsled runs at St. Moritz had developed into a more serious interest, and he had been talking to a number of people about the up-coming Olympics in Cortina. As the family had been having winter holidays in Switzerland for many years, since Alfonso was a child, it was both familiar to him and the source of even more adventures. Thus he had learned to ski at an early age, though he was not a competition skier as some reports had suggested. The one-man cresta run was also a measure of a man's sense of daring, and it would appear that Portago first gave this a try during a visit in the winter of 1953/54, and was possibly egged on by Ed Nelson. There are tales of amazing achievements on the cresta but in fact these didn't come until later. However, during late 1955, Portago had convinced some St. Moritz bobsledders to give him a trial run on the hill, and that was leading to another adventure scheme, one which would turn out to be quite serious, and where the outcome would be glory rather than gold. In the meantime, Portago was intent at repeating and improving on his 1954 success in the Bahamas.

The Nassau Development Board had decided to increase and improve their publicity for the 1955 Speed Weeks. Two hundred applications were duly received for the nominal 100 places available. The number was nominal because some drivers brought more than one car, and some cars were for more than one driver. What was spectacular for

1955 was that 17 Ferraris were entered and that would be more Ferraris than had ever appeared together anywhere outside of Europe. Cars, drivers and teams started to arrive on Tuesday December 6 aboard the SS Queen of Nassau and the SS Evangeline, with the first party not starting until that evening! It was clear by this stage that the Speed Weeks were well on the way to becoming the most significant social event for racing people. Some people remember the racing as good, and some don't remember it at all!

Portago and his wife Carroll on their way to Nassau in 1955. ***(Credit - Petrie Collection)***

Thursday provided a practice opportunity for almost all the cars and drivers, but it was wet and that was a problem for the first-timers. There were a number of fairly minor incidents, though some drivers found that their cars suffered harshly if they got off the Windsor Field surface. Some drivers also wanted to abandon Le Mans-type starts but the organisers prevailed on 'safety grounds'. Racing got underway on Friday, December 9 with events for 500 cc. F3 cars on a course especially laid out by the five drivers, and then there were over and under 2-litre production car races. The over 2-litres saw a straightforward fight between three D-Type Jaguars of Sherman Johnston, Wallace and Erickson and the newly acquired Ferrari Europa GT (chassis 0415) of Alfonso de Portago. These were significantly different cars and though these were 1955 production D-Types, they were a different breed than the Europa. Portago finished 4th overall and 1st in class behind the Jaguars with Stirling Moss in 6th in an equally outclassed but rapidly driven Austin Healey.

Portago races his Ferrari 250 GT past one of the marker barrels on the Nassau circuit.

The Governor's Trophy race over 30 laps was also on Friday, and was the race won the previous year by Portago. This time he set out in his own Monza in pursuit of Sherwood Johnston's Jaguar D-Type, Phil Hill's Ferrari Monza and the Ferrari 375MM of Lou Brero Sr. There were 57 cars in this race and the competition was fast and furious, but the speed and driver ability differential was enormous. There were many, many incidents with cars going off, and several over-turning as a result of being hit by another driver. As Portago moved past Brero, then Phil Hill and was ready to make a move on Johnston's Jaguar, Johnston braked on the quickest part of the fast bend just before the start-finish line. Portago had intended to stay on Johnston's tail and then pass him down the straight. The two cars spun an enormous distance but collected themselves and carried on. Brero had gone into the lead but the Spaniard went past him. This was at the halfway point and Portago and Phil Hill fought for the lead for the remaining distance, with Fon taking an important win against the future World Champion.

As was customary at Nassau, Portago had lent his brand new Ferrari Europa to New York photographer Bill Derujinski for this race. It would appear the New Yorker was out of his depth. He missed a corner and plowed into the undergrowth, which flipped the new car onto its roof, inflicting serious damage. The story goes that Portago arrived at that corner to see his car in a sad state and promptly spun himself!

Portago managed to bend the front of the Ferrari on an errant Austin Healey. ***(Credit - Tom Burnside)***

Portago was off to celebrate his victory at a fabulous party hosted by Lady Greta Oakes, and that went on for many, many hours. The mechanics' work went on even longer as there was a great deal of repair work to be done. Much of it was bodywork, but the Windsor Field undergrowth damaged suspensions, fuel tanks and numerous other parts. Having learned this in 1954, a much larger supply of spares had been brought in 1955.

Though Saturday was an overcast and damp day, the race programme was bright, with short 5-lap races, a second 500 cc. event, a race for local residents, and marque races for Jaguars, Porsches and then finally, the more significant one for Ferraris. Twelve Ferraris were entered for the Alberto Ascari Memorial Trophy race. This was only a five-lapper but it was hard fought between Portago's 750 Monza, the 857 Monza of Luigi Chinetti driven by Phil Hill, Brero Sr. and two more 375 MMs, and Masten Gregory in another Monza, though one which was ill-handling and uncompetitive. Portago put on another demonstration of strong driving and won the short race from Phil Hill.

First race on Sunday was at noon, just as well as the partying didn't finish until pretty early in the morning. After a further 500 cc. race, it was time for the major event of the Speed Weeks, the Nassau Trophy race, a tough 210-mile event which had something like 60 starters. The drivers rushed across the track for the Le Mans start and the predictable leaders were the Ferraris of Phil Hill, Portago, the 300S Maserati of Gregory and Sherman Johnston's D-Type Jaguar. There were early retirements and Moss' Austin-Healey broke a stub axle after ten tours. Johnston's Jag dropped all its oil, and retired and there were then a number of sliding cars going off. Phil Hill held the lead but Portago was right behind him, setting fastest lap, and not only finishing second but winning the Index of Performance as well. Phil Hill enjoyed his race but had bounced off several other racers trying to stay ahead of the Spaniard.

Portago with his good friend Porfirio Rubirosa at Nassau. ***(Credit - Bahamas News Agency/ Terry O'Neil Collection)***

At the festive awards party at the British Colonial Hotel, Portago seemed to get the most trophies after winning the Governor's Trophy, second and Class D in the Nassau Trophy and the Alberto Ascari Memorial Trophy. It had been another successful Speed Weeks and in spite of the social nature of the event, it had been another opportunity to perform and perform well in good company. Kenneth Rudeen wrote in Sports Illustrated that Portago's choice of the number 13 for his race number was an indication of the "dash with which he drives", number 13 almost always being avoided by overly superstitious racing drivers, then and now. Rudeen managed to interview Portago after the Governor's Trophy race when Portago and Johnston had clashed: "I tried to slip-stream him; I wanted to ride the partial vacuum behind his car to save power and then take him on the curve. But he hit the brakes before I expected it. If you cannot avoid hitting a car it is best to do it exactly from behind." Rudeen also quoted Phil Hill as commenting "that Portago, he drives like a demon." (Rudeen in Sports Illustrated, Dec.19, 1955,p.39) He had also commented on the positive way in which Portago's driving had been viewed by the crowds, and after being beaten by Phil Hill in the Nassau Trophy race that he really wanted the car that Hill had driven.

Ferrari Europe 250 GT Long Wheelbase Berlinetta Chassis 0415GT

This car was completed on November 16, 1955 and it was the last PininFarina competition Berlinetta with a 250-MM body. It had flat, covered lights, bonnet louvers and a door for access to the radiator cap. Portago won one race with it at Nassau 1955, and another driver crashed it quite seriously. Some records had this car at Oporto in 1956 but that is inaccurate. The works test driver Sighinolfi is said to have crashed the car while testing at Modena in September 1956 though this is contested. It passed to Hassan and then to D. Beach in 1960, and then Roschmann bought it in 1993 and it has run in a number of Mille Miglia retro runs and other historic events.

The Ferrari 250 GT, chassis 0415 GT, currently races in historic events.

Ferrari 750 Monza Spyder Scaglietti Chassis 0496M

Portago had ordered this Ferrari in time for the Goodwood Nine Hours, where he shared it with Mike Hawthorn where they ran very well but eventually retired with rear end difficulties. According to some records, this was the car that Portago then had a string of excellent results with: second in Caracas in November 1956, first in the Governor's Cup at Nassau and first in the Ferrari race there as well, and then second in the Governor's Trophy. However, it is thought these results were achieved by 0602.Sometime between the end of 1956 and 1958, the car was sold to Gary Laughlin in Texas via Luigi Chinetti. Charles Peck then raced it through 1959 and 1960. It was not seen between 1961 and 1970, and then did some historic races before changing hands several times, and is now thought to be in Italy.

The Ferrari 750 Monza, chassis 0496, as it is today.

ENTER THE OLYMPICS - 1956

Very few people, and even fewer men, ever got close to Alfonso de Portago. The journalist and writer Robert Daley doesn't claim closeness, but almost by accident he was the person who helped to turn the tale of Portago from a story about a very prolific sportsman into a legend:

"I paid my own way to the Winter Olympics at Cortina d'Ampezzo in 1956 and the New York Times was going to pay me $50.00 a story and I think they figured on using about three or four. I ended up writing fourteen and earning what to me was a fortune that year. I had to pay $255.00 in advance to the hotel in order to guarantee getting a hotel room. I was counting up the number of stories I would have to do just to pay the hotel as I was riding in a 3rd class train carriage from Nice to Venice and from Venice to Cortina. I was looking for stories and I was fascinated by the bobsledding because it was so sensual and I just wanted to get close to it, and I was able to. The skiers were way above you when they started out but the bobsledders were standing there and you could just talk to them. The fast bobsledders were the Italians...Eugenio Monti...and there were one or two Americans. I remember a guy called Tyler. But what I do remember clearly was that Portago came out of nowhere and he was 4th fastest after the first run, and I thought maybe he was going to win a medal. I could see a good story here and a chance to get my first fifty bucks."

Alfonso de Portago at the 1956 Winter Olympics at Cortina.
(Credit - Petrie Collection)

"He was fascinating to talk to. Every question I asked him, he gave me some outrageous answer back. I don't remember all the specific questions and answers now, but I used them at the time and wrote about them over and over again. I remember how easy it was to talk to him, and how I found it so easy to do. His wife was there, a very good-looking woman who was eight years older than Portago as I recall...as were Linda Christian and Dorian Leigh. There was something about these women...I never dared go after a woman who was eight years older than me in my life! He wasn't interested in fishing around for publicity. I had no feeling of that at all. He was just interested in giving outrageous answers to questions, and in talking and enjoying himself and expressing his enjoyment. Gurner Nelson was there too, a much more sober type. Gurner was a good interviewee as well...they had lots of stories to tell. Portago's wife Carroll...I remember her fondly after all this time because I talked to her too. Now why did I talk to them as well? I couldn't talk to Monti because of the language, and the Americans wouldn't have cared about talking to me anyway. Nelson spoke English. Carroll spoke English and Portago spoke very good English."

Robert Daley helped the author separate some of the Portago myth from the reality, especially in relation to the Spaniard's variety of sporting accomplishments and the extent of his skills. While history has tended to record Portago's achievements in motor racing, horse racing and in the bobsleigh arena as being relatively equal, the truth is somewhat different. In horse racing, Portago competed a great deal, but his success was limited, especially in major events. As 1956 progresses we are beginning to see the skill he developed behind the wheel of Grand Prix and sports racing cars. When it comes to his exploits on ice, however, he did very little but nearly attained the ultimate prize, and for that he is recalled as something of a bobsledding 'expert'...and he wasn't.

Daley has written that Gurner Nelson introduced Portago to bobsledding, probably sometime in the winter of 1955/1956, though an understanding of the rather 'subservient' nature of Nelson's relationship to Portago would indicate that it was more likely that Nelson was really Portago's guest in Switzerland during the winters there, and may have encouraged him to try a bobsled run. It remains uncertain.

Whenever they did have their first run on a two-man bob at St. Moritz, Nelson had suggested he steer and Portago be the brakeman. Portago refused, and impulsively took the wheel and headed off down the run, having instructed

Nelson not to touch the brakes. Robert Daley quotes Nelson as saying Portago's first ever run on that day, the first run of his life, was a full fifteen seconds faster than what was achieved by then World Champion Franz Kapus on his first run of the new season, done on the very same day under the same conditions.

Edmund Gurner Nelson was acting as the coach for the Spanish bobsled team. *(Credit - Petrie Collection)*

It was this achievement and Portago's suspicion that this was another sport where he could do very well, that was the spark of an idea for a Spanish bobsleigh team. No Spanish team had ever made any impact on either the two-man or four-man bob.

It all had started for Portago at St. Moritz during family holidays. The Olympic bobrun there is the only remaining run in the world that is still made of natural ice, and many European and World Championships as well as two Olympic Championships have been decided on the icy path from St.Moritz down the 1600 meter hill to Celerina at the bottom. This run opened in 1904, the oldest in the world, at the same time the St. Moritz Tobogganing Club was formed. Though techniques and equipment changed dramatically over a hundred years, the run itself has remained very much the same. Changes to improve safety and the general layout in recent years have been helped through the efforts of the St. Moritz Bobsleigh Club, and funds raised by family and friends of...the Marquis de Portago. There is now a Portago Corner near the finish line, and the current length is just short of one mile, though the original configuration of 19 turns has been retained.

Portago had admitted that he only had three or four runs before he became convinced that he should embark on setting up a Spanish Olympic squad to contest both the two-man and four-man bobsleigh. Sometime between the races in Caracas and Nassau and the middle of January, Portago had set actions in motion which would shock the elite world of bobsledding. He approached the Spanish Minister of Sport, to whom he had reasonably easy access through his family connections and status, and proposed that he be given the responsibility of organising a team to contest both the two-man and four-man bob at the 1956 Olympics at Cortina. With this granted, it was relatively easy to get an entry from the Olympic Committee as the bobsled event was one of those which were not oversubscribed, and the presence of nobility, even at the expected lower end of the entry, was good for the crowds. He then recruited his team: Vicente Sartorius, a cousin of his, Gonzalo Taboada, who would appear to have been a friend of Sartorius, and another cousin, Luis Munoz. Munoz would be the brakeman and would also be Portago's partner in the two-man bob. The coach for the Spanish team was not Spanish. It was in fact Edmund Gurner Nelson. Most of the 'squad' had met at one time or another, and it is possible that they even may have shared winter holidays, but they certainly had never been down a bobsled run together, and Sartorius and Taboada had not apparently even seen one before. Portago then went off and purchased the team's sleds for each event at a cost of some $1100 each from a Swiss supplier, and had them painted in his own interpretation of the Spanish colours. There were no committees, no sports grants, Portago just put up the money and they went to the Olympics. The 1993 Disney film *Cool Runnings* dramatized the real-life experiences of an equally improbable but generally realistic Jamaican bobsled team, which started out as something of a joke before it surprised some of the more serious teams.

Portago and Munoz prepare for a practice run in the two-man bobsled. *(Credit - Autopresse)*

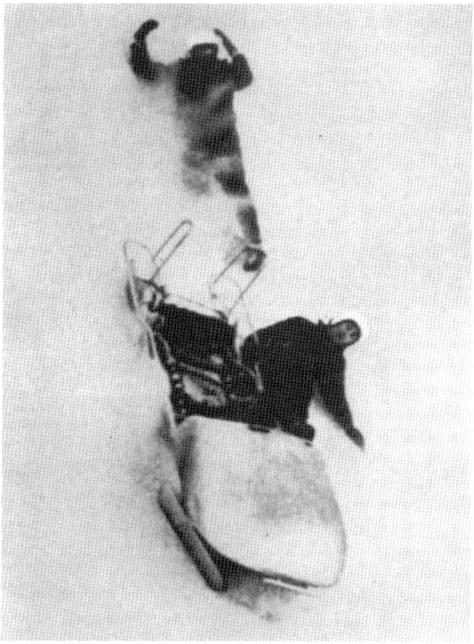

Portago and Munoz in one of their many crashes at Cortina in the trial runs. ***(Credit - Petrie Collection)***

It wasn't that the Spaniards were treated as a joke. It was just that they weren't taken very seriously, but nor were the Poles, the Romanians or the French as well as the second teams of some of the more experienced nations. In the early days of the Cortina Olympics, as 25,000 people were expected to 'jam' into Cortina D'Ampezzo, most attention was focussed on the practice sessions for the skaters, the well-known international hockey teams and the skiers. On January 21, Robert Daley was up early in the morning watching the bobsledders carrying out the dawn patrol, loading the heavy sleds onto the trucks which would carry them up to the start line. For two hours, Daley watched as the teams flew down the icy chute to be carted back up to the top again and again. The session was then over just before the first rays of the sun could start to melt and soften the glistening run. On January 24, Daley reported on the first timed practice runs before the official start which would take place in a few days time. He recorded a new record by the favourite, Italian Eugenio Monti in the two-man runs, with an American Bud Washbond second quickest. Another Italian Umberto della Costa was 3rd, Swiss Max Angst 4th and another American Art Tyler 5th. A French sled had hurtled over the wall at the Belvedere Curve, without injury to the riders. Britain's Keith Schellenberg went over the crest at this curve with his right rear runner but managed to pull the sled back onto the ice and finished his run. The total of the time on the two runs would determine the qualifying order, with twenty teams to run, in two 'flights', the slowest five teams last and therefore unlikely to post quick times as the ice deteriorated.

Hurtling down the Cortina bob run. ***(Credit - BRSCC Archive)***

Portago and Munoz on one of their fast final runs on January 25th. ***(Credit - Farabola)***

What Daley didn't mention in this report was that in one of his runs, Portago had managed 4th fastest time. His second run wasn't so quick so he was down the order, but it suddenly made Daley think the Spaniards had a chance and he decided to spend more time with the loquacious Portago. In his January 27 Special Report to the New York Times, Daley put the Marquis squarely before the public for the first time:

"Alfonso Cabeza De Vaca De Kavaca (sic) y Leighton, Marquis of Portago, is an utterly improbable young man. The 27 year old Spanish nobleman, who has made fewer than thirty trial runs in a bobsled, was in fourth place tonight after the first two of the required four runs. None of the experts had figured him in the first twenty. Quite frankly, Portago intends to finish third tomorrow; he hopes to do even better with his four-man sled. Portago's sports career has had almost as many twists and turns as Cortina's bob run. He has taken part in almost every kind of sporting event. Twice he rode his horse in Britain's Grand National steeplechase. He drove twice in Mexico's grueling Pan-American road race. He used to fly his plane." (Daley, in the New York Times, Jan.27, 1956)

Daley provided a portrait of the Spaniard to a much wider audience than he had had before. He was also contributing to the legend, accepting on face value many of Portago's tales of his achievements. He also stirred up the interest of other journalists who would draw on Daley's profile…and add to it:

"Portago is 6 feet tall, weighs 172 pounds, He has dark hair and intense dark eyes. Ed Nelson, the American coach of the Spanish bob team describes him as a natural athlete. 'He is the type who would have made a great halfback in American football. He has the ability to relax under pressure, which all great athletes have. He can learn anything,' Nelson said. 'If I said to him he had to become good at ski jumping, in three weeks he'd be marvelous. When he was a jockey he trained down to 138 pounds. He was probably better at that than anything. He was the best amateur jockey in France and that means the world. The pro jockeys used to say what a pity the marquis is so tall. If only he had been a normal size what a jockey he could have been' ". It would appear that Nelson was also helpful in contributing to the 'all-conquering' image that began to grow around Portago, long before the days of professional public relations and image-making specialists.

Daley also perceived Nelson as a coach having some difficulty in controlling his headstrong nobleman. Nelson told the Times reporter that Portago didn't like to go to bed at night, that he didn't drink, but he would be likely to stay up all night working on his sled or his car or whatever he was interested in at the time. Nelson also reported that Portago was a long-time chain smoker, though he didn't inhale, so the 'coach' was not unduly concerned!

The New York Times report carried Portago's comments to Daley about meeting his wife, Carroll McDaniel. When asked how he had met his wife, Portago replied that one 'doesn't meet an American woman, she meets you.' Daley asked Portago what his wife thought of his racing, and got the subsequently oft-reported reply ' I don't ask her, I am Spanish.' This comment struck a macho nerve in many journalists then and later, as it appeared in almost every biographical story on Portago.

By January 27, Daley reported that Portago had only had one accident on his practice runs. Portago told him that he had overturned at Bandio Curve during his second run. "It was Belvedere Curve. If you get into trouble at Belvedere, you overturn at Bandio." Portago also explained that he felt he was still "groping" his way down the Cortina run, but credited the famed Italian Eugenio Monti with helping him develop his technique. He said that Monti had been helping him everyday, and that he now wanted to buy a sled similar to the Italian's which he felt would be more competitive. One of the interesting interchanges between Portago and Daley concerned his preference for motor racing over bobsledding. "A bob run lasts only a minute and twenty-three seconds. An auto race may last twenty-four hours. There is another important difference. One likes to think one controls a car 99 per cent of the time. One doesn't control a bob, one helps it." (Daley in New York Times, Jan.27, 1956)

The report of January 31recorded Monti's record breaking run in the four-man bob, setting a time of 1:18.18 with American Art Tyler second on 1:18.91. The runs had already become severely rutted when these two set their quick times. Portago continued to amaze bobsled experts with a qualifying run of 1:20.94. This secured him a good starting slot for the final runs. His time had been set on only his twelfth ever run on a four-man bob. Portago said: "Driving a four-man sled is like driving a truck. There is very little skill to managing the big sleds. In the small sleds, a good driver makes all the difference. I like the small sleds better. If my brakeman hits the brakes, I'd hit my brakeman. Every curve has its safety factor. Say you're driving a car through a curve that is safe up to 100 miles an hour. A great driver like Juan Fangio will take that curve at 99.9. I am not so good as Fangio. I would take that curve at 96 or 101. If I take it at 101 I have an accident."

When the bobsled competition was finally over, Portago had not quite achieved his announced ambition of a medal, but the Spaniards had managed an amazing result.

In the four-man competition, the Swiss team of Kapus, Diener, Alt and Angst had the gold medal, with the Italian team of Monti, Girardi, Alvera and Mocellini getting the silver. The bronze went to the USA, Tyler, Dodge, Butler and Lamy. Then came the Swiss and Italian second teams, the German and Austrians, Germany 2, and in ninth the very surprising quartet of Portago, Sartorius, Taboada and Munoz. Twelve other teams , including the two British squads, were behind them. It was a staggering result for rank amateurs. They had been seventh, tenth, seventeenth and sixth in their four final runs.

But if that was impressive, the two-man results were stunning. Italians dalla Costa and Conti had a total of 5 minutes 30.14 seconds for the gold medal, countrymen Monti and Alvera were on 5 minutes 31.45 seconds for silver, and the Swiss pair Angst and Warburton had 5 minutes 37.46 seconds for the bronze. Portago and Munoz had managed seventh in the first run, equal third in the second, third in the third and fifth in the fourth run. Their time was 5 minutes 37.60 seconds, giving them fourth place and missing the bronze medal by fourteen hundredths of a second.

Carroll Petrie had clear memories of the 1956 Winter Olympics:

"I had very positive, happy memories from that period. We had very good times when we went to St. Moritz, which we did regularly. When we went to Cortina for the Olympics, it was more or less the case that he asked his Spanish cousins to come with us and that he was going to enter a team for Spain in the Olympics. There were the Sartorius cousins and Luis Munoz that he did the events with. We had gone to St. Moritz every winter with his mother. That was a regular occurrence. She was English, and as I have said, she was very encouraging about sports, and that included winter sports. I remember Harry Schell being there with us as well. Anyway, it became one of Fon's plans to do something with a bobsled team, and with his determination and competitive nature, I wasn't surprised that they did well. I guess I just didn't think about it very much, and wasn't that surprised that they did well. I sort of expected it, but it turned out that they did something no one else expected."

Portago and Munoz on the way to an amazing 4th place in the two-man bobsled.
(Credit - Getty Images)

"Fon was very well coordinated as an athlete, and he could learn to do things very quickly. When he first saw the cresta run, which was before the Olympics, sometime before, he just wanted to do it. He only did a small number of runs on it, maybe a dozen or fourteen and he did what he set out to do, set a new record. That was amazing but it was the kind of thing I got used to. He fell off most of the times on the cresta so he only made it to the bottom on a few occasions, but one of those was with a new record. Whatever he did required coordination, which he had, otherwise he wouldn't have done it well. I can't say what he thought about risk. He never discussed motor racing with me...he would not have. I don't think I would have negated it. You just have to take people as they are. You can't take them and try to change them around. That was true about the bobsledding and the motor racing. I think that is why we had the marriage we had, and I know that is why I had the very happy second marriage I did with my late husband Milton Petrie. He was as focussed on his business as Fon was on his. They both excelled in what they did. Milton Petrie was very successful and very dedicated in a different way, but they both had wills of steel."

Perhaps this summary related to the author nearly half a century after Portago's death was the most succinct and accurate summation of his character that anyone had ever managed to put into words. It captured the quintessential nature of the man who could turn his inner resources and determination to some amazing achievements.

Portago himself later said to historian Hans Tanner: "Everyone wants to do his best and I know I am best as an athlete. I knew that before I raced I would drive well, and I do. I don't get scared, so I have an advantage in taking up sports where others might be afraid." (Tanner, H. in Motor Racing June 1957, p.149) Portago said on some occasions that he didn't experience fear, and on others that he certainly did. Was this an example of his inconsistency, or were in fact both true? He also said in some interviews that a good driver didn't have fear, and this may well have meant to him that a good driver didn't fear his job or his task, but experienced fear at appropriate times, such as when he was the passenger with Chinetti, or when a car got out of control.

Buoyed up by the Olympic glory, and without a race coming up until March, Portago got an entry for himself and Luis Munoz in the Swiss Two-man Bobsled Championship, organised by the St. Moritz Bobsleigh Club. The practice and finals took place on February 10, 1956. Eighteen teams had been entered, and the Italian teams had set unofficial practice times in good conditions at 1 minute 19.17 seconds and 1:19.56, but the practice and finals took place later in the day and by then the ice was softer and rutted. The Swiss pair Angst and Gartmann had a slowish 1:28.21 for their first run but very quick 1:23.69 and 1:23.47 for their second and third runs. The British team of Keith Schellenberg, who was becoming a good friend of Portago's, and J. Rainforth had a 1:25.83, 1:24.10 and 1:23.63. Portago and Munoz did their first run at 1:27.15, followed by 1:24.55 and then 1:23.76, so they finished third in this competitive event. Their third run was the fourth fastest of all the 54 runs down the hill. Just over a second had separated the first three, again very impressive as the Spaniards were the only 'amateur' bobsledders, in the sense that they had virtually no experience.

This photo was taken in February at St. Moritz during the Swiss Championship. British bobsled rider Keith Schellenberg is second from the left.

Many years later, Grand Prix driver Robin Widdows would reflect that he was always proud of the fact that he, along with Alfonso de Portago, had been one of very few Olympic bobsled competitors who had driven Grand Prix cars. Widdows drove for Cooper in 1968, and had been a successful F2 driver, and had been in the four-man bob in 1964 for Britain. Keith Schellenberg himself gained a measure of fame in motor sports as well, though he was not a Grand Prix driver. He preferred adventures and would take his pre-war Bentley on the London to Sydney Marathon in 1968, as well as many other rallies for historic cars. Probing through Olympic statistics reveals a number of racing drivers who made at least one Olympic appearance.

Australian Frederick McEvoy was a voiturette racer in the pre-war years. He competed for Britain in the 1936 Olympics, winning a bronze medal in the four-man bobsled. Italian Alfa Romeo driver Antonio Brivio was also in the 1936 games, in both the two and four-man events. That would make McEvoy the only racing driver to win an Olympic medal, and Portago, McEvoy, Brivio and Widdows the only racing drivers to take part in the four-man bob. Other drivers, some relatively little known, include: Karl Ebb in the 1924 3000 meter steeplechase in Paris, Asser Wallenius in speed skating at Chamonix in 1924, Argentine Roberto Mieres in yachting in Rome in 1960, Widdows was also in the two-man bob in 1964 at Grenoble, Davina Galicia in skiing at Innsbruck in 1964, Grenoble 1968 and Sapporo in 1972, Dutchman Ben Pon in shooting at Munich in 1972. Franz Klammer the skier dabbled with racing and rallying, as did Jean Claude Killy, though he was a bit more serious about it than

Portago was back at Sebring for the 3rd time in 1956. ***(Credit - BRSCC Archive)***

Klammer. Other Olympians who did some racing or rallying include Luc Alphand, Kristian Ghedina, and Annamarie Moser Proll, all skiing stars. Robert Daley had quoted Portago as saying at Cortina that he would be doing a sports car race at Daytona. Daley admitted he knew little about motor racing at that time, and this was probably an error, as the next race on the calendar was the Sebring 12 Hours. A brief note appeared in the motoring press in late January which said that British driver Lance Macklin would be driving Portago's Ferrari 625. Where that came from isn't known and it didn't happen. Meanwhile, the sports car racers were getting ready for Sebring. Dorian Leigh's biography reports that she met Portago at Sebring, but this seems dubious, and in spite of occasional contacts between them in Paris and New York, they clearly drifted apart, though Dorian was still maintaining an unrealistic belief that Portago might still divorce his wife.

A very high quality entry had been received for the 1956 race, the best so far. Nine Jaguar D-Types were down to battle works cars from Ferrari, Maserati, Aston Martin and a competitive range of privateers including some potent looking Corvettes. There were three works Ferraris, two 860s for Luigi Musso/Harry Schell and Juan Fangio/ Eugenio Castellotti. There was also a works 857 Monza (chassis 0578M) to be driven by Portago and American Jim Kimberly. This was the car which Phil Hill and Olivier Gendebien had driven to second place at Buenos Aires. Phil Hill would be sharing a private George Tilp-owned 860 with Masten Gregory. The three Corvettes were entered 'privately' but clearly had Chevrolet backing and technical support.

A wonderful portrait of Juan Fangio at Sebring in 1956. ***(Credit - Eveleth)***

In the practice sessions for Sebring, Bill Grauer of Riverside Records was prowling through the pits and caught up with Portago and asked him how it was that he was driving for Ferrari, to which Portago replied that as Spain had no competition cars, Ferrari was the logical choice. Grauer tried to engage him in a conversation about Pegaso as a racing car which Portago wouldn't rise to. When asked who he thought the competition would come from, he was clear that he thought Fangio would win, Hawthorn had a good 'second' chance and he admired the American drivers Phil Hill and Masten Gregory. Portago's predictions were pretty accurate.

A grim looking Luigi Chinetti listens in on a Portago discussion. ***(Credit - BRSCC Archive)***

In spite of the threat to their dominance, Ferrari managed to control virtually the entire race. Portago and Kimberly had set solid times in practice, and the 857 looked potentially capable of running with the newer cars. However, Musso/ Schell led after the first hour, Fangio and Castellotti taking control during the second. They relinquished the lead at the changeover to the D-Type of Hawthorn and Titterington, but once the Fangio/Castellotti Ferrari got back in the groove, it held the lead all the way to the end. Portago and Kimberly were a good pairing and they ran a steady race, 8th in the first hour, then 7th, then 5th, 4th, 5th, 4th, 5th, 6th and 6th at the end of nine hours. As a number of cars struck problems, the pace looked like they would work their way closer to the

Portago was clearly enjoying the Ferrari in practice at Sebring.

Carroll Portago is amused by something her husband has said. Sebring 1956.
(Credit - Petrie Collection)

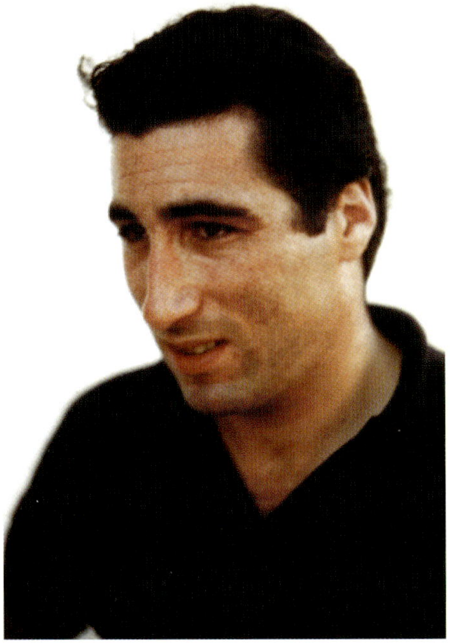

Portago at Sebring 1956.
(Credit - Ferrari)

Fangio, Musso, Castellotti, Schell and Portago all get up to no good at Sebring. ***(Credit - Petrie Collection)***

Another shot of Musso, Schell, Fangio, Castellotti and Portago. ***(Credit - Bernard Cahier)***

Stirling Moss and Briggs Cunningham at the end of the Sebring race. ***(Credit - Eveleth)***

Fangio and Castellotti on the winners' stand with Musso. ***(Credit - Eveleth)***

front. It was not to be, as the car coasted in with a dead engine and no result, but it had been a good and restrained race by Portago and the American driver.

Portago's performance at Sebring had impressed Ferrari back in Italy and he was nominated as one of the works drivers for the Nurburgring 1000 Kilometers race on May 27. He was to be paired with long-distance specialist Olivier Gendebien in the Ferrari 290 MM (chassis 0628M). This was a car which was new for the Mille Miglia in late April and was driven to second place by Peter Collins accompanied by the adventurous photographer Louis Klementaski. The Mille Miglia was won by Eugenio Castellotti who drove to victory single-handed. Castellotti was named as a third driver with Portago and Gendebien at the Nurburgring, and he would only drive in practice as he was teamed with Juan Fangio in an 860 Monza (chassis 0602M).

Portago had now met Enzo Ferrari on at least two occasions. He would later describe him as a dictator, in that if he didn't like someone, he wouldn't sell them a car. But Portago personally said that as far as he was concerned " he was a wonderful guy." He was aware that Enzo Ferrari had the final word on everything that happened at the factory. On a day to day basis, the drivers including Portago worked with two managers, a technical manager and a sporting manager. He described himself at that time as being one of the 50% of drivers in the team who had no mechanical knowledge. He said at the early stage, until he had become more experienced as a works driver, he could not tell what the car was doing except by his times. He said these things retrospectively, acknowledging that he probably would not have wanted to make those things so obvious at the time. Portago said that if he wanted to terrify the mechanics, he would pick up a screwdriver!

Portago and Olivier Gendebien check the Ferraris before practice at the Nurburgring 1000 Kilometers. ***(Credit - Walter Baumer/The Nurburgring Collection)***

Portago and Gendebien keep an eye on Castellotti in practice at the Nurburgring. ***(Credit - P3 - Motorsports)***

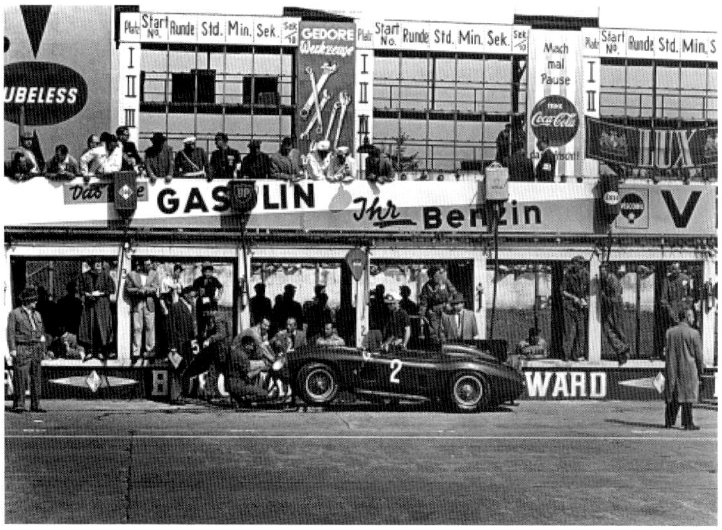

Portago watches work on his car during practice. Castellotti stands on the pit counter two pits to the left. ***(Credit - Walter Baumer/The Nurburgring Collection)***

This race had attracted much attention and had the best entry ever seen at a sports car race at the 14-mile circuit in the Eifel Mountains. At first it was thought that three days of practice was far more than necessary as this race traditionally had a Le Mans start with the cars lined up in order of engine size rather than practice times. However, for 1956, it was decided to run according to times in practice, so as the drivers would run across the tarmac for the start it would be the quickest car at the front. This didn't necessarily mean it would be the fastest driver, and all the major teams had most drivers trying most cars. As the weather was occasionally wet and looked likely to remain changeable, the focus was on getting all drivers acclimatized to the conditions. Portago still had relatively little experience in the wet, but this never appeared to be an issue with him, and his long stint at Reims in the 12 Hours had taught him a lot about driving in the dark and the wet.

A large crowd turned out for the practice days, and some 70,000 fans appeared for the race, a round of the World Sportscar Championship. Best practice time was set by Fangio and Castellotti in their Ferrari 860 in 10 minutes 3.6 seconds. Musso and Trintignant were second in a 290 MM and Phil Hill/Ken Wharton third in another 290 MM (chassis 0626), followed by Moss and Behra in their works Maserati 300S. The Mike Hawthorn/ Desmond Titterington Jaguar D-Type was some 13 seconds off the pace of the pole-sitters, but big gaps were much more prevalent in the long-distance races in the period, especially at the Nurburgring. Paul Frere was sharing a D-Type with Duncan Hamilton, but Frere had a big crash in practice, damaging the chassis. Jaguar test driver/racer Norman Dewis brought another car across to Germany by road, something he was accustomed to doing. Dewis, who had been one of the works drivers at Le Mans in 1955, told the author recently that he did an enormous amount of testing of the D-Types. He would have used the trip across to the circuit to set the car up for the race! Unfortunately he arrived too late for practice so Frere/Hamilton would start at the back of the field.

The sun came out just before the 9.00 a.m. start, providing a colourful spectacle for the huge crowd. "Achtung! Achtung!" blared over the loud speakers, interrupting a relaxed conversation going on between Moss and Hawthorn as they waited to dash across the road, while veteran Louis Chiron was seen setting his watch a minute before the off. Star sprinter Moss was, as usual, first across the road and first away in the Maserati. He was chased out of sight by Hawthorn's Jaguar, Collin's Aston Martin, Portago's Ferrari in fourth, Fangio, Musso and the rest of the 58 starters. The field included some stunningly fast sports cars and a few oddities...the Ford Thunderbird of Isenbbuegel/Rathjen, a pair of East German EMW 1500 cc. sports cars, and hordes of smaller Porsches and Alfa Romeos.

Hawthorn got his Jaguar past Moss briefly before the cars disappeared out into the country, but then Fangio got in front, with Moss following him through. After nearly ten and a half minutes, Moss blasted past the pits in front, and it was several seconds until Hawthorn, Fangio, Collins, Musso, Phil Hill, Taruffi, von Trips, Peter Walker, Reiss, Frere and the pack came streaming through. A Ferrari was seen to be missing which sent up an alarm in the pits. It was Portago's car, and after a few minutes he came rushing into the pits with the front bodywork badly damaged. The bonnet was pulled off, a detached radiator hose was replaced, and several works mechanics started removing bent metal and making repairs, and Portago was sent back out on his way. He had made an attempt to pass Peter Collins on the outside of a corner and had slid or understeered off the road, and gotten well stuck into a big and tough hedge. He got a number of people...twelve policemen apparently...to drag him out in short order.

On lap three, Luigi Musso was on Hawthorn's tail as they approached the South Curve past the pits. He lost control of the Ferrari which spun and rolled into a ditch, trapping Musso underneath. Fortunately, marshals got him out quickly, soaked in fuel, but he was very lucky to have only suffered a broken arm.

Moss had a 20 second lead by lap 10 of 44, with Fangio second. Hawthorn had been called into the pits, apparently to be warned for "overtaking on the inside". This strange incident would come back to haunt Hawthorn. He left the pits in third still ahead of Phil Hill going steadily in fourth. Portago was back up to speed in his battered Ferrari but he was called in as he been disqualified for accepting outside assistance. A Ferrari team decision had already been made to put the Portago/Gendebien pair into the 290 MM with Hill (chassis 0626). This meant Ken Wharton wouldn't get a drive, and that Gendebien didn't get any race laps in his original car. Phil Hill would go on to be a very successful F1 and sports car driver, and in a year or two, it would be less likely that someone of Portago's stature would be moved into his car. But at that point, Portago was looking very good as a Ferrari team member, no doubt assisted by his aristocratic heritage in the eyes of Enzo Ferrari.

Portago's Ferrari heads out into the country at the Nurburgring.
(Credit - Bill Bean)

Phil Hill described his feelings about his entry into the European scene with Ferrari:
"I was at the end of the bench and I felt very inferior to most of my competition over there in '56. Fangio was a god to me, and most of the others were in the idol

category. My self-confidence completely disappeared. As a result of this attitude, my lap times were affected. In a sense, I was still a fan in Europe driving against the famous professionals. I found it quite difficult to adjust, mentally, to this situation." (Nolan, 1996,p.76)

Roy Salvadori drove well yet again in the works Aston Martin DB3S.
(Credit - Bill Bean)

Not long after being called in to be disqualified in one car, Portago was put into Hill's Ferrari and he carried on. Moss brought the Maserati in on lap 15 to hand over to Behra who returned to the pits after a short drive to report suspension failure so the leader from the beginning was out. This put Castellotti in front with Portago/Hill/Gendebien now a good second, and Hawthorn/Titterington in the D-Type third. This was turning out to be a very quick and competitive race with some of the best drivers of the decade fighting against each other. Portago would later reveal how pleased he was with this race, as the Nurburgring was his favourite circuit. Maserati team manager Ugolini brought Harry Schell's Maserati in and put Behra into it, and by half distance he had gotten past Hawthorn, with von Trips/Maglioli in the speedy little Porsche fifth overall. Gendebien had replaced Portago and then the Spaniard was back in the car on lap 23. When Fangio/Castellotti stopped for fuel, Behra/Schell moved closer in second place. Moss took over from Behra on lap 32 and sat a minute behind the Ferrari. Moss cut the deficit in half in six laps, and then Hawthorn tangled with a Porsche and lost a lot of time. When Fangio came in for a top-up of fuel, Moss went by...and the great Fangio could not close the gap. Thus victory went to the Maserati of Moss/Behra/Taruffi/Schell, with Fangio/Castellotti second, and Portago/Hill/Gendebien a reasonably close third. Portago had been seen as the 'main' driver in this trio, so in spite of his trip into the hedges in the other car, he improved his status at Ferrari.

Stirling Moss hurls his Maserati into the corner at the 'Ring'.
(Credit - Bill Bean)

Peter Collins drifts his Ferrari tidily through a quick corner.
(Credit - Bill Bean)

Phil Hill described the race as he saw it: "Then they called me in to hand over the car to the Portago/Gendebien combination. Fon got in and kept up the pressure, with Gendebien in turn relieving him at the wheel. At the windup our Ferrari got third overall with only the Moss and Fangio cars ahead of us. I felt pretty good about this but my jubilation didn't last long. (Nolan, op. cit.)

Both Stirling Moss and Mike Hawthorn were critical of poor marshaling at the Nurburgring, complaining that while there were many officials around the pit area, there were few on some of the remote corners. Moss said he saw a blue flag only once during the race, in spite of considerable amount of overtaking he was engaged in.

Autosport announced that the entry for the Paris 1000 Kilometers, scheduled for June 10, only two weeks after the grueling race at Nurburgring, would include Mike Hawthorn joining Portago in a Ferrari. Again there was a good entry, though this was not a championship round, over 129 laps of the 7.78 kilometer/4.8 mile Montlhery track, which featured the dangerous banked section. This was the first running after an attempt to run a 24 hour race in 1955 had failed. There had been a history of many Bol d'Or endurance races at the French circuit.

When the cars arrived at Montlhery, there was no sign of Hawthorn, or of any Jaguars and only one Aston Martin, a DB3S for Ken Wharton and Tom Kyffin. There were only a few Porsches, unlike at the 'Ring', but there were two Gordinis which might surprise a few people as well as the two EMWs from East Germany, which had surprised people at the Nurburgring with their speed. This meant the race should be a straight battle between the Ferraris and the Maseratis as in Germany. Maserati sent a 300S, the Nurburgring winner, for Jean Behra and Louis Rosier, and one for

Chico Landi/Gerini. There was the works Ferrari 857S (chassis 0584/0578) for Portago and Phil Hill, and three 750 Monzas for Trintignant/Picard, Schell/Lucas, and Meyrat/Munaron, as well as Ferrari 500TRs for Pilette/Milhoux, deChangy/Dernier, and Rousselle/Bianchi, as well as one of these for the female pairing of Thirion/Peduzzi. There was a mix of Maserati 200S and older A6GCS models as well, with Maria Teresa de Filippis sharing a 200S with Carlo Tomasi.

Much of practice and virtually all of the race took place in appallingly wet conditions, and although there were many incidents on the narrow and slippery circuit, none of these were serious. The two Ferraris of Trintignant and Schell took advantage of their good grid positions to lead the opening lap, but Behra then took the Maserati into a comfortable lead, and he opened up a gap of a second and a quarter by the 40th tour. Behind the Maserati, Portago was engaged in a hard fight with his old friend Harry Schell for second place, trying to uphold Ferrari honour. The surprise was that they were being given a hard time by the Gordini of Manzon, Pilette's Ferrari, the second Gordini being driven by da Silva Ramos and Barth in the EMW. The top speed of the 2-litre Gordini and 1.5-litre EMW was something of a shock to everyone. Behra led Trintignant after two hours, and the Ferraris of Dernier and Munaron had both slid off the road in the poor conditions. One of the EMWs disappeared. When Behra handed over to Rosier at their first stop, they were leading Schell/Lucas, Trintignant/Picard, Manzon/Guelfi and Portago/Hill, who had dropped a lap behind the leaders. In the second half of the race, the jubilation which Phil Hill had described at the Nurburgring was gone as the Ferrari suffered a fractured fuel line. This dropped them back into the clutches of the 'lesser' runners, but Hill's annoyance was immediately converted to speed. Autosport states that he broke the existing lap record six times as he fought to regain position. Hill himself remembers it as nine times, and given his modesty, that is likely to be accurate. It was slightly annoying that Behra should have set fastest lap of the race on the final lap, taking away Hill's new record. But Hill and Portago had pushed very, very hard as a pair, and brought the car back up to fifth at the finish behind Behra/Rosier, Schell/Lucas, Trintignant/Picard and Pilette/Milhoux. It was disappointing to them and doesn't look that impressive in the record book, but it was a superbly driven race in terrible conditions.

Phil Hill in the Ferrari he shared with Portago at the Paris 1000 Kilometers at Montlhery.
(Credit - Autopresse)

The winning Maserati ran out of fuel on the slowing down lap, and if that had happened two minutes earlier, the perennially second Schell would have had a rare win. The race was judged such a success despite the awful weather that many French commentators now held out hopes for the revival of a full Grand Prix de Paris. Though sports car racing continued into the early 1970s at Montlhery, the Paris Grand Prix never happened. Then recently, after a number of years of historic events, the circuit has now closed to racing…the loss of yet another site of some very important motor racing.

Five days later a number of the sports car brigade were in Portugal for the Oporto Grand Prix, on the mouth of the River Douro. There were to be two main races on the 4.6-mile Boavista road circuit which would later attract Grand Prix cars. The first race was on Saturday for up to 1500 cc. sports cars, and this gave a fairly easy victory to Roy Salvadori in a works Cooper-Climax sports car. He was chased by Porsches and Maseratis but never lost the lead over 20 laps, taking the Oporto City Cup. The works Porsche of Portuguese J.F. Nogueira was second, with Reg Bicknell's Lotus-Climax third. Jack Brabham had been in a strong second when his gearbox let him down and he retired. Lotus driver Cliff Allison had also been going well when the rough roads of Oporto loosened a fuel pipe and the Lotus caught fire. Cliff Allison: "This was one of the races I remember seeing Portago. I don't know why I remember it, because I was so concerned that I had managed to set myself on fire. The interesting thing is that Portago was one of the people who came over to me after the race to see if I was ok. That stuck in my head."

Sunday June 17 saw the main event, the Oporto Grand Prix for sports cars over 1500 cc. This brought a good entry for a relatively minor race, including a number of works cars. The Ferrari factory sent cars for Portago and Phil Hill, Portago getting the same 857S he had driven with Hill at Montlhery (0584/0578). Some reports had Portago driving his 250 GT (chassis 0415GT) at Oporto but there is no evidence of this. Maserati sent a 300S for Schell and other cars from the two Italian manufacturers were present for Pilette, Nogueira, Godia Sales, Mascarenhas, Musy and the loyal Maserati driver Baron de Graffenried. The British Whitehead brothers Graham and Peter were there with an Aston Martin DB3S and Maserati 300S respectively. Even a couple of Pegasos showed up. Schell was the initial leader in the 40-lap race, but the Portuguese driver Nogueira got past him. Schell dropped out with Portago on his tail, looking poised to strike, as the Maserati had steering failure. Though Portago got the quick Ferrari past the Portuguese driver's similar car, he wouldn't let the Spaniard get away. They had a tremendous duel after many laps of flying in close company. Nogueira hit a kerb and suddenly flipped, injuring him seriously. Phil Hill kept Portago in sight to finish second with Musy in a 3-litre Maserati third. Portago set the fastest lap at just a fraction under 100 mph in a stirring drive. Phil Hill said that he might have done better "except for my feelings regarding the circuit. There was one fast downhill stretch through the trees that really had me bugged. I kept losing the tail of the car, and my adrenal flow was something awful. I'd heard about two drivers who'd gone into those trees the previous year and were in asylums, and that little bit of information sure didn't help to settle my nerves." (Nolan, 1996,p.76) The author wondered who might have circulated that seemingly unfounded story, but couldn't determine the culprit. Phil Hill was always a gentleman and was reluctant to point a finger at any likely parties. In fact, it was often difficult to get Phil to comment on his fellow drivers, either positively or negatively.

The same journals that reported the Oporto race announced that Fangio/Castellotti, Collins/Gendebien and Portago/Trintignant would form the basis of Ferrari's attack at the following weekend's 1000 kilometer Supercortemaggiore Grand Prix to be held at Monza.

Portago had rather suddenly become a 'professional' racing driver, having been signed as a regular sports car driver for Ferrari for which he was paid a fee as well as part of the prize money. He was also racing more intensively than he had done at any time previously, now almost every weekend, and he was getting more time behind the wheel in these few months than he had altogether in his two earlier seasons.

The Ferrari driver announcements, as often happened, turned out to be inaccurate.

The Supercortemaggiore Grand Prix was sponsored by Agip-BP fuels, and the race got its name from the big oil refinery at Supercortemaggiore. This race demonstrated once again how popular sports car racing had become in 1956, and 62 cars were entered for what was predicted to be a very high-speed clash at Monza, with 41 being allowed to start. The full road circuit and banking combination was to be used for this event which had usually been run for 3-litre sports cars. For 1956, however, it had been decided to limit it to 2-litre cars, with a class for up to 1500 cc. engines. The decision was made to slow the cars down and as practice commenced, the organisers would be surprised at how quick the 2-litre cars were going. Like some of the recent races, there were masses of Maseratis and Ferraris, Maserati entering no less than nine works cars as well as looking after several private machines.

Maserati had a pretty difficult series of practice sessions. They had few new cars, the most competitive for Stirling Moss who was to be paired with Nino Farina who had just returned from a rather unsuccessful attempt at the Indy 500. The Maseratis were struggling on the combined road/banking and the tyres were pounded against the body on the banking, and nearly all the cars had to have larger bulges hammered out to make more room. Moss set some very quick times, and then Farina went out and almost immediately rolled the new Maserati into scrap. Another car, though older, was then brought over for Moss to share now with Piero Taruffi. The team had assigned Belluci as his co-driver but Moss argued he needed someone more competitive. Farina was carted off to hospital with a broken collarbone. Jo Bonnier/Mackay Fraser and Jack Fairman/Marie Teresa de Filippis were in 1.5-litre Maseratis.

Ferrari had an entry of four works cars, and like Maserati, would be tending to some of the private owners as well. Mike Hawthorn was down to drive a Lotus Climax with Duncan Hamilton but gearbox problems forced its withdrawal and suddenly Hawthorn found himself in a competitive works Ferrari which he would share with Peter Collins. However, the Scuderia were not faring much better than Maserati with Fangio having a rear axle failure, and then a piston broke in his replacement car. Von Trips and Hans Herrmann were added to the Ferrari driver strength, but when Hawthorn and Hamilton were available they were brought in as well. Then the cars started breaking down so Phil Hill, Herrmann and Hamilton were without a drive. Hill's self-confidence wasn't helped by this move, and as he would have been in the car with Peter Collins, the final result didn't make him feel any better.

Portago was sharing a Ferrari 500 TR (chassis 0652 MDTR) with Belgian Olivier Gendebien. They had a relatively quiet practice period, both going through the mandatory learning stages that the organisers set in place for all drivers. This meant a period of lapping at set times to practice the entry and exit from the road and banked sections of the circuit. Some of the 'veterans' complained but Portago hadn't had the experience so he spent as much time on it as possible.

The Ferrari 500 TR was a new car, having the same chassis, engine and rear axle as the production Testa Rossa model, but with a sleeker body by Touring. The new 2-litre, 4-cylinder car had sturdy chassis tubes, coil spring and wishbone independent front suspension. The engine was based on the F2 engine and the car had a four-speed gearbox in unit with the engine. The rear axle was one-piece, using coil springs, radius rods and A-bracket location. The 500 was lighter than the Mondial 2-litre which had the DeDion rear end.

A Le Mans start was being used, with the fastest cars at the front of the long line parked down the Monza pit straight. As the flag fell, Gendebien starting the car he was sharing with Portago, was first off the line and into the lead, pursued by Collins, Moss, Schell and da Silva Ramos in the Gordini. As the dust cleared, it became apparent that several cars were still sitting there, and these included Fangio's Ferrari, the Chiron/Cabianca OSCA, Rosier's Maserati, de Filippis, and the Ferrari of the other two women drivers, Peduzzi/Thirion. They all eventually got started and charged off after the rest of the field.

Stirling Moss, who had already been having a hard time at Monza, had even more trouble when his prop shaft broke on the very first lap while he was going very quickly. The shaft ripped through the fuel tank located in the cockpit, and Moss managed to get the car stopped safely. When he made his way back to the pits, he would be teamed up with Cesare Perdisa for the rest of the race. Peter Collins slipped past Gendebien and they were being followed by Carini, Gerini, and Villoresi, though the attention was on the progress of Juan Fangio. He was cutting his way through the field at a good pace, but not actually gaining on the leading Collins/Hawthorn Ferrari. Portago would say later in one of his interviews that this was one of the races where he watched Fangio's progress and technique for pressing on even though he was well behind. He said several times that he learned a great deal from Fangio, watching and driving behind him. A bit later, Fangio would say how highly he thought of Portago's ability.

The start of the Supercortemaggiorie Grand Prix with Portago in car # 65 ahead of a large field. *(Credit - Largada)*

The veteran driver Luigi Villoresi was driving a very impressive race in the 1500 cc. OSCA and was holding 5th overall. Considering Monza's reputation as a circuit that rewarded big engines and high speed, the little OSCA was doing amazingly well. In spite of the banking, the full circuit layout at Monza

Peter Collins about to lap Jean Guichet's Ferrari on the Monza banking. ***(Credit - National Motor Museum)***

required very precise driving, so the good drivers were doing well in the circumstances. Bonnier was getting the most out of his Maserati on the long straight sections of the track. Schell's gearbox broke on only the second lap, and that meant von Trips didn't get a drive. He and Portago had been sitting on the pit wall waiting to take over and planning the battle they would have with each other. Von Trips, a 'fellow' nobleman, was another driver to find Portago easy to get on with, and like Fangio would predict Portago to become an eventual World Champion. Perdisa was pushing his 2-litre Maserati very hard and he also went past Gendebien. At ten laps, it was Collins, Perdisa, Gendebien, the flying Fangio, Villoresi, de Graffenried, Barth, Lucas, Bonnier and Cornacchia. Louis Chiron, in the OSCA he was sharing with Cabianca, was seen to be shaking his fist at everyone he could in traffic, in his usual style. History has always treated Chiron as a 'gentleman driver' who had achieved much in the pre-war period, but he certainly had some 'quirks' which others resented. He had more or less publicly declared the pre-war French woman driver Helle Nice a Nazi collaborator, something for which many people never forgave him. When drivers were interviewed about other drivers they liked or didn't like, there were often comments about a certain driver who always waved his fist at others, but these drivers always kept the name of that person anonymous!

The Gendebien/Portago Ferrari on the Monza banking. ***(Credit - J.Uribe)***

On the 29th lap, Collins set an astonishing new sports car record of just over 200 kph, and Fangio had moved past Gerini's Ferrari into third. A few laps later Gerini retired, as had de Graffenried. Gendebien had slipped back to 5th, and there was a fuss in the Maserati pits as Piero Taruffi objected to Perdisa's car being handed over to Moss instead of him. He was then assigned to partner Andre Simon, whose co-driver Sgorbati was told by team manager Ugolini that he would replace Jack Fairman in the Maserati Fairman was driving with de Filippis...which was barely running at this point...very confusing for the spectators and the drivers! Moss took over from Perdisa on lap 49 during an overlong stop, and Hawthorn went in for Collins on the following lap, also making a slow stop. Then it was Castellotti in for Fangio who had gotten into second place from starting 30 seconds behind the field at the start. Mackay Fraser retired the Bonnier car before the halfway point after going well, but one of the carburetors had fallen off. On lap 82 Hawthorn was brought in for more fuel and Collins got back behind the wheel. This was an over-cautious pit stop and cost them 30 seconds. Moss had put the Maserati into second and now he reduced the gap by several seconds and was only 22 seconds off the lead. A few laps later it was down to 9 seconds, but Peter Collins then kept the gap at that, and Moss couldn't get any closer.

Portago had taken over from Gendebien and went quicker and more consistently and brought the car back up to 5th, having had it drop to 6th. When Carini stopped, Portago got into 4th where he stayed. Collins/Hawthorn won from Moss/Perdisa, Fangio/Castellotti, Portago/Gendebien and Villoresi/Maglioli, this last pair winning the 1.5-litre class.

Ferrari had managed to take a win from Maserati on home ground, and it was another steady performance from Portago.

An interesting photo appeared in the motoring journals after the Italian race. It showed a group of drivers before the start at Monza, and they included Fangio, Harry Schell, Stirling Moss and Peter Collins. A smiling Fon Portago is just to the back of Juan Fangio. It demonstrates two things about Portago: the illustrious group of star drivers he had joined, and Portago's possible ambivalence about his presence in this group, as there are several similar photos over the years where Portago appears smiling but always slightly to the rear or the side. One could speculate, and it would only be speculation, that Portago was very much in awe of a number of the drivers. It was clear from later interviews that this was true in relation to Fangio, and probably Alberto Ascari. Duncan Hamilton reported that there was a contingent of himself, Portago, Hawthorn, Musso, Collins and Castellotti, which set out to visit every nightclub in Milan after the race. At some point, Hawthorn and Collins cut a cake that had been presented to them by Enzo Ferrari himself in recognition of their victory. Hamilton said he couldn't quite remember when or where that had occurred, such was the state of the celebrations. (Hamilton, 1960)

Another photo of Portago on the edge of the group of top drivers at Monza: Fangio, Schell, Moss and Collins. ***(Credit - Petrie Collection)***

Ferrari 500 TR Chassis 0652 MDTR

Portago drove this new 2-litre car only once, sharing with Gendebien to finish 4th overall at the 1956 Supercortemaggiore Grand Prix at Monza. This works car was only completed shortly before the race at Monza. It was sold almost immediately after the race to Luigi Chinetti and then went directly to John Edgar. Carroll Shelby drove it two or three times before Temple Buell bought it for Masten Gregory who campaigned it at Thompson Raceway in Connecticut, in Wyoming and Sacramento before it went to Nassau. It was the car Gregory used in the Ferrari race at Nassau, beating Portago into second place. Masten Gregory had four races with it at Nassau and then raced it in Cuba in February 1957. Chet Flynn bought it in 1957, raced it himself until 1959. Bill Burroughs bought it and used it though 1959. It changed hands several times, raced regularly, and now is owned by John Bosch in the Netherlands.

The Ferrari 500 TR, chassis 0652, driven by Portago and Gendebien at Monza as it is today.

In another confluence of complex factors, Portago would find himself facing the next most important change in his motor racing career. The first had been his inclusion in the works Ferrari sports car team. The next big move was into the Ferrari Grand Prix line-up, which took place at the French Grand Prix at the super-fast Reims circuit. There hadn't been a French Grand Prix in 1955 after the Le Mans crash so this race had added significance.

Ferrari entered five cars for the French race, the Lancia D-50s for Fangio, Castellotti, Collins, Portago and Gendebien. The Lancia D-50 had first appeared in late 1954 when Gianni Lancia brought the company, which had been doing very well in sports car events, into Grand Prix racing. The new car was stunningly different with large side fuel pods and a beautiful sounding V-8 engine. Ascari put the new car on pole for its first race at the 1954 Spanish Grand Prix but retired with a clutch problem. Everyone present thought they were seeing Lancia getting ready to rule the world. The cars didn't finish the first race in 1955 in Argentina, but then Ascari won the non-championship F1 race at Valentine Park in Turin, where Portago had made his Formula 1 debut in his own Ferrari 625. He had been impressed by Ascari's performance, and was happy to be driving his own Ferrari. There is no indication whether he suspected then that it wouldn't be that long before he would be driving a D-50.

Ascari had finished 5th in the 1955 race at Pau where Portago was 8th, and then Ascari had won the Naples race. He was leading the Monaco Grand Prix when he crashed at the chicane and he and his Lancia flew into the harbour. They were both rescued but a few days later Ascari was killed in a still unexplained practice crash in a Ferrari sports car at Monza. Gianni Lancia was crushed by Ascari's death. Though Lancia was in serious financial difficulty, the prospect of Ascari winning the World Championship had kept Lancia going and fending off the creditors. When Ascari was gone, so were Lancia's hopes. The entire team's equipment was sold off to Scuderia Ferrari for virtually nothing. This was a tremendous boost for Ferrari whose 553 and 555 Grand Prix cars were just not working very well, and not many of the drivers liked them. The Lancia 'gift' gave Ferrari a new lease on life with a 2.5-litre car which was well capable of winning.

Eugenio Castellotti had begged Lancia to let him run the team's car once more at the 1955 Belgian Grand Prix where he covered himself in glory by putting it on pole, an emotional tribute to Ascari and Lancia, though he retired in the race. Two D-50s were entered by Ferrari along with four 555s later in the season at the Italian Grand Prix. Two cars also showed up at the Gold Cup at Oulton Park at the very end of 1955, which had clearly been Mercedes Benz' season. For 1956, there was a mix of D-50s and 555s at the two South American races but for the rest of 1956, the Lancia D-50 was Ferrari's Grand Prix car. This extended well into 1957 until the F2-based Dino 156 first appeared.

There was no public announcement of Portago's move into the Grand Prix team, and indeed that would have been unlikely in the period anyway. It was very likely to be on a trial basis, possibly without a written contract and with no guarantee of permanence in the arrangement. The proven drivers would have had contracts but the 'new boys' had to demonstrate their competence. It was also common practice for Ferrari to provide a car for a 'local' driver at their own Grand Prix. Andre Pilette drove a D-50 painted in Belgian yellow for the 1955 race at Spa.

The French Grand Prix was significant for other teams as well. A new Grand Prix Bugatti was making its debut, and a great deal of fuss was made about it and its driver, Maurice Trintignant. Trintignant was always game for a challenge and for many years worked at being the great French driver, and was perhaps disappointed towards the end of his life not to be officially recognised for his very important achievements in motor racing. At Reims, he was lucky to get the Bugatti ahead of Pilette's little Gordini and Simon's private Maserati. It disappeared early in the race and was never seen again.

Another surprise was the sight of Lotus principal Colin Chapman behind the wheel of a Vanwall in practice. Chapman was a very fast driver as well as brilliant designer, but he had a big crash in practice and that was the end of his F1 driving career. Ferrari produced their own surprise with a streamlined body. This was impressive looking but Reims was not the place to be testing untried aerodynamics. Portago did several laps in this car, but it wouldn't handle, lifted, and generally could not be made to run quickly so was put aside. It was another car not to reappear.

Mike Hawthorn had moved to the BRM team but the car was not ready, so he was loaned to the Vanwall team, which seemed to be getting into its stride. He joined Schell and Chapman, but that was reduced to a two-man team when Chapman was out. That happened when he smote the back of 'new boy' Hawthorn when the brakes didn't work!

The aerodynamic bodywork was tried on this Lancia D-50 by Portago at Reims but it wasn't raced.
(Credit - D.Thirlby)

The Ferrari drivers in their garage before practice for the French Grand Prix; from left, Collins, Gendebien, Portago, Fangio and Castellotti. *(Credit - Reims Archive)*

The cars lining up for the race, Portago's to the far right. ***(Credit - Author's Collection)***

There were five works Maserati 250Fs, the five 'Ferrari-Lancias'…whatever they were called by the team, they were Lancia D-50s…four works Gordinis and a handful of privateers. Hawthorn got the Vanwall around for the first ever 200-kph lap at Reims, for which he was given 100 bottles of champagne. He had just beaten Harry Schell to the bubbly, and Schell was immediately going very well in the Vanwall.

Portago put a very impressive lap in that first session on Wednesday of 2 minutes 30.9 seconds in the D-50 (chassis 0007), making him 4th quickest behind Collins, Schell and Hawthorn, some five seconds faster than teammate Gendebien. Fangio was fastest of all on Thursday, and Castellotti had this honour on Friday. When the practice was all over the grid read Fangio, Castellotti, Collins, Schell, Hawthorn, Behra, Moss and Portago in 8th spot. Gendebien was two places and two seconds further back. Eighth of twenty in his first 'proper' Grand Prix car as a member of the Scuderia Ferrari must have been satisfying for Portago.

Portago was just behind Stirling Moss' works Maserati 250F on the grid, which must have also given them both something to think about. The author sat in the Monaco Historics paddock recently with Sir Stirling to talk about his recollections of the Marquis de Portago:

"One of my outstanding memories of Portago was at the Tour de France. I was with a guy who was a good crumpet chaser, but Portago really had that department all sorted out. He was a good-looking chap, swarthy, fast in a car, probably very good as a polo player; he was quite the desirable bloke from the ladies' point of view. I remember when he came on the scene, he was certainly competent. I didn't think then that he would become a lead driver in a team, but it was clear that he was competent enough to get an invitation into a very good team, and that is what happened. Of course, he had a lot of aura around him, and a good bit of publicity, and that was one reason why the organisers would like to have him in a race. And Fon was a really nice bloke as well as a competent driver. We were in some of the same races in the early 1950s. I think he was at Sebring in 1954 but I can't remember what he was driving, but I do remember meeting him. Yes, he was with Harry Schell, wasn't he? Well, they were a combination and Harry and Fon were inseparable. They had something of a reputation as gamblers…I think they would go off for hours at a time trying out some plan to make big money gambling! I remember Fon at Nassau, the one year when he won most of his races. I think I was driving an Austin Healey. That was an ideal race for him, especially in his early days, he was certainly good enough to win those sort of events. When you turn the pressure on in Formula 1, well then he didn't show quite the same results, but I remember him as being very competent."

" I wasn't personally close to him, though we chatted often, and discussed what was going on. His circle of friends was more Harry Schell and Nano da Silva Ramos. I was much too young! I was a bit immature. I would chase the girls and then stop. They would chase them, catch them…and have really big parties. I was being very serious about being a racing driver! I do remember some of the things he got up to…his affair with Linda Christian for one. But he was one of those guys who when you met them, you couldn't help liking them. He was a very likeable, friendly, affable guy. You have to remember that motor racing in the '50s was very different. Racing was still a sport, the drivers were friends. We were going from one circuit to another every week, so we met each other and were doing things together, and it was a lot more enjoyable. I think my quality of life when I was racing was much higher than Michael Schumacher's is today. There's no humour around now, and guys like Portago lived on that. I think Portago was serious about his racing but I don't think he would have let it ruin his life. I think racing was one of his ambitions, and if he had taken it more seriously, Portago wouldn't have enjoyed it as much. I was similar, though I took it much more seriously than he did. I think of myself as a professional driver and he wasn't in that sense. But I enjoyed it very much and so did he. I remember being in some scraps with him in sports car races, more so than in Grands Prix, and I knew he was quick. I believe Enzo Ferrari was quite happy to have him in his team for the publicity. It was lucky that he also turned out to be very capable."

Portago in his works D-50 getting ready for the start. ***(Credit - Reims Archive)***

When it came time for the start at Reims, Portago had a box seat for the chaos created by Moss' engine failing to start. It had to be pushed to get it going, and it was pushed all the way to the front, stopping Charles Faroux from bringing the flag down, and then Moss just managed to get back into position when the engine kicked over and they were off. Villoresi, however, was also struggling to start and he was left behind until all the others departed. The race was over 61 laps of the five-mile circuit, a total of 314 miles. As they came down past the pits from the tight Thillois hairpin after the first lap, three Ferraris led, with Collins in front of Castellotti and Fangio, with Schell, Hawthorn, Moss and Portago. Harry Schell had second gear jam on the Vanwall on lap two and he dropped to ninth while the mechanics sorted it out. On the third tour, the three D-50s still led, with Hawthorn and Portago desperately trying to stay on terms with them. Soon Fangio got into the top spot, and five D-50s were in the first six places, Gendebien having towed up behind Portago.

The start of the 1956 French Grand Prix with Collins in front. ***(Credit - Author's Collection)***

Just as Hawthorn started to lose ground in his Vanwall, Schell came into the pits in his. He did another lap but retired with terminal gearbox damage. On lap eleven, Hawthorn came in, apparently feeling the results of having driven in the 12 hour sports car race only a few hours before. Schell jumped in and rejoined the fray, but Portago had moved into fourth and the D-50s had all the leading positions. Moss also retired his car but immediately took over Perdisa's 250F. Moss came back out in front of Portago who had the advantage of using him as a 'pace-maker' and he began to set some quick lap times. He began to catch his three leading teammates as the Ferrari pit had signaled the leaders to take it easy. They totally missed the fact that Harry Schell was embarking on the Grand Prix drive of his life. On lap 14 he was 42 seconds behind the leader, but he soon caught and passed Gendebien. On lap 16 Portago slowed on the entry to Thillois. The gearbox had broken. Portago pushed it down the slope towards the pits as far as he could, stopping with exhaustion just before he reached the pits.

Fangio leads a group down the long straight at Reims. ***(Credit - Author's Collection)***

By lap 28, Schell had reduced the gap to Fangio to a mere 8 seconds, and was right up with the three D-50s. He had shot past Moss, and then the 'faster' board went out to Fangio. Schell charged past Collins and Castellotti to head past the pits on Fangio's tail, setting a new lap record on lap 30 of over 201 kph. On lap 35 he was right behind Fangio, and then started to slow, coming into the pits where frantic work went on attempting to repair a ball joint in the throttle linkage which had sheared. He resumed but the engine wouldn't run properly. Then Fangio was in for a stop, and had to set out after Behra's Maserati, which he couldn't catch. Collins took the win from Castellotti, Behra and Fangio. Schell only managed tenth but had earned the respect of everyone present. But it was Fangio who set a new record of nearly 205 kph. The crowd had seen another riveting Grand Prix.

Portago leads the second group in the early laps at Reims.
(Credit - Author's Collection)

Portago driving as hard as he could at Reims.
(Credit - Ferret Fotographics)

Juan Fangio at 175 miles an hour past the pits at Reims. ***(Credit - Author's Collection)***

Immediately after the Grand Prix, many of the teams and drivers journeyed west, either through or around Paris, to Rouen, where the city of Joan of Arc was celebrating a huge festival, and hosting stages of the cycling Tour de France. There were two sports car races scheduled, the Coupe Delamare-Debouteville for up to 1500 cc. cars, and the Grand Prix of Rouen for the bigger machinery. The festive atmosphere had captivated the whole area on the weekend of July 7/8, and the appearance of the Tour de France at the circuit on Saturday morning brought vast numbers of spectators to the beautiful 6.5 kilometer circuit which sweeps up and down through a forested area a few miles from the cathedral city. Sadly, this is another great track no longer used for racing, and only recently the last of the remaining pit buildings have been torn down.

There were two practice sessions for each race, starting at the unbearable hour of 6.00 a.m. This was definitely not popular. Colin Chapman had bounced back from his shunt at Reims and was on the front row with a 1500 cc. Lotus, the very car which had just run in the Mobilgas Economy run in England. Mike MacDowell was in a Cooper and Harry Schell in a Lotus. Phil Hill was in a works Cooper-Climax but not long into the race, a rod came through the block. Cliff Allison in the second works Lotus soon joined boss Chapman at the front and these two proceeded to move away from the field. Schell in a third Lotus completed a fine day for the then Tottenham-based firm.

This British win gave hope to the many British fans present that the Aston Martin team might do the same in the main race, but the proximity to the Reims race the week before meant there was a large and competitive entry. Ferrari had sent three cars and Maserati two. Peter Collins had switched to an Aston for the race, and was joined by Tony Brooks, Roy Salvadori and Stirling Moss. Perdisa and Behra in their Maseratis bracketed Castellotti's 3-litre four cylinder Ferrari on the front row, followed by Moss and Collins. Castellotti had taken over Fangio's car as he was on holiday, and Phil Hill was in a private 750 Monza, on row three with Brooks and Schell, also in a private Ferrari. Behind them were Salvadori and Portago in the third works Ferrari. This was a 3-litre 290 MM (chassis 0626M) with a V-12 engine, unlike Castellotti's. Portago had expressed his unhappiness with the car, or specifically with the V-12 engine, which he felt, was unresponsive under 5000 rpm. Portago had been described by British journalist Maxwell Boyd as part of the colourful atmosphere at Rouen: "De Portago, the professional amateur, drove up in his works Ferrari, a cigarette hanging from the corner of his mouth." (Boyd in Autosport July 13, 1956, p.42.) There was an Ecurie Ecosse D-Type Jaguar for Desmond Titterington just behind Portago, followed by ten privateers in Maseratis, Ferraris, a Gordini and two Mercedes Benz 300Sls. The Mercedes were at the back of the grid and looked unlikely to offer any competition on this circuit, which demanded good handling and a dose of agility.

At the flag, Perdisa, Collins and Moss shot off downhill through high-speed bends to the tight and slow Virage du Nouveau Monde at the bottom end of the circuit, before heading back uphill through faster bends, trees and some daunting corners before bursting back out onto the top of the main straight above the pits. Frenchman Jean Behra was desperate to do well 'at home' and tagged onto Moss, while Collins put the Aston in front on lap 5. Five laps later, Portago was engaged in a mighty battle with the Swiss privateer Musy who was trying to force his Ferrari past the Spaniard. The field started to string out at this point and the first of the retirements came. Harry Schell appeared on foot, and six laps later, Peter Collins was missing, only to appear a few minutes later, the telltale on the rev counter stuck way above where it should have been. Behra got past Perdisa and Musy moved in front of Portago, but only for a lap as Portago tried to keep the V-12's revs high enough to out-run Musy. The D-Type was sitting behind this pair, rather bemused by the tactics. Portago got back past the other Ferrari by the halfway point but was finding the car was just not running cleanly. He came flying into the pits, and some oil was added to the engine and some orange juice to the driver, and he set off again a lap behind.

Behra had a 20 second lead over Perdisa by this stage, driving as well as anyone had seen, forcing the Astons into some ragged maneuvers to keep up. On lap 37, Perdisa suddenly pulled in and retired his Maserati 300S, and then Castellotti was seen to be catching Behra. Then both the Italian and Moss went by Behra who had a broken shock absorber. Despite a huge effort from Moss, the Aston Martin couldn't catch the Ferrari and Castellotti won, with Behra hanging on for third. Portago finished in 9th, behind Musy after his stop. He probably regretted the stop because Musy had spun and Portago might well have beaten the Jaguar into 7th, but these were the minor placings. Phil Hill finished a good 6th in his private 750 Monza, which brought murmurs from other customers about how well it was prepared. The fact was that Phil was just driving superbly well.

Ferrari 290 MM Chassis 0626

This works Ferrari, a 290 MM Scaglietti Spyder, first appeared as Juan Fangio's car, number 600, at the Mille Miglia at the end of April, and ran in red with a nose-band in Argentine colours. It was the car entered at the Nurburgring for Phil Hill and Ken Wharton, and was shared with Portago/Gendebien finishing 3rd. After Portago's 9th place at Rouen it was driven to second place at the Swedish Grand Prix by von Trips/Collins. Temple Buell bought the car in 1957 and it won the Buenos Aires 1000 Kilometers with Musso/Castellotti/ Gregory and Perdisa. In August 1957 Masten Gregory was second at Spa, and in December Jo Bonnier was 6th in the Governor's trophy and 4th in the Nassau Trophy in the Bahamas. Paul O'Shea was 9th in the Cuban GP. It passed through the hands of Americans Bob Williams, James A. Flynn, Bob Dusek and Kirk F. White before going to Pierre Bardinon in 1970 for 17 years. It went to Ron Stern in the UK via Terry Hoyle.

The Ferrari 290MM, chassis 0626, which Portago drove at Rouen, as it is today. ***(Credit - Keith Bluemel)***

In the days when drivers would take part in a Grand Prix, a sports, touring or lesser formula race, sometimes at the same meeting, their schedule was indeed very busy. Portago found himself amongst those leaving Rouen and heading straight for Silverstone, the scene of his crash the previous year in practice for the International Trophy race. The British Grand Prix was to take place on July 14 on the 4.71 kilometer ex-airfield circuit in Northamptonshire. There were 31 entries of which three did not appear, one of these being the Ferrari-entered Lancia D-50 for Olivier Gendebien. To be accurate, the car appeared but Gendebien didn't. After Reims, it was expecting a lot to think that Silverstone could provide a very exciting spectacle. Very few of the Grand Prix races run at Silverstone have offered great drama, though some fine driving has been characteristic of this race. Many of the spectators were there to see the British teams, which generally were disappointing, or to see Fangio…who wasn't.

Ferrari had what had to be seen as the 'regular' driver squad with Fangio, Castellotti, Collins and Portago. Most of these would race their usual cars, with Portago in 0007 as he was at Reims, though virtually all the drivers tried all the cars in the set-up periods on Thursday and Friday. Maserati had four works 250Fs and the team was looking after some of the private cars as well. The British entry was promising, with BRM bringing cars for Hawthorn, Brooks and Flockhart, and Connaught had three cars as well for Archie Scott-Brown, Desmond Titterington and Jack Fairman. Tony Vandervell's Vanwall team also had a trio of cars for Harry Schell, the hero of Reims, Maurice Trintignant, and amazingly he talked Froilan Gonzales into the third team car. Then there was a batch of private entries.

Timing was the subject of much argument after practice, as times hadn't been made available, and then were only given to the nearest second. The cars which looked to be going well were the Maseratis of Salvadori and Moss, Hawthorn's BRM, Schell and Gonzales. Fangio, of course looked good, and so did Collins but the D-50s were far less happy at Silverstone than they were at Reims. The Connaughts weren't going well, and when it rained on Friday, it was the Thursday times which would count for the grid. When some more detailed times were finally published, it was Moss on pole from Fangio, Hawthorn and Collins, with Schell, Gonzales and Salvadori next. There was still a lot of arguing about the timing, however.

Portago was one of those not looking very comfortable at Silverstone, and he was in 12th spot on row four, behind some of the Connaughts which didn't please him. Portago was apparently now feeling the pressure of being a regular team Grand Prix driver and he was reported as looking concerned about his practice times.

Drivers gather at the British Grand Prix at Silverstone, from left to right, Schell, Perdisa, Gonzales, Behra and Portago at the rear on the right. *(Credit - Author's Collection)*

Race day was very gray but it wasn't raining, and when the flag went down, Mike Hawthorn had revved the BRM perfectly and shot away into the lead, followed by Tony Brooks who also made a brilliant start from row three. He had to dodge past the Vanwall of Froilan Gonzales, the 'Pampas Bull' having a drive shaft break on the line and he went nowhere as the rest of the field swarmed around him. There were echoes of previous terrible failures of British cars on the start line at Silverstone! Hawthorn and Brooks then pulled the two BRM P25s away from the rest as they crossed the line for the first time. After three laps they stretched out the gap to Fangio to five seconds, a serious morale booster for the British fans. Portago had thrust his Lancia D-50 past both Scott-Brown and his teammate Castellotti. Flockhart's BRM stopped, not a good omen, and so had Jack Brabham's ex-BRM Maserati 250F. Fangio managed to catch and pass Tony Brooks, and the Vanwall weak link was showing as Schell came into the pits with a broken shock absorber. Archie Scott-Brown wouldn't let Portago and Castellotti get away, and he began to push the Connaught very hard. Scott-Brown was an amazing driver who had birth defects, including a severely withered arm and a short leg, and he had to overcome serious prejudice before he was allowed to race at the top level. He was often a virtually 'magical' driver to some fans in the way he could handle very high-powered cars, especially Lister-Jaguar sports cars. In the Connaught, he was a tiger.

Peter Collins was in the lead in this car at the British Grand Prix.
(Credit - Author's Collection)

Fangio had an uncharacteristic spin, a result of having to push too hard to keep up, and he rejoined after Collins and ahead of the big battle between his two fellow D-50 drivers and the flying Connaught. By the end of lap 14 of 101, a British BRM was in the lead and the first four drivers were Brits. Then Moss passed Hawthorn and Fangio did the same to Brooks. Sadly, the hub assembly on Scott-Brown's Connaught broke as he had gotten ahead of the two D-50s. Moss led Hawthorn and Salvadori, driving one of his best races, and then Fangio who was working very hard to make any progress. Fangio was described as looking as tense as Tony Brooks appeared relaxed. The Lancia D-50s were tentative on the corners and seemed to lack grip, unlike at Reims. The Vanwalls were in disarray, some of the privateers started to stumble, and then Hawthorn was caught by Salvadori. Hawthorn flew into the pits at the end of lap 23, all the grease gone from the transmission joint. Moss was way out front, and Roy Salvadori looked happy in second, and Fangio was back in third, looking untidy as he overtook slower cars any way he could. MotorSport captured the dice between Castellotti and Portago: "The duel between Castellotti and de Portago was still going on, the Italian leading, but with his mouth open and looking very harassed, while the Spaniard was sitting right behind wearing a wonderful 'poker-faced' expression, and every time Castellotti nipped by a slower car, his 'shadow' would follow through, regardless of whether they were on the straight or in the middle of a corner." (MotorSport August 1956, p.455) In fact, Castellotti was so intimidated by the attention he was getting from Portago that he pulled into the pits on lap 33 for an investigation to see if something was wrong.

Eugenio Castellotti in the car eventually taken over by Portago at Silverstone.
(Credit - Castellotti family)

This is the car which Portago started but handed over to Collins so they finished second.
(Credit - Ferret Fotographics)

The race seemed to have settled into something of a procession with Moss and his Maserati at the front, until Tony Brooks brought about a change. He had stopped to have a faulty throttle attended to and then got out again. The rear end seemed to lock solid as Brooks lined up for Abbey Corner, and the BRM just went end over end, shooting Brooks out of the car and then immediately burst into a mass of flames. Brooks had received facial injuries but was very lucky to be alive. This was followed not many laps later by poor Roy Salvadori's Maserati having the fuel tank strap break, so he had to stop for repairs, losing his superb 2nd place to Fangio. Moss' lead over Fangio was then reduced two laps later when he stopped for oil. The Maserati engine was now down on power and the gap dropped to five seconds, though Moss managed to hold it there. All of this had moved Portago up into 5th spot and he seemed to be the only D-50 driver not looking terribly worried about his car. The circuit was very slippery from the covering of oil it was getting from all the cars in trouble. Peter Collins joined this bunch as his oil pressure disappeared altogether and he came into the pits.

Jean Behra was now breathing down Portago's neck, so the Ferrari pit decided to call Portago in and give his car to Peter Collins, and Collins immediately discovered that Portago's car had been handling much better than his own! Salvadori soon retired altogether and on lap 69 Moss was in the pits and out of the lead with a further loss of power. He was back out on the track behind Fangio but ahead of Collins in the Portago car, which had moved up to third. Jack Fairman had undramatically moved the Connaught up to fourth as other cars dropped by the wayside. Then an amazing thing happened as Castellotti was called in to hand over to Portago (chassis 0009) to see if he could do any better than the Italian in catching the Connaught. Having spun and buckled a wheel,

Castellotti thought he was being retired and was fairly amazed to see Portago leaping into the cockpit of what he thought was a dead car. The final drama came when Moss stopped out on the circuit on the 93rd lap.

Collins leaves the pits having taken over from Portago. *(Credit - Petrie Collection)*

In the meantime, Portago was driving what looked like a wounded crab around the circuit at high speed. He 'missed' the black flag the first few times it was shown, and when he finally came in, he got involved in a serious argument with the steward Harold Parker, contending that the car was still driveable, even though it appeared that the chassis had been bent. He won the argument and was allowed to drive round slowly, stopping before the line to wait for the finish. His determination earned him a lot of supporters that day. As the flag dropped, Fangio won, and Collins and Portago shared second place, Behra was third and Fairman fourth, and Castellotti and Portago were credited with eleventh place. As was the tradition in the period, Moss won the supporting sports car race and Salvadori the F2 race!

Castellotti comes in with his damaged car and Portago considers what to do next.
(Credit - Alan Smith/Klementaski Collection)

Portago flings the almost undriveable car around Silverstone.
(Credit - Ferret Fotographics)

Portago leaps into Castellotti's car to attempt to make the finish.
(Credit - Ferret Fotographics)

Portago argues with the officials who have black flagged him.
(Credit - Autosport)

Portago pleads with Eason-Gibson to be allowed to complete the race, which he did.
(Credit - BRSCC Archive)

Portago pushed his car over the finish line to win the cheers of the crowd.
(Credit - Ferrari)

Autosport (July 27, 1956, p.105) added a further insight to Portago's role at Silverstone:
"Peter Collin's original car lost its oil pressure, but as lubricant was dripping from the undertray when it stopped at his pit, the car's abandonment may have been due to a more sinister reason. Alphonse (sic) de Portago showed great sportsmanship; he saw Pete's car stationary and next time around came in and jumped out like lightning, vacating the seat for his teammate. As it seems unlikely that there was time for Sculati to give him a come-in signal, the Spaniard must have taken it on himself to hand over to the Championship aspirant. Anyway, it is the sort of thing that de Portago would do. Also one cannot forget his gesture in taking over Castellotti's rather bent machine, determined to get it to the finish."

July 22 would mark the sixth of ten consecutive racing weekends for Portago in a season that was not yet one third over. To a large extent, this explains the dearth of material which ever appeared in the press and society magazines of the period about Marquis de Portago and his family. He would have seen them only occasionally and briefly on the way to and from the next event, and as Carroll Petrie said, she did not attend many of these races. To some extent, it must also cast some doubt on Portago's reputation as a compulsive woman-chaser. While there would have been parties and social gatherings around these races, the rest of the time was spent getting to the next one. In this case, the next one was in Bari, a long way from Silverstone. In the meantime, the motoring press carried the story that Juan Fangio was unlikely to race at Le Mans later in the month and that his place would be taken by Portago.

Bari on the Adriatic coast of Italy was seen by the motoring journals of the day as one of the last bastions of real racing through city streets. Bari only ran one event each year by 1956, but the whole life style of the port city shifted to accommodate this big event, with tram tracks being covered with tarmac, and huge advertising posters filling the region. The Gran Premio itself would consist of two races, one for sports cars up to 2000 cc. and one for over 2000 cc. cars over the 5.5-kilometer Lungomare circuit. The organisers were well aware of safety issues and located the pits away from the circuit and the drivers had to access it by a kind of bypass, and the straight had been shortened by the inclusion of a new twisty section.

Maserati and OSCA sent works cars to Bari but Ferrari decided to leave it to privateers. The incentive for the drivers in the 27-lap first, smaller car race was that the first five would get into the main 36-lap event. Behra and Perdisa in the factory Maserati 200S entries and Cabianca and Villoresi in OSCAs were the class of the field. Munaron, Cortese, Starabba and Carini had 2-litre private Ferrari Testa Rossas. Perdisa led Behra at the start and they had a magnificent battle for the full 27 laps, though Behra got back in front and won from his teammate, and Cabianca, and Gino Munaron's Ferrari.

The Modena Maserati factory sent 300S machines for Stirling Moss and Piero Taruffi and two 3.5-litre Maseratis also showed up. Ferrari then decided to send a works car for Portago, and this was the same car he had driven at Montlhery with Phil Hill, the 857S (chassis 0584/0578) with a three-litre engine, not 3.5 as reported in the journals of the time. Phil Hill had his 750 Monza there but it blew up in practice so he was out. Duncan Hamilton came with a D-Type Jaguar and Graham Whitehead with an Aston Martin DB3S. Jo Bonnier brought his rarely seen 1953 Alfa Romeo 6C 3000CM, which couldn't escape being called a 'Disco Volante', though technically that is incorrect. This is one of the ex-works cars, which ran at the Mille Miglia and Le Mans in 1953. Behra, Perdisa, Cabianca, Munaron and Giardini's Maserati A6GCS would also get another race for finishing in the top five in the first event earlier in the day. The OSCA team, however, decided not to run Cabianca's car after its exertions in race one.

Stirling Moss was lucky to get away ahead of the two smaller Maseratis, which managed to tuck in behind him in the main race. Behra and Perdisa were ahead of the larger car of Taruffi. The D-Type and Aston Martin just could not cope with the tight nature of the circuit but Portago had gone well in practice. Moss had done a 2 minutes 32.6 seconds in practice and Portago 2 minutes 34.5 seconds. Portago then got pushed into some of the many hay bales lining the course and lost many places. He was trying desperately to catch up but had the grill bent and stuffed with hay and was overheating and then the oil pressure sank and he was out. Indeed, those present had seen Portago as clearly the main rival to Moss as he was quicker than Taruffi, Behra and Perdisa. Moss opened up nearly a whole lap on the 2-litre Maserati teammates, and Taruffi completed the quartet of Modena cars with Musy, also in a Maserati 5th, and Duncan Hamilton came through in a praiseworthy 6th.

A rare photo of Portago at Bari in the Ferrari 860 Monza. ***(Credit - Ferrari)***

A big post-race party ensued at one of the sea-front hotels where the prize-giving took place, with awards to just about everyone, including first and last retirement, longest distance traveled to the race, best official…everyone got something. No wonder the teams and journalists loved going to Bari.

From Bari, all the sports cars teams and drivers headed back across Italy towards Le Mans to be joined by many more for the next edition of the 24 Hours. While it was expected that there would be considerable changes to track layout for safety reasons after the disaster the previous year, a lot more attention had gone into a variety of complex rule changes governing engine sizes, and what could be considered 'standard production' cars. In the end, these regulations served only to prompt entrants and manufacturers to be much cleverer about what they entered and what they said on their entry forms. The two new rules which affected everyone concerned the mandatory use of a full-width windscreen and a flexible-material tonneau cover, and a ban on refueling before 34 laps of the races, no further refueling in less than 34 lap intervals, and fuel tanks could be no larger than 29 gallons. This meant that cars had to achieve at least eleven miles per gallon, which was fine for the small cars, and a bit more difficult for Jaguar, Aston Martin, Ferrari and Talbot, which could just about squeeze 12 miles out of a gallon with no reserve. The result of all this was that the Jaguars and Aston Martins were detuning their engines, and all the teams were trying to produce windscreens with wipers that worked. Many of these would be impossible to see through, so drivers were getting ready to peer over the top.

The three works Ferraris were described in the journals as 2.5-litre TRs, though in fact they were 625LMs, and they were for Portago/Duncan Hamilton (chassis 0642LM), Phil Hill/Andre Simon and Maurice Trintignant/Olivier Gendebien. Fangio and Castellotti were not at Le Mans, and Peter Collins was with Aston Martin. Duncan Hamilton was in the team after being sacked by Jaguar for 'disobeying orders' at the Reims 12 Hours. Aston Martin had a 2.5-litre prototype for the new rules, based on the DB3S engine, but with many improvements, and Gordini also had 2.5-litre cars. What the race was turning out to be was four races in one: the larger cars if they could reduce their fuel consumption, the 2.5-litre prototypes, the up to 1500 cc. cars and the Index of Performance. The Jaguars were quickest of all in practice in spite of the engines being detuned.

The Ferrari Portago was to share with Duncan Hamilton at Le Mans, seen in scrutineering.
(Credit - Archive Gasnerie)

Portago in night practice for Le Mans. (Credit - Vintage MotorPhoto)

Rain fell before the 4.00 p.m. start when the drivers ran across the circuit to their cars. Mike Hawthorn's D-Type was into the lead right away, but disaster was awaiting some of the cars on only the second lap. Hawthorn was leading Moss, Ron Flockhart, Peter Walker, Paul Frere, Jack Fairman, Portago in 7th, and Phil Hill. Paul Frere in his D-Type shared with Desmond Titterington had attempted to pass the Fairman/Ken Wharton D-Type, and had spun. Fairman did his best to miss Frere and hit the bank, and bounced back onto the track. He was trying to restart when Portago came through the corner and hit the Jaguar fairly but apparently not terminally hard! However, he had broken the oil tank. He tried to get back to the pits but the oil was gone and the engine seized at Whitehouse Corner. Fairman managed to drag his Jaguar back but didn't go any further. That meant that two, possibly three potential winners had been eliminated in a flash.

Duncan Hamilton in practice at Le Mans. ***(Credit - Petrie Collection)***

Portago hits the Fairman Jaguar and three important cars are out of the Le Mans 24 Hours. ***(Credit - Petrie Collection)***

Phil Hill had a front-row seat for the debacle at the Esses, as he was on Portago's tail, keen to beat the Spaniard who was quickest Ferrari driver in practice: "Frere had spun into the bank. The circuit was as slippery as a bar of soap that year, and both Fon and I began to climb onto our brakes, desperately trying to cut down our speed before the Esses. Immediately Fon got out of shape; he couldn't slow up enough, and he wrote off both Jags, hit both of 'em and split his own tank in the bargain, spilling oil all over the track." (Nolan, 1990,p.76)

Duncan Hamilton recounted the 1956 Le Mans race, where he had set up his caravan behind the Ferrari pits:

"The Ferrari drivers were: Phil Hill, Trintignant, Manzon, von Trips, Portago and myself. They were all old friends and our team spirit was splendid. Mike Hawthorn was always resting in our caravan, particularly when the Marquise de Portago was present, a fact which greatly amused Portago himself….Portago and I were the fastest pair in practice, if one took the collective times of the two drivers in each car, and we were hopeful of doing well. Jack Fairman had taken my place in the Jaguar team which was led, of course, by Mike Hawthorn. Stirling Moss and Peter Collins were leading the Aston Martin team. It rained before the start of the race, and the Ferrari team manager asked me to drive first. I did not want to do this, feeling that I was, after all, the new boy of the team. He saw my point of view and allowed Portago to take the first stint. Portago made a good start but was involved in, unfortunately, a triple crash at the Esses when a works Jaguar, driven by Paul Frere, skidded and brushed a teammate, the Jaguar of Jack Fairman. Portago, unable to miss these two cars, wrecked the front of Fairman's car, and then rammed Frere's car broadside on. Both Jaguars and our Ferrari had to retire from the race, so not only had Jaguars kept me out of their team, they had also, indirectly, prevented me from driving a Ferrari. Portago's first words when he came into the pits were: 'I have written off the Jaguar team. It's just as well you weren't driving Duncan, or they'd have said you'd done it on purpose.' Come to think of it they might have at that." (Hamilton, 1960, p.182-3)

The rain continued until early Sunday morning. The race remained a long consistent battle between the Ecurie Ecosse D-Type of Flockhart/Sanderson who held the advantage from Moss and Collins throughout the 24 hours. Phil Hill's works Ferrari broke its transmission, but Trintignant/Gendebien finished a good third overall in the Ferrari with a 2.5-litre engine against the bigger Jaguar and Aston Martin. The Jaguar's time on the straight was measured at 153 mph, some 28 mph slower than in 1955, so the fuel regulations had certainly slowed things down. The windscreen rules were universally criticized as dangerous, in fact making vision almost impossible for some drivers.

Ferrrari 625 LM Spyder Touring Chassis 0642MDTR
This is another works Ferrari which Portago drove on only one occasion. It was the car Fangio and Castellotti had brought to 3rd at the Supercortemaggiore race in June, and it was sent to Le Mans for Portago and Duncan Hamilton. Later in the year it was sold to Bob Publicker who took it to Nassau. Then Lucky Casner raced it in Florida in early 1958. It passed through the hands of several Americans, appearing at the Mille Miglia Retro in 1987 with Steve Barney.

The Ferrari 625 LM, chassis 0642, which Portago crashed at Le Mans in 1956, as it is today.

The German Grand Prix was the following weekend at the Nurburgring. Something of a serious row had broken out in the British press about the exclusion of Mike Hawthorn from the Grand Prix. Whether the non-appearance of all the British teams was a result of this was not made clear. Hawthorn had been refused insurance for the Grand Prix on the basis that he had made a rule infraction at the Nurburgring 1000 Kilometers for 'overtaking on the inside'. Journalist Tommy Wisdom took up the case on behalf of Hawthorn in the daily Herald in provocative terms, reminding the Germans that they had only recently "been allowed" back into motor racing. Wisdom argued that Hawthorn had been cautioned and that should have been the end of the matter, and that he himself had seen Germans making the same move in that race. He intimated that Hawthorn was really being punished for his alleged role in the 1955 Le Mans crash. Wisdom called on the RAC to take action against the German organisers. None of the manufacturers admitted that they took heed of this furore but nevertheless they didn't show up. Eleven years after the end of World War II, Wisdom's language and tone was very anti-German and emotive, but it may have worked.

The German Grand Prix had not been run in 1955 as a consequence of the Le Mans crash, so now that Mercedes had retired from competition, there were no German cars for the August 28 race. Terrible weather in the days preceding the race kept the Sunday crowd down to a relatively small 100,000, but they were welcomed on race day by warm sunshine and a party atmosphere returned to the great Eifel Mountain circuit. Without German and British entries, the field was a modest 19 cars, quite small by usual standards. This included the five Ferrari entries for Fangio, Collins, Castellotti, 'new boy' Luigi Musso, and Portago, who was again down to drive his usual chassis 0007 D-50. There were the three Maserati 250Fs for works drivers Moss, Behra and Maglioli, two Gordinis for Manzon and Milhoux, nine independent Maseratis and an old Scuderia Centro Sud Ferrari 500 for Giorgio Scarlatti.

The Ring lap record had been in place since 1939 when it was set by Hermann Lang in a Mercedes, and that must have been one of the most long-standing records of all. This was broken in practice by both Fangio and Peter Collins, and Collin's improved performance was evident to all. In one of the sessions, the timekeepers made a serious error, recording Collin's time as some ten seconds down on Fangio. Collins went out and drove his heart out, and was still listed as way behind his teammate. So out he went again and went even quicker. It was then realised that the timing was wrong and in fact he had been within .3 of a second of Fangio. These efforts had dragged the first two cars three seconds ahead of Castellotti and a full twelve seconds ahead of Moss, with Musso fifth and Portago on row three in ninth place some 46 seconds behind Fangio. His previous good performances notwithstanding, the Spaniard was finding driving a fast Grand Prix car around the Ring was different than driving a sports car. He was, however, encouraged when it was discovered after practice that his quickest time had been set with the rear part of the chassis completely fractured. It didn't say a lot about his sensitivity to what the car was doing, but indicated how he would press on regardless!

The cars in the Nurburgring paddock before the German Grand Prix.
(Credit - Archive Fodisch)

This discovery led to all the cars being completely stripped and gusset plates were welded around the shock absorber mounting points. As the Lancias were being run at the Nurburgring for the first time, it was not surprising that some weaknesses were being found. The cars had often been described as 'over-engineered', meaning they were built very strongly. However, even they had some critical weak spots.

Fangio, Collins, Portago and Musso before practice for the German Grand Prix.
(Credit - Musso Family Archive)

It was a thundering horde of red cars first into the South Curve, with Collins ahead, but Fangio, Moss and Collins changed places more than once on the first lap, and as they came past at the end of the first of 22 laps, Fangio led his teammate and Moss, with Salvadori, Behra and Portago next. Portago had moved from ninth to sixth on the opening lap and was finding the race conditions a real spur to setting faster lap times. Castellotti had gone off on lap one and came by the pits with a dented front cowling. Scarlatti and Manzon retired pretty quickly, and Salvadori went out on lap three as Fangio and Collins broke the lap record. Castellotti was in the pits, retiring the following lap but was told he would take over Musso's car. Collins then came in after 8 laps with a severe fuel leak, and he was nearly unconscious from the fumes. Castellotti moved to take over from Collins but the car was finished, so he then jumped into Musso's car as he too came flying down the pit lane. The engine hadn't been turned off and the Maserati team protested this. At the halfway stage, Portago had now moved into a promising 4th place behind Fangio, Moss and Behra, and he was now turning lap times much faster than his practice times, pulling himself closer to his teammate's times.

The cars are brought to the grid.
(Credit - Author's Collection)

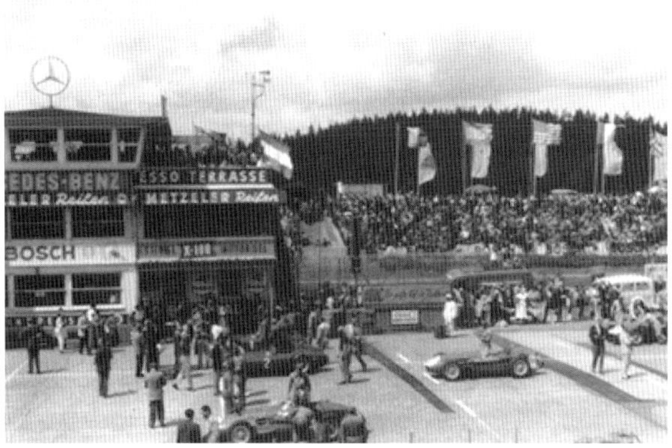

Mechanics push the cars to the grid.
(Credit - Author's Collection)

Much to Portago's chagrin, Collins had recovered and the team decided to call Portago in to hand the car over to Collins as he was close enough to finish well up the order. Fangio had gotten the record down to 9 minutes 44 seconds, way below the old record. Fangio went another three seconds quicker after that, and there was no chance Collins would catch him, and Behra had stopped to have a loose fuel tank repaired. Nevertheless, Collins was flying, and that resulted in him losing it between the Karussel and Schwalbenschwanz and he went into the ditch. As Castellotti also went off, Portago was right to be indignant, an unusual response for him. He had been doing well and would have finished third behind Fangio and Moss.

Portago in the early laps of the German Grand Prix.
(Credit - Author's Collection)

After the race it was revealed that when Collins had come in, Castellotti thought it was Musso's car, and was surprised to find he had jumped into the wrong car. It didn't slow him down as he was then hopping aboard Musso's car when it arrived. Portago argued after the race that Collins should have pushed the car back onto the road and continued. The two took a road car, Collin's road going Ford Zephyr, and went to collect it. It turned out that it required a tow and the assistance of many people to get it out

Portago pushes the D-50 through the Karussel at the Nurburgring.
(Credit - Oldtimer Markt)

of the ditch, so Portago withdrew his argument, still bitter about not being on the podium. But Collins was still in the Championship hunt so he would also have been aware where the priorities were.

There was not a lot of time for Portago to brood over his misfortune at the German Grand Prix, as once again the racers were packed and on their way north to Sweden for two races a fortnight apart. The first was the Swedish Grand Prix for sports cars at Kristianstad, at the Rabelov circuit. The August 12 race was a big event, the second since the success of one in 1955. The entry included no less than 21 works drivers from Ferrari and Maserati alone! This was a Championship round and Ferrari led Maserati in the Championship by ten points but would have to drop points as only three of the five rounds counted. Ugolini and Maserati brought no less than five 300S models and the new and largely untried 450S, a brutish 4.5-litre V-8. The drivers were Moss, Behra, Taruffi, Schell, Maglioli, Villoresi, Musy, Godia, Bonnier and Simon.

Maserati had to win the race and Ferrari gain no points to win the title. This looked very unlikely but Ferrari wasn't taking a chance so there were three of the 290 MM V-12s, and a pair of 860 Monzas. The Ferrari drivers were Fangio, Castellotti, Collins, Gendebien, Portago, Hill, Trintignant, Hawthorn, Hamilton and Manzon. They were backed up by eight private Ferraris…the Scuderia was taking no chances. One of the privateers was the 750 Monza of Picard and Vidilles (chassis 0568M). In practice, both works teams swapped most of the drivers between most of the cars so it was virtually impossible to tell who had recorded what time in what car. Stirling Moss, Harry Schell and Piero Taruffi thundered around in practice in the new Maserati 450S which was spectacular and rapid but had little stopping power and it was decided not to race it. It clearly was going to be Maserati's front runner for 1957.

Portago was down to drive one of the Ferrari 860 Monzas (chassis 0602M), but the final pairings weren't settled until just before the race started. His nominal partner was Le Mans co-driver Duncan Hamilton, who never got a race at Le Mans and was hoping for better here in Sweden. It was to be another Le Mans start, again by practice time rather than engine size. In fact, most of the organisers using such a start had abandoned the old tradition of lining the cars up by engine size. Peter Collins in the Ferrari 290 MM he was sharing with von Trips got away first of the 27 cars, a couple of the privateers having trouble getting their machines started. Taruffi didn't come around after the first lap, as Flockhart in one of the three D-Type Jaguars present had slid into Taruffi and the Maserati was out. Amazingly, there were virtually no changes in the order for the first of six and half-hours. Collin's leading Ferrari was a bit smoky but sounded healthy. Mike Hawthorn had started the Ferrari he was now to share with Portago and Hamilton. He was the only one to get into a bit of trouble in this first hour, having a moment which let von Trips past him into third place behind Moss' Maserati. The Godia-Sales/Bonnier and Musy/Simon Maseratis retired on laps 25 and 26 with axle and gearbox failure respectively.

Just before the first scheduled stops for fuel and driver changes, Hawthorn was off the road again into some hedges and when the Ferrari came back, it had to have large clods of earth removed from the bottom and the suspension. After all the stops had been made, the Behra /Moss Maserati was in the lead, with the Fangio/Castellotti car now second, with Gendebien/Collins third, Phil Hill in the other 12-cylinder 290 MM fourth, and Portago in the 4-cylinder 860 Monza 5th. Even though Maserati had suffered the first casualties, their car in the lead still gave them some hope of the Championship. Then things changed. Behra had brakes that weren't working and he had to make a stop for repairs. The Gendebien/Collins Ferrari which had had a small oil leak now had a bigger leak and stopped for a top up, letting Manzon get a drive in the car on lap 76. He didn't go far as the engine blew and he stopped, and his oil on the road put Hill on the grass and Portago into a long and lurid spin, which Flockhart was lucky to avoid. Hill took some time finding his way out of a cornfield. Fangio maintained the lead, with Hill still in second, and Portago was now in third, with Collins who had moved into the car with von Trips fourth. He had also been off into the cornfield. Schell was now the first Maserati in fifth and Moss was then put into that car to speed things up. Flockhart had blown up the Jaguar engine. One chaotic Maserati pit stop was followed by another, so when Behra came in, all the fuel and oil they had poured on the ground went up in flames.

Portago had gotten his car up into a fine second place behind Fangio, and then the Ferrari team decided to do another complex series of driver changes, the time lost dropping Portago to third with Hamilton now driving, and Castellotti had blown up on the circuit. That dropped the great Fangio out of the lead he had held for much of the long race, making Phil Hill and Maurice Trintignant the rather surprised winners. Von Trips and Collins were next in the second V-12 290 MM and then came the 860 Monza of Portago/Hawthorn/Hamilton. Three private Ferraris followed the fourth placed D-Type of Graham and Peter Whitehead, which had been lent to them by owner Duncan Hamilton, and that meant Ferrari had won the Championship, and Portago had rather unfairly been deprived of another good position for no good reason.

Duncan Hamilton's autobiography provides something of a feel for what the post-race evening was like. Before the race, when asked during the medical check what his blood group was, he had answered 'whiskey and Perrier', and which the doctor had written down. In the event of an accident, Hamilton wasn't sure what he was going to get! The drivers were set to have a party, and attempted to buy a case of whiskey from their hotel, as they had found it sitting under a drinks table in the dining room. Refused their offer, Hawthorn, Collins, Hamilton, Castellotti, Musso and Portago created a distraction for the staff and as a result of this, the whiskey found its way to their rooms. This eventually led to the rather famous tale of Mike Hawthorn and the hotel fire hose. Having had a bucket of water poured over his head by Hawthorn, Hamilton took the fire hose from its wheel, delivered it to Hawthorn's room, and turned it on. This started a period of some chaos at 4.30 in the morning as the hose blew Hawthorn's pajamas off, and as he couldn't control the hose which had gone berserk, he found himself trying to get into other peoples' rooms. At one stage Hamilton, Hawthorn and the hose entered the room of another driver who was doing something with a woman friend which did not include sleeping. The hose knocked them to the floor and the party continued. The Swedish Automobile Club secretary arrived a few hours later to negotiate a financial settlement with the rather perturbed hotel staff.

The Swedish Grand Prix had been the final and deciding round in the World Sportscar Championship. After this race, the drivers dispersed to a number of other events at Nurburgring, Messina, Caen, Shelsley Walsh or Ollon-Villars. Salvadori, Manzon and Schell were racing in the Grand Prix de Caen, which Schell won in his Maserati 250F. Portago was either still in or had returned to Sweden for the weekend of August 25-26, to take part in the fifth running of what were known as the International Cannon Races, or the Cannonloppet, at Karlskoga. This was another street circuit, a short, 2-kilometer twisty affair in the centre of Karlskoga. There were to be six races, of which the Over 1500 cc. Sports Car Race was the most significant. Portago was the best known of the drivers present, and he was down to drive the Ferrari 750 Monza (chassis 0568M) which had been run at the Swedish Grand Prix by Francois Picard and Jean-Claude Vidilles, where it had retired.

Portago was up against Curt Lincoln's D-Type Jaguar, Mike Head's Cooper-Jaguar, and several local Ferraris, one driven by Gunnar Carlsson. Carlsson and Jonas Kvarnstrom, both in Scuderia Bjurstrom Ferraris took the lead in wet weather in front of a rather small crowd. Portago took second at the halfway point in the 30-lap race, and finished four seconds behind Carlsson. The circuit was tight but the drivers seemed to like it, and the spectators thought it was great because most of it was visible from a central point.

Ferrari 750 Monza Spyder Scaglietti Chassis 0568M

Portago had a one-off drive in this Monza at the Cannonloppet races, it being lent to him by the owner Francois Picard. Picard had driven it in February in the Agadir Grand Prix, and at Dakar and the Paris 1000 Kilometers by Picard and Trintignant, and at Rouen by Picard. In 1957 it was raced by Eric Lundgren and by Carl-Otto Bremer. Bremer raced it throughout 1958. It was run in Swedish ice races through the early 1960s, and earned its nickname…the 'Ice-Racer' then. It disappeared for 20 years, reappearing in 1988, found its way to the USA. Harry Leventis bought it in 2000 and then Carlos Monteverde took it over and has raced it in historic events ever since.

The Ferrari Monza, chassis 0568...the Ice Racer...which Portago raced in Sweden. This car is regularly raced today.
(Credit - Peter Collins)

Although the motor racing schedule had been very full for several months, Portago did manage to find time for other activities, including making contact with Dorian Leigh. She had returned to Paris with her son Kim, who was now nine months old, and still seemed to have remained a secret to her own family. Dorian Leigh had started a model agency in Paris, a novel initiative at the time, and this was prospering. She says that she was seeing Portago off and on during this summer, though keeping him at a distance from the child. She claimed that they were seeing each other 'in secret'.

It was also in the late summer or early autumn of 1956 that Portago first encountered Linda Christian. There was a certain element of déjà vu about their meeting, and perhaps not a little scheming, as it took place in exactly the same nightclub, the Elefant Blanc in Paris, where Portago had met Dorian Leigh. Linda Christian was an actress who had attained a certain reputation in several films, few of which were ever critically acclaimed. They included The V.I.P.s (1963), Tarzan and the Mermaids (1948), and The Devil's Hand (1962). She was, however, strikingly attractive. She had been born Bianca Rosa Welter in Mexico, and lived in Palestine in her youth. After making a few second rank films, she met the American star Tyrone Power, and they married in January 1949. They soon had two daughters, Romina and Taryn. After an on-again off-again affair with another actor, Edmund Purdom, Linda Christian and Tyrone Power were divorced, though on seemingly amicable grounds, where he had relatively free access to their children, and they appeared to remain on good terms.

In her autobiography, Linda Christian gives an account of her meeting and the early days of the relationship with Portago through the tragic ending. (Christian, 1962) Like the memoirs of Dorian Leigh, there were evident flaws, especially in relation to the timing of some events. It would also seem that the first meeting with Portago was less of an accident than it may have seemed. Christian had arrived in Paris and met a man on the way into Paris who worked to get her attention. This turned out to be Edmund Gurner Nelson, and it seems he may have alerted Portago to her arrival.

From what Linda Christian has written, there are some difficulties in judging just how long the period covered by their first few encounters was. She describes Portago as charming and persistent, and says that he phoned her non-stop until she agreed to meet with him. Unlike Dorian Leigh, who made no mention of his hygiene and other personal habits, Linda Christian takes pride in tackling his preferred pattern of not shaving or bathing or ever going to the dentist. Her account includes forcing him to do all these things, which may have happened but would have been out of character according to many other reports of the way he behaved in a disdainful manner towards women. It also seems fairly early in the relationship that he was informing Linda of an impending divorce, something which Carroll Petrie denied had ever been likely or started.

Whatever the details of Portago's relationships were, they took place against the backdrop of an immensely packed racing programme. After the race at Karlskoga, Portago headed for Monza for the Italian Grand Prix on September 2, joined by his teammates and the rest of the Grand Prix 'circus'. This was the last round of the 1956 World Championship for Drivers, and it looked like only BRM wouldn't appear at Monza. Ferrari entered an amazing six Lancia D-50s for their squad, which now included Wolfgang von Trips as well as the recent addition Luigi Musso. Enzo Ferrari must have been very happy to have two noblemen in his Grand Prix *equipe*. Portago was down to drive his usual car, chassis 0007.

This race turned out to be a difficult one for Ferrari, and almost a very costly one. Fangio was favourite to take the title but Stirling Moss was threatening. Ferrari had decided to use 16" Engelbert tyres for this race as they had experimented with them the previous year. The high speeds on the banking were not kind to these tyres and they started to experience treads lifting. Fangio had set a quick time, as had Moss and Behra. On Saturday, Fangio was cruising around setting reasonable times, with von Trips taking to Grand Prix racing very comfortably. He was not that far off Fangio's time on his debut. Then he suddenly spun into the trees in the middle of the Curva Grande just past the starting area. He was doing about 130 mph at the time, and was thrown out, very lucky to get only minor injuries. The car was written off, and when he explained that the car had suddenly veered right, the Ferrari team just smiled and put it down to inexperience. The team's failure to check the car and the other cars in the team was a serious omission and they would pay the price for this, and the price could have been much higher.

On race day, Fangio was on pole from teammates Castellotti and Musso, with Taruffi's Vanwall next, and the Maseratis of Behra and Moss following. Collins and Villoresi were on row three just quicker than Portago who was ninth fastest. Von Trips, of course, wouldn't be taking part. Musso, recovered from his recent broken arm, was leading a Grand Prix for the first time as the field headed off into the distance. He was being chased by Castellotti and Fangio, Moss and Collins, soon to be joined by a flying Harry Schell, again pushing the Vanwall on very purposefully. Team tactics seem to disappear, and the growing rivalry between Italians Musso and Castellotti was coming to a head. The first group had broken away in their furious battle, and there was a gap back to another fight, this time between Behra and Portago, the Spaniard giving nothing away to the wily French driver. On lap five, the total disregard of potential tyre troubles for the Ferraris had reaped its reward, and both Musso and Castellotti threw rear treads. They flew into the pits demanding new tyres. Portago had been running a slightly more restrained pace, but he also lost a tread. He slid wildly down the banking at 160 mph and made his way back to the pits for new tyres. However, the high-speed sideways slide damaged the rear suspension and he could do nothing but retire. Schell and Moss were now having a real go for the lead, with Schell proving

Castellotti leads Collins at the Italian Grand Prix in 1956.
(Credit - Castellotti Collection)

Portago comes into the pits with a shredded tyre after his lurid slide on the banking. ***(Credit -Bernard Cahier)***

faster in a straight line. This was the cause of great hope in the Vanwall pit which was beginning to see all their work pay off.

Castellotti and Musso were making up ground but the loadings on the tyres on the banking were too much for the Engelberts, and Castellotti lost another tread and had a lurid time avoiding a major crash, but he hit a small wall and stopped. Collins also had a tyre failure and went into the pits. Schell had a Vanwall leading a Grand Prix for the first time, though Moss and Fangio were right behind him. On lap 19 Fangio trickled into the pit-lane with the steering arm broken, and then a rain shower soaked the circuit, putting Moss in front. A steering arm was taken off Portago's car and put on Fangio's car and Castellotti went out again in that car. Fangio stood by as Castellotti and Musso were called in for tyre checks and changes on lap 30. Not long after this stop Moss was leading Musso, Collins, Flockhart in a Connaught, and Behra in Maglioli's car. Schell had sadly retired with a seized rear end after another wonderful race. When Collins came in for a new tyre on lap 35, Fangio took over though there was no chance he was going to catch Moss. This meant that Collin's chance of winning the title was really gone but Fangio's wasn't so it was a logical decision. Nevertheless, Collins and Portago were praised in the motoring press for their consistent sportsmanship throughout the season as well as Collin's at Monza. Then Moss ran out of fuel and as he coasted, Piotti brought his Maserati up behind and pushed him to the pits…those were the days! Musso now led, but then he too had a steering arm break and headed towards the pit wall as he came off the banking. He managed to end up in the pit lane, and sat there having lost the Italian Grand Prix. Moss had his lead over Fangio drop from 20 to 6 seconds in the last few laps but he was well aware of what was going on. He came across the line the winner with Fangio second, sharing with Collins, and winning the World Championship. Flockhart was third and Godia a non-stop fourth. Ferrari very nearly had thrown the World Championship away for Fangio. It was discovered on the following Tuesday that steering arm failure had caused von Trip's practice crash. Had this been checked earlier and discovered, the other cars could have been modified.

There was now a two week 'break' for the first time in many months before the next event. As the next race was a further two weeks away, there was a chance to have a month away from racing. Portago decided, having gotten so immersed in almost non-stop motor racing since the beginning of a year which had included some glory in the Winter Olympics at Cortina, that he would continue. He had arranged purchase of a new Ferrari 250 GT Tour de France (chassis 0557GT). This was to be entered in the Tour de France, with Edmund Gurner Nelson again acting as co-driver/navigator. This would be the second of these cars Portago had owned; the first, chassis 0415GT, had been raced at Nassau at the end of 1955. This was also a long wheelbase berlinetta with body by Scaglietti. The car was completed at the factory on September 10, 1956 and had been consigned to the American market, which means it might have been ordered through Luigi Chinetti. One of the reasons Portago bought the car was that he intended to enter it at the 1957 Mille Miglia, after seeing how well Olivier Gendebien had done in the 1956 race.

Portago's 250 GT before the start of the 1956 Tour de France. ***(Credit - Autopresse)***

Portago had apparently used some of the time since the Italian Grand Prix driving some of the roads to be used on the Tour this year. The event would run from September 17 through 23rd, and cover over 6000 kilometers. It was one of the hardest Tours on record, and for 1956 would have only two night stops, and the hardest road sections over the Alps would be run at night. To demonstrate what kind of event it would be, there were entries for Grand Prix drivers Stirling Moss, Harry Schell, Olivier Gendebien, Maurice Trintignant, Louis Rosier and Jean Behra as well as Portago and a number of very competent sports car racers.

Portago smiles from his 250 GT before the start. ***(Credit - E.Jiminez)***

105 cars started at Nice, all being either Grand Touring or Touring cars in two groups, Strictly Series or Non-Series, which allowed a degree of modification. The rules governing the entries were complex, but with much factory interest, a great deal of thought had gone into picking the car most likely to survive and possibly win.

The cars departed from Nice and headed north and west, arriving at the Mont Ventoux hillclimb for the first test, a timed run up the 21-kilometer hill not far from the city of Avignon. Jacky Pollet's Mercedes 300SL set fastest time, indicating that the battle was likely to be between the Mercedes and the Ferraris. Future Grand Prix driver Willy Mairesse was second, also in a Mercedes, with Moss's similar car third. The cars went up the hill at one-minute intervals and then continued onto the road section after getting to the top. Fast cars seen on the road sections on the way to Nimes were the Porsche of Jean Behra and his brother Jose, Paul Frere and Harry Schell, both in Alfa Romeo Giuliettas, and then came the production series Ferraris of Trintignant, Louis Rosier, Portago, and Gendebien. Gendebien was driving a Farina-bodied car, less agile and heavier than the Scaglietti-bodied cars, and looking harder to drive. Pollet, who won the 1954 Tour, looked very smooth in his Mercedes 300SL at Mont Ventoux, while Willy Mairesse was on the ragged edge. Those watching the event had some difficulty determining who was leading, especially in the classes. The difference between standard and modified was small on some cars…the removal of bumpers…to large on others. One report said that the only thing standard on the factory Renault Dauphines was the name badge! Portago's Ferrari was in the Grand Touring and Series Touring Class while Moss' Mercedes 300SL was in the Special Series Touring and Modified GT division, yet the performance was quite similar.

Mercedes were looking good after the opening period of one test and a lot of road miles. None of the top cars had any road penalties, so the order was: Pollet, Mairesse, Moss, Cotton, Portago, La Caze, and Trintignant. The field left Nimes and headed across the Massif Central in the direction of the Pyrenees in the southwest. Most of the Monday night was spent in reaching St. Gaudens, the site of the old and famed Comminges road circuit where great racing had taken place before and shortly after WWII, though sadly no longer. Stirling Moss put on a superb performance here during a tough five-lap race. The cars immediately departed to the Peyresoude hillclimb, which is right on the French-Spanish border, where the four and a half-kilometer hill suited the Mercedes once again. It was looking already that the Tour de France would be a total Mercedes benefit. Pollet was quickest here, with La Caze and Moss right behind. Portago and Trintignant kept the flag flying for the Ferrari drivers and remained well up the overall list. Former Panhard Monomille driver Claude Storez had his Porsche Carrera ahead of all the smaller cars. He was in the Modified group, and led Behra who was running in the production class.

The cars wound up the West Coast of France on the second night, over entirely secondary and small roads. The average speed was around 60 kph and there were secret checks to make sure no one was averaging more than 80 kph. Although the roads were minor ones, the cars were not struggling to keep to the required speed, in spite of large crowds out at some points in the middle of the night. At checkpoints, large numbers of locals came out to see the exotic field going through, or stopping at the brief rest points. The early morning arrival after the long night was to be at Le Mans for a hard flat out race of twelve laps. By the time the Tour had arrived at Le Mans, it was beginning to look like the striking new Ferraris entered would be overshadowed by the pack of Mercedes. However, Portago and Trintignant set that right at Le Mans, moving right up the field. The Frenchman's car had the engine begin to seize at the end of the race, so the mechanics were set to work to do a rebuild. The more 'production' Ferraris of Gendebien and Louis Rosier could not match the pace of the other two, especially Portago. The Ferrari progress was aided by problems for the 'Mercs', as Moss lost power, Rene Cotton had a tyre burst and frightened himself, and Mairesse finished the race with a broken piston. Storez' speedy Porsche blew its engine at Le Mans and he was out, though Harry Schell's Alfa Giulietta was flying, and Guelfi's similar car hit a herd of cows!

By the end of the Le Mans 'test', the drivers had been on the road for 60 hours, and fortunately or otherwise, they were not able to work on the cars in parc ferme until 6.00 a.m. the next morning, so a good rest was guaranteed. The Mercedes mechanics were all getting set to change wheels and tyres, as the tyre wear on these cars was now obvious. Pollet's performance at Le Mans kept him as the overall leader.

The field had now been reduced by 33 cars, and it proceeded cross-country for the short trip to Rouen. Portago and Trintignant now really began to demonstrate how much better the Ferraris were than the Mercedes on a tough circuit like Rouen. They beat them soundly, and Moss was still down on power, with even Rosier's heavier Ferrari performing well here. Jean Behra's production Porsche Carrera was quicker than the bulk of the bigger cars and moved up the standings, and the Alfas went well on the twisty circuit. After Rouen, the Tour moved right into the northwest corner of France in the Pas de Calais before heading southeast towards Reims and another major circuit test. A major organisational disaster came close to seeing many cars thrown out on lateness, as the decision had been made to locate the check-in control in the Reims paddock. As the event was open to the public, the competitors were stuck in a huge traffic jam on the approach to the circuit, and several desperate competitors took to the local fields to find a shortcut through the mess. Because it was so obviously an impossible situation, the organisers were forced to lengthen the time allowed to check in. By the time the cars were parked up, the current standings were published and Portago had moved into the overall lead after the Rouen race.

With Gurner Nelson beside him, Portago drove very quickly to win the Rouen special stage.
(Credit - LAT)

Nelson, Portago and the Kessler Sisters at the Reims race stage.
(Credit - DR Photo)

Of course, it was now night-time, but the circuit was floodlit for the series of 12-lap races. While Pollet was able to give Portago some semblance of competition, he was slower, and Stirling Moss' engine problems in the car he was sharing with George Houel were getting worse and he was dropping down the field. Portago was driving brilliantly, and the Ferrari clearly was happy in the cool night running. This put Portago further ahead in the overall standings. His winning performance at Reims did not distract him from some of the other things going on at the circuit. The organisers brought in a number of stars and celebrities to improve the show, including the Kessler Sisters. Ellen and Alice Kessler were German twins who performed at the Lido in Paris from 1955 to 1960 with a song and dance act. They both made a number of films and became rather iconic figures. Spanish filmmaker Pedro Almodovar would include twins in some of his films based on the Kessler Sisters. The attractive pair did not fail to get noticed by Portago and Nelson, and it seemed no accident that they also showed up at the finish of the Tour.

Both Kessler Sisters find Portago a good target at Reims on the Tour de France. *(Credit - DR Photo)*

Things get passionate at Reims. *(Credit - DR Photo)*

Around midnight on Thursday, the Tour de France moved northwest again towards the German border, covering a large road mileage through the Vosges, then the Jura and on south towards Aix-les-Bains. This was not the most difficult part of the road section but was very challenging and some effort was now required to keep to the average. The weather conditions remained fine, and the route was not difficult to follow, so it can be assumed that Edmund Gurner Nelson was not having a hard job in the cockpit next to Portago. It appears that Nelson did drive part of the route, but not much, as Portago was well wound up and driving brilliantly. The special test at Aix was a straightforward drag race, a standing start run over a half-kilometer. Portago should have added this to his list of wins but didn't. He made a superb start in first and then second gear and as he attempted a speed shift to third, he knocked off the ignition switch and ended up coasting over the line. As each second was worth 10 points in penalties, he got 28 points, as Pollet had done a 1 minute 18.1 seconds and Portago 1 minute 20.9 seconds. La Caze was second behind Pollet. This error was costly, as it put Pollet back into an overall lead and stung the Spanish pride. Hemard's Index-leading Panhard went onto one cylinder as he went over the start-line and his time of over one-minute cost him a massive 632 points.

The cars now headed for Grenoble as darkness arrived, and this marked what was the most difficult road section, the complex of passes over the Alps between Grenoble and Briancon, all in the dark. 26 cars failed to make it to the end of this long and arduous section. Poor Maurice Trintignant collided with a non-competing car coming the opposite way down one of the cols, and he was out, a blow to the growing Ferrari hopes. The competitors who included rally drivers or navigators in their team seemed to make up time and have an easier run on this part of the Tour. As the route wound its way out of the mountains to St. Etienne, a 20-lap race greeted the survivors. At the start of this stage, Pollet was holding on to his overall lead, with Portago next. Stirling Moss, by dint of some repairs and remarkable determination, had kept himself and George Houel in third place. The Mercedes of La Caze, which had been holding third, had retired when the gearbox broke in the mountains and couldn't be repaired. Rosier was in difficulty with his Ferrari, having to repair brake pipes.

Portago had control of the St. Etienne street race, and he was lapping slower cars fairly quickly. One of these threw a rock up which shattered the Ferrari's windscreen, and he was forced to ease his pace. Moss had found some power in the Mercedes…virtually everything had been changed…and he was second behind Portago as Pollet experienced a broken valve rocker. The cars then turned north towards the finish at Paris. There was a second night stop at Vichy, with the cars again locked up until early Sunday morning. Sadly, Pollet was able to repair his Mercedes but it took too long to reach the Vichy stop in time and he was forced to quit, after having been a leader for much of the way. This had now reduced the field to only 37 cars, and then showed just how tough this Tour was. The order as the cars left Vichy for Montlhery was now Portago, Moss, Gendebien Behra, Cotton, Schell, Frere and Mlle. Thirion. It was interesting that the MotorSport report mentioned the trials being experienced by the co-drivers, and described Nelson as "a friend named Nelson, who was completely inexperienced and was suffering the ardours of night-and-day motoring philosophically". (Motorsport, November 1956, p.703) This ignored the fact that the pair had driven an OSCA in the 1954 event.

The final race stage was to be twelve- lap races at the Montlhery circuit. The unbroken spell of fine weather had continued through the final day, and that had helped the big cars considerably, though Behra and Schell would have liked some rain. Stirling Moss had finally gotten the Mercedes to run properly and he was very fast at Montlhery. Portago had managed to get a sheet of Perspex to replace the broken Ferrari windscreen, and he only needed to have a reasonable finishing position to take victory. While Moss was uncatchable during this last race, Portago was not far behind. Some of the front runners ran into trouble at the last moment. Mlle.Thirion was going slowly on three cylinders and the Alfa battle between Schell and Frere ended when Harry ran out of fuel. This meant he lost the small class race but won the class overall.

Portago pushes on one of the long road stages. ***(Credit - Author's Collection)***

The start of the Montlhery race stage with Portago shown here just leading Stiling Moss' Mercedes. ***(Credit - E.Jiminez)***

Moss and Portago have a chat before the start of the next stage after the Montlhery race. ***(Credit - E.Jiminez)***

The final standings had Portago/Nelson on 7307 penalty points with Moss/Houel some 100 behind on 7405, leading Gendebien/Ringoir(Ferrari), Cotton/Leclerc (Mercedes), Behra/Behra (Porsche), Schell/Vidilles (Alfa Romeo), Frere/Schied (Alfa Romeo), Peron/ Bertrammier (Ferrari), Renel/Bessey (Porsche). Thirion/ Polensky won the Ladies Trophy and were 11th overall. Only 37 cars arrived at the finish, and there were very few complaints from the teams about the quality of the event. Portago had enjoyed the race stages, having won five of the six. There were some noises about the fact that certain manufacturers had produced less cars than the rules had specified, but this was a fairly minor complaint which would get attended to the following year. As the festivities at the finish in Paris and the prize-giving came to an end, Portago and Nelson were spotted in company with the...Kessler Sisters!

Autosport celebrated Portago's win by putting him on the cover.

There was again a short break until the next race, the Coupe du Salon, scheduled for October 7 at Montlhery. There were races for up to and over 1300 cc. special series and grand touring cars, which attracted some of the surviving and repaired cars from the Tour de France. These were 16-lap races and a 24-lap event, the Coupe du Salon, was for up to 3-litre sports cars in three classes. The small car race attracted more Alfa Romeo Giuliettas, Roger Loyer winning in his Alfa followed by two more.

Then it was time for the over 1300 cc. race, and Portago entered his Tour de France winning long wheelbase Ferrari 250 GT (0557GT), often referred to as a Europa in contemporary reports. Jacques Peron in another Ferrari, his Tour car, led initially with Portago right on his rear, and Behra continued pushing his 1500 cc. Porsche amongst the bigger cars. George Houel was driving the Mercedes 300 SL with which he and Moss had finished second in the Tour. Houel showed his own ability as a driver, finishing third behind the two Ferraris and staying ahead of Behra. Boulan's Alfa was fifth, and Behra took the class for up to 1500 cc. cars.

The Coupe du Salon, over 24 laps, was run in soaking wet conditions. Swiss driver Benoit Musy had his new Maserati 2-litre on pole, Duncan Hamilton had his D-Type, as did Andre Pilette. Da Silva Ramos put his 3-litre Gordini into the lead at the start followed by Pilette, Musy, Godia and Behra. Louis Rosier's Ferrari spun under braking and flipped into the air, as Hamilton passed underneath. Rosier was very seriously injured, and died three weeks later from his injuries. Musy eventually took the lead and looked like the winner when he was suddenly seen fighting the car. The car rushed up the banking and vaulted over the top, plunging some 80 feet to strike several cars below. Musy was killed instantly, and Francisco Godia led until the end in his Maserati, as Hamilton took second. Rosier's death in his fifties was a shock to the French racing establishment.

Autosport of October 19 ran a report of the editorial staff's pick of the top 15 Grand Prix drivers of the 1956 season. They used a star rating system: 5 stars-Fangio, Moss; 4 stars-Collins, Behra; 3 stars-Hawthorn, Castellotti, Schell; 2 stars-Brooks, Portago, Salvadori, Musso; 1 star-Trintignant, Scott-Brown, Flockhart, Fairman. There was no report of the drivers' response to this judgement, but presumably Mike Hawthorn was not enthralled! It also seems likely that Portago's good all-round performances of late helped in this little popularity contest. (Autosport, October 19, 1956, p.507)

Portago back at Montlhery in October for the Coupe de Salon which he won. *(Credit - Archive Fodisch)*

On October 20-21, the Italian 'Due Giornate' took place at the Castelfusano circuit near Rome. This was a very fast 4-mile circuit, which had not been used for two years. There were six races on the programme for this 'two-day' event for touring, special touring, grand touring, sports racing, Italian 750s and British F3 cars. While OSCA dominated in one of the sports car races, Mackay Fraser's Lotus won another, though clearly the Italian crowd was enthralled with the Lotus and Cooper bunch. The main race, the Rome Grand Prix on Sunday, was won by Behra's 2-litre Maserati from Harry Schell in a similar car. Gigi Villoresi's Maserati was forced off the road into the hay bales and overturned. Villoresi was seriously injured, with a broken leg and arm and other injuries, and this accident overshadowed the rest of the meeting. There was a Grand Touring race in three classes and this was won with some ease by Portago, again out in his Tour de France long wheelbase 250 GT. He beat another Ferrari and Mercedes, while Bonnier took the small class in an Alfa. So far, Portago had three wins out of three races in this car.

Portago was back in Paris after the Castelfusano race, and getting ready to set off to Venezuela. He had been persistently pursuing Linda Christian according to her autobiography, and she insists that she fixed a date with him for a friend Elga Anderson. Late one night he telephoned to thank her for arranging the date, and now he wanted to come and see her. She reports that she saw him briefly the next day before he left for the airport. He was accompanied by Eugenio Castellotti, and she describes a great deal of boyish bantering between the pair, and also that Portago said he would be back after arguing with his wife over a divorce. It either was a repeating pattern of using the possibility of a divorce to further a new relationship, or the women involved had invented this pattern. Given how many times it was quoted by Dorian Leigh, there does seem to be a case that Portago tended to use this tactic on a regular basis.

Portago before the start of the Coupe de Salon race at Montlhery, the car unrepaired from The Tour de France a few weeks earlier. *(Credit - Autopresse)*

The Venezuelan Grand Prix was the destination for Portago and Castellotti as they took their leave from Linda Christian in Paris, the race to take place on November 4 in Caracas on a 4-kilometer road circuit. Stirling Moss dominated the entire weekend, getting pole position in a Maserati 300S. Something of a surprise was sprung by Portago who put his Ferrari 860 Monza (chassis 0602M) next to Moss, ahead of the Ferrari of World Champion Juan Fangio. It was this event which helped to consolidate Fangio's high opinion of his younger teammate. Moss led from the start, followed by Portago, Fangio and Harry Schell in another Ferrari. Portago's car was the same car Musso and Schell drove at Sebring, Musso at the Mille Miglia, and Fangio, Castellotti, Peter Collins, Mike Hawthorn and Duncan Hamilton had also driven it. Portago had shared the car with Hawthorn and Hamilton in Sweden so it was a very well developed car with a strong record, and one with which Portago was very familiar.

The Rome Grand Prix at Castefusano, where the public roads presented hazards in practice for Portago. ***(Credit - Actualfoto)***

Castelfusano provided a challenging road circuit...with the trees. ***(Credit - Actualfoto)***

Portago and Collins have a laugh before the Le Mans start at the Venezuela Grand Prix sports car race. ***(Credit - Autopresse)***

Portago is pensive in the Ferrari at Caracas. ***(Credit - Autopresse)***

The start of the Venezuelan Grand Prix. ***(Credit - J.Uribe)***

Stirling Moss took a lead at the beginning of the two and a half-hour race, which it looked like he would never lose. In the early stages of the race it was Portago who kept him in sight with Fangio next ahead of Schell. Then Portago caught Moss, put him under pressure and held the lead for eight laps. Moss told the author that he had been very impressed by Portago's ability in a sports car and the race at Caracas made it clear that "Portago had really emerged as a fine and competent driver. It wasn't that I wasn't trying either, he was just quicker at that stage of the race." On lap 15, Moss got back in front of the Spaniard and from that point he wouldn't be headed. Fangio had closed up during the battle between Moss and Portago, and after several more laps, he moved into second. Schell was holding fourth and Bonnier was further back in his venerable old Alfa Romeo 6C 3000CM.

A few of the runners had already dropped out, including the quick Gordini of Da Silva Ramos whose engine failed, and Isabel Haskell De Tomaso had trouble with her Maserati. The only woman driver had been going quickly, much to the delight of a crowd, which rarely saw a woman racing driver. Portago was then suddenly in difficulty and was then called back into the pits. An argument ensued with the officials over some kind of infringement, which was not specified. Portago roared out of the pits but on lap 70 he was back as the car was unhealthy and wouldn't restart. Schell's retirement around this time as well allowed American Masten Gregory in another Ferrari to move into third spot with Carini's Ferrari fourth. Fangio put in a hard effort to catch Moss to no avail, and in fact his car started to show signs it might not finish, and Gregory in the 2-litre Ferrari was winding the Champion in but couldn't catch him. Behra only managed a quiet and unspectacular fifth.

The Venezuelan race was followed by a relatively lengthy interval, during which Portago stopped off in the USA before returning to Paris. He also spent some time in this period making arrangements for his return to bobsledding at the end of the year, and organised a new two-man bobsled to be prepared for himself and Luis Munoz. The World Bobsled Championships would be held in St. Moritz and Portago was intent on improving on his result in the Olympics.

It was at this point that Linda Christian says that she put a great deal of pressure on Portago to change some his personal habits. She also made a number of observations about him which she later recorded:

"Had Fon followed in the mold his friends had known for so long the spoiled selfish young man with too much money, a family position and a great appeal to women, and who exploited all three, then our friendship would have been brief, soon forgotten, But underneath was not the man his friends knew. Nobody had ever pulled him up on anything. At sixteen, he found out that he didn't have to go to school any longer, and just stopped. He used to say simply that he was completely amoral. Women had refused him nothing, and it was evident in his attitude toward them, reflected even in his aversion to sending flowers. Fon was not really selfish, and he was not a taker, or he would not have changed. He was a thoughtless man who became a thoughtful man. And somewhere in that transition process, I began to realize that what had started out in fun and laughter now seemed close to real affection." (Christian, 1962, p.216-17)

Autosport had Portago back on the front cover for a second time in 1956 after the Nassau Speed Weeks.

Then it was time for the racing crowd and their more affluent followers to head off for the Bahamas for the next running of the Speed Weeks at Nassau. The 1956 races were to be sandwiched between two major power boat meetings from December 6 to 9. The popularity of the week had increased internationally and the committee sent out an increased 120 invitations, most of which were responded to very quickly. The number of tourists was up dramatically over the previous year, and the association with the power boat races kept a stream of visitors coming into the Bahamas. There were some difficulties with New York dockworkers that year and a few people took their cars by road to Florida, while others didn't worry, and paid the price of not having a car show up! Many of the American entrants were taking this year's meeting very seriously, and Chinetti's North American Racing Team garage in New York was busy preparing several Ferraris. Some specially prepared Corvettes were put together for Nassau, and although they arrived under the guise of private entrants, they were very much products of Chevrolets 'non-competition department'.

Seen here at Montlhery, Moss and Portago became closer friends at Nassau. *(Credit - Autosport)*

Portago follows the policeman's directions to the circuit in his Ferrari 860 Monza. *(Credit - World Wide Photo)*

A holiday atmosphere was soon evident, and parades of cars through the streets of Nassau got racing fever to a fairly high pitch. There were many more 'team members' accompanying the cars and drivers this year, as this had become *the* race meeting to attend. The Windsor Field circuit had been improved to a degree this year, though by the time the cars showed up for first practice, it had a covering of local sand which had to be swept away. Phil Hill was worried about the abrasive nature of the circuit and how tyres would be chewed up at a rapid rate, something that wasn't quite so big a concern in the first races in Nassau as the cars were less powerful. Now the cars and the drivers were getting more serious. There were, however, many light-hearted moments and Portago was at one point seen being directed by a policeman from the British Colonial Hotel out to the circuit...he was driving his Ferrari 860 Monza at the time!

Both Phil Hill and Portago tried to take a professional and diplomatic line with race director Red Crise, expressing concerns about safety, especially the very wide approaches to some corners where smaller cars would take a very different line into a corner. Portago emphasized some of the FIA safety directives regarding numbers of starting cars, to which Crise responded that "the FIA does not tell me how many cars I start!" (O'Neil, 2006, p.65) Crise took a very autocratic and heavy-handed approach, something he felt he was entitled to for inventing the Speed Weeks, and he tended to treat the drivers with some degree of disdain. Moss, Gregory, Hill and Gurney pressed Crise on some issues and were reassured that an RAC official would rule on their concerns on race day. Despite the disagreements with the organisers, scrutineering took place at the Windsor Field circuit on Wednesday, which also marked the start of the on-going round of parties and social events. Thursday was set aside for practice which was due to begin in the morning but had to be delayed for many hours. Terry O'Neil describes the wonderful tale of how five miles of communication wire had to be inspected when the public address and radio systems wouldn't work. It turned out that one of the workers had tied the two strands of wire together rather than splice them! (O'Neil, 2006 p.66) Many drivers decided to do only a minimal number of laps as there was still a lot of sand on the circuit.

Carroll Shelby said that Portago spent a lot of time "banging fenders with me" at Nassau. *(Credit - Eveleth)*

Racing started on Friday with five-lap heats and prelims for the various classes of the Governor's Trophy race followed by the two 20-lap races for the Governor's Trophy itself. While Masten Gregory won the heat for Class E & F, it was the Class B, C & D heat which had the serious runners, including Portago in the works Ferrari 860 Monza which he had last raced a few weeks before in Venezuela (chassis 0602M). The main contenders included Carroll Shelby in a Ferrari 410S, Phil Hill in an 857S, Jon von Neumann in an 860 Monza, three D-Type Jaguars and the 'non-works' Corvettes. Interesting names found on the entry list were Richie Ginther, Loyal Katskee, George Constantine, the Breros, Jim Jeffords, and Dick Thompson.

Carroll Shelby quickly took control of this short race and led John Fitch across the line. Phil Hill hadn't started very well but was just behind Fitch at the end. Portago had the brakes locking on the Ferrari and he struggled to an uncharacteristic seventh place. Portago hadn't earned many friends at the start of this heat when he accelerated away from eleventh starting spot before the flag dropped, touched a couple of the cars on the way through, and was in front of the field as the front row left the grid. In retrospect, it appears the brakes were locking on the grid and Portago was trying to free them off. The speed with which Shelby caught him indicated the Ferrari wasn't working properly. Stirling Moss should have been in this heat but his own car didn't arrive from Venezuela, so he was offered Bill Lloyd's 300S. He had soon found that the tyres were unsuitable for the surface so Lloyd drove it himself in the heat, and didn't make the finish, being hit by another car, which caused severe damage to the radiators and the body. The car needed extensive repairs and then would be saved until the main Nassau Trophy race in two days time.

The Governor's Trophy race for classes E, F, G & H followed later in the day, much later in the day. There were several indicators of the organisers' lack of experience, one being the inability to keep to the timetable. The second was more serious, and that was not recognising the difficulties they would encounter in the final race of the day, which would start as it got dark. In the meantime, Masten Gregory looked like he would win the 20-lapper for the smaller cars, but a puncture dropped him to fourth, giving the win to a happy Howard Hively and his Ferrari.

So as darkness approached, the 29 cars in the class B, C & D Governor's Trophy race lined up on the grid. Most either did not have lights or had them taped over, as there had been no thought that they would be driving in the dark. To add to the problem, the many large drums used as course markers were all painted black! Interestingly, O'Neil has the Portago flag-jumping incident in the main 20-lap race, while Autosport said that it was in the shorter heat. In any event, this race settled down to a fight between Carroll Shelby's Ferrari, the D-Type Jaguar of John Fitch, and Portago's works Ferrari. The setting sun was proving a problem for the drivers, and von Neumann was off the circuit at the outset. Portago squeezed past the D-Type of Fitch on lap four and set out after the Texan, but it was quickly getting dark as the leaders started to lap the backmarkers. While Portago had lights on the Ferrari, Shelby and Fitch didn't, and the organisers were desperately straining to read the numbers on the cars. On laps 8,9 and 10 Portago drew closer and closer to Shelby, as Phil Hill had moved up to 4th. George Constantine hit one of the barrels very hard but kept going, just as Portago got past Shelby. There were suspicions that Shelby had allowed the Spaniard past so that he had the benefit of his lights. That didn't go quite to plan as Portago slowed for some of the numerous incidents on the track. Then Portago tapped the Austin Healey of Stiles and that cost him his headlights. With just about no visibility, Shelby and Portago crossed the line together, the Texan in front, at an average speed of just under 100 mph. Lou Brero Sr. was third in a D-Type, Fitch who couldn't see at all, Constantine in the 3rd D-Type and Ginther in the Ferrari. Phil Hill had spun his Ferrari and the tyres had thrown up a large piece of jagged coral, which broke Hill's goggles. He came into the pits, blinded and bloody and retired, though fortunately the damage to his eye was not serious. The Corvettes fared somewhat better in this race than in the heat, finishing 7th, 9th and 10th though they really didn't seem to be competitive in spite of their power.

There was a rather mixed field for some of the Nassau races. *(Credit - Speed Age)*

Portago had a less successful year at Nassau in 1956 compared to the previous year. *(Credit - BRSCC Archive)*

Lady Oake's cocktail party at Hillcrest House was scheduled for 6.00 to 8.30, so there was a lot of scrambling as drivers and entourages attempted to get away from Windsor Field in order to get ready for this big bash. Speed Age magazine was one of the few which had commented that Portago's wife Carroll was with him at Nassau, and she joined him for the glittering event that was considered the important and exclusive party to go to…except everyone was invited!

Saturday was sensibly reserved for a series of seven five-lap races, which was welcomed by the somewhat hung over Friday night survivors. Those who didn't show up at Lady Oakes, and even some who did, were also seen at Dirty Dick's, the Junkanoo Club, Cumberland House or Blackbeard's, all legendary Nassau hangouts. The Resident's race number one went to Albury's C-Type, and race number two to Crise's own Porsche 550 Spyder. John Fitch won the Jaguar race which only had four cars in it. There were nine starters in the Ferrari race in three classes, with ten second intervals between the classes. Portago was in the Ferrari 857S, which was variously described as a works car, a works car hired for this race by Portago, and a car belonging to Luigi Chinetti, though it was the car Portago had raced before (chassis 0584/0578). It was the Ferrari driven in the 5-lap heat on Friday by Hill, and may have been the car that Hill or Ginther used in the Governor's Cup. It was fairly banged about by the time Portago got into it on

Saturday. Portago was just about to go past the slower Masten Gregory car when one of the carburetors starting leaking a lot of fuel, and the engine wouldn't pull more than 3000 rpm. This kept him in second but well ahead of the other runners.

The five-lap Porsche race went to M. Marshall's 550 Spyder, the first Ladies' race to Denise McCluggage in a similar Porsche, and the second Ladies' race to M. Lowe's D-Type borrowed from Lou Brero Sr. There was enough time left for a bizarre football game played with a coconut, and Carroll Shelby was more than surprised when he was piled into by Denise McCluggage with this heavy weapon, and it looked like he had received a serious shoulder injury, though it wouldn't stop him from racing on the following day.

The RAC steward decided that the main Nassau Trophy race on Sunday should be limited to 50 runners, rather than all those who had wished to take part. This was a sensible decision, especially as a 15-lap consolation race was then laid on for the 42 who didn't qualify as fast enough for the main race. This went to the Mercedes 300SL of M. Malarkey from Jan de Vroom's Ferrari 250GT.

Bill Grauer from Riverside Records was at Nassau as he had been at Sebring, peppering drivers with simplistic questions, which everyone took in good part. He asked Moss, Hill and Portago about their tactics, especially with tyres and this was reduced to something of a shambles as they were all listening to each other, so they were trying to record and not give away secrets at the same time. There was a great deal of back and forth between Moss and Portago, something Moss remembered and would comment on to the author many years later.

Then came the main event, with 42 of the 50 eligible cars lining up for the Le Mans start. Bill Lloyd's Maserati 300S was repaired for Stirling Moss who had been fairly relaxed and was seen out water skiing. Moss and Shelby's Ferrari set off together, Shelby's shoulder strapped up after the 'coconut incident'. Shelby had been third in the line and Moss 18th but they were soon out in front of the field. They came across the line with Shelby in front but Portago had latched onto Moss for third. Portago then had a spin on the second lap trying to hold Moss, and Constantine was third, and the Corvettes had moved up. Portago was driving brilliantly to recover from his spin, moving into 5th by lap 5 and 4th by lap 6. Then he caught and passed Constantine, with Phil Hill following him through. Moss got by Shelby who then suddenly disappeared. The 4.9 Ferrari then limped into the pits with a puncture and returned to the fight in 29th place. Hill had slipped past Portago, but the Spaniard repassed him.

Moss had a 42-second lead over Hill on lap 17 as Portago came in for tyres. Fitch had taken third when his gearbox locked in 2nd. Portago unlapped himself from Moss and started pulling away. Phil Hill, who had been saving his tyres, was off line for one of the corners and hit a heavy marker barrel, splitting the fuel tank. He admitted that the sight of the rubber peeling off Portago's tyres had made him slow down to save the car and he would have been better going quicker. By lap 25, Shelby had worked himself back up to third behind Moss and Brero, with Gregory, Constantine, Portago, Lunken and Boynton behind. Portago came back in a lap later for another tyre, and Shelby had a second puncture. The Spaniard had another spin at Victoria bend, just as Shelby retired with no steering. As the race moved towards the end of the 60 laps, Portago again drove through the field. He finally made it up to third, though Gregory was a long way ahead in second, well behind Moss. Portago would have had second but for his spins and tyre problems, though it looks like he wouldn't have caught Moss in the 300S.

500 people showed up for the International Motor Ball at the British Colonial Hotel. There was one person missing from the prize-giving ceremony. Red Crise came forward when Portago was to receive his trophies and announced: "I want you, ladies and gentleman, to excuse Alfonso. He had to make an urgent trip to Paris this morning for his annual haircut. Now you will excuse him, won't you?" (O'Neil, 2006, p.75-76) Crise also announced that the racing would move to Oakes Field in 1957 as Windsor was being reactivated as the Nassau airport. As for Portago, it seemed that he had to return to Paris, not for a haircut, but to make arrangements for his next bobsled adventure.

Portago had arranged his usual winter holiday at St. Moritz, which extended over the Christmas period. Linda Christian and her two daughters Romina and Taryn accompanied, or were at least part of, the Portago party...or at least were there, whatever their 'status' was. Dorian Leigh records that Portago had come and asked her to allow their son Kim to come to St. Moritz over Christmas. Leigh herself either was not invited or didn't wish to go, but sent Kim with his nanny, Ursula. She later stated how angry her sister Suzy Parker, who was also in St. Moritz, was when she saw

Portago making a fuss of Kim, and was also paying attention to Linda Christian. Leigh claims that Kim was introduced to his paternal grandmother, Olga, which undoubtedly he was. Portago's mother was then said to have telephoned Dorian to say what a nice boy he was. Dorian says she resented Olga's opposition to Portago's divorce from Carroll, but she would allow Olga to see Kim when she wanted. She declared that the relationship with Portago was over, though he tried to revive it some months later.

Amongst the activities going on at St. Moritz was the usual attempts on the Cresta run. Portago said to Linda Christian: "This year I intend to break the world record, which has been standing since 1931." At the time, it wasn't clear to her whether that was a bit of bragging or a serious threat. It wouldn't take long to find out.

Portago dances with Linda Christian at St. Moritz in December 1956. *(Courtesy of Linda Christian)*

Another relaxed moment...in a suit...at St. Moritz. *(Courtesy of Linda Christian)*

Virtually everyday after Christmas, Portago would make at least one practice run, which he seemed to very much enjoy. The official record setting day was on December 31...New Year's Eve. He had a practice run which was impressive but still left him off the record. Linda Christian claims she saw him hit a bump and told him that might be slowing him down. He is said to have acknowledged this and headed off for his next attempt. Christian's comments often seem rather patronising, and she took credit for actions and changes which seem somewhat unlikely. Nevertheless, she had managed to establish what she thought was a very close relationship with Portago. He would later claim to Dorian Leigh, according to Leigh, that he knew she was 'just there for the publicity she could get'! Linda Christian was, however, moved by his attention to Kim at St. Moritz, a child she referred to as belonging to 'some American girl'!

The first Autosport of the new year heralded Portago's achievement: "That versatile sportsman, the Marquis de Portago, who has ridden twice in the Grand National and is an expert skier, apart from being a member of the Ferrari works team, added another laurel to his achievements last Sunday when he broke the 25 year-old record for the bobsleigh Cresta Run at St. Moritz. He covered the 568-yard run in 28.9 seconds, traveling over the snow at more than 60 mph, .1 of a second faster than the old record held by John Crammond since 1931, He had already equaled the old record six times, before succeeding in his seventh attempt. Incidentally, Portago's motor racing contract forbids him to ski because it is too dangerous." (Autosport, January 4, 1957,p.4) William Shand Kydd, who was another of that rare breed of Cresta runners and steeplechasers, remembered Portago's achievements very clearly. Shand Kydd was also proud of the fact that he had done the Cresta and ridden at the Grand National. In another announcement in that same magazine, it was announced that the Ferrari Grand Prix team would be represented at the Argentine Grand Prix by Mike Hawthorn, Peter Collins, Eugenio Castellotti, Luigi Musso, Wolfgang von Trips, and Alfonso de Portago. This formidable team made Ferrari's chances for 1957 look very good indeed. Two of these drivers would be gone by the end of the year, four by the end of 1958, five by the end of 1959 and all by the end of 1961.

Portago sets a new record for the Cresta at St. Moritz. ***(Courtesy of Linda Christian)***

Ferrari 860 Monza Spyder Scaglietti Chassis 0602M

This very well raced works Ferrari first appeared at Sebring 1956 where Musso and Schell were second overall, and then Luigi Musso took it to third overall in his solo drive in the Mille Miglia. Fangio took second at the Nurburgring 1000 Kilometers, Castellotti won the Rouen race with it, and he and Collins retired in the Targa Florio. Portago drove it for the first time at Kristianstad in Sweden where he, Hawthorn and Duncan Hamilton took third. Portago was third again in this car in Caracas, and then was at Nassau with this car and 0578M as well. He took 0602M to seventh in the Preliminary race, 2nd in the Governor's Cup and 3rd in the Nassau Trophy. It was sold to Mr. Gelder in the USA, and went to Pierre Bardinon twenty years later, where it remained for eight years. It changed hands a number of times between 1984 and 1994, finally going to Fritz Grashei, who raced it occasionally at important historic events.

The Ferrari 860 Monza, chassis 0602, as it is today, seen here in the retro Mille Miglia.

THE MILLE MIGLIA - 1957

The motor racing year was about to get off to an early start with the Argentine Grand Prix on January 13. Autosport on January 11 reported that Portago had just led the Spanish bobsled team "in the Winter Olympiad in Cortina this week". (Autosport, Jan.11, 1957,p.34) There must have been very few winter sports fans working on the magazine at the time, as the magazine which usually came up with interesting and accurate news stories got it wrong this time. The Olympics had been held the previous January and it was the Bobsled World Championships, which were to take place at St. Moritz, not Cortina. The mistake was interesting in the light of the next news item, which was that Formula 3 driver Henry Taylor would be a member of the British bobsled team at St. Moritz. Taylor had won a number of Cresta events in 1956.

The Argentine Grand Prix was the first of the season, and the first round of the 1957 World Championship. It was thus a substantial disappointment that not one British team appeared in Buenos Aires for this event. Ferrari and Maserati more than made up for it, Scuderia Ferrari sending no less than six Lancia D-50s and eight drivers, while there were four works Maseratis, and three Scuderia Centro Sud cars. Two of these were Maserati 250Fs and the third was an older Ferrari 500 for Alessandro de Tomaso. Luigi Piotti was the only true privateer with his own 250F. Thus there were only fourteen cars in total. Ferrari had entered cars for Collins, Musso, Castellotti, Hawthorn, Cesare Perdisa and the 'Pampas Bull', Froilan Gonzales. Portago and von Trips were there as reserve drivers, in what was expected to be a race run in record temperatures. The D-50s had not been dramatically changed, but most of them now had 'one-piece' body sections, that is the fuel pontoons were no longer separate from the car as in 1955 and 1956 but were fared into the main body. Variations on the size and number and location of the actual tanks within the body changed on a regular basis.

Fangio, Collins and Portago before practice at the 1957 Argentine Grand Prix. *(Credit - Archive Fodisch)*

Maserati had cars for Fangio, Behra, local Menditeguy and Moss. But Moss was no longer a Maserati driver, so what was this about? Stirling Moss had signed his name to a contract with Tony Vandervell's Vanwall team, which was going to make a major attack on the World Championship, except that they weren't ready for Argentina so Moss was lent to Maserati. That was not unusual in the period, but imagine a team these days lending out their top driver to score points for the opposition, points that might cost you the title at the end of the season. The Centro Sud Maseratis were for Schell and Bonnier. Maserati had even more to be happy about because they had lured Fangio away from Ferrari, even though the 'great man' had won the 1956 Championship. He had had enough of life in the Ferrari team and was seemingly quite happy in his new team. Portago had said at one point that he was happy he had been in team in 1956 so that he had the chance to drive against Fangio in the same car, both in Grand Prix and sports cars.

Moss set fastest time in practice in preparation for the 100-lap race, over a second a lap faster than teammate Fangio. This set people speculating about whether Moss and Fangio would be allowed to fight amongst themselves for the lead. Behra was next and Castellotti got the only Ferrari onto the front row, though they had the whole second row. Any thought that there might be a fabulous race about to unfold were soon swept away. A huge crowd was on the grid when the starter was trying to get the race under way. He had the cars sitting for ages with their engines running, and it seems that he may have used a flag to wave it at the crowd. Some of the drivers saw this and they were off. Moss didn't, shearing a pin in the gearbox and bending the throttle linkage. He was straight into the pits and spent nine laps there. He would make up some of this and set fastest lap, but that took the sparkle out of the race.

Portago leads one of the Maserati 250Fs at the Argentine race.
(Credit - Autosport)

Behra was in front from Castellotti, Fangio, Hawthorn and Collins, and then Castellotti put a Ferrari...that is, Lancia...in front on lap three. Behra was back in the lead on lap nine. Four laps later, Collins had pushed himself passed everyone else, where he stayed until his pit stop on lap 26. This was now looking like it might be a very exciting race after all, with the Maseratis being swept aside. Gearbox trouble stopped Collins after only one more lap. Behra was then first, but not for long as Fangio had decided that it was time to go, and he did. Musso was then out, and Collins took over Perdisa's car, and then the D-50 clutch weakness struck Hawthorn and he was out, having had a good battle with Gonzales. Gonzales then came in on lap 42 and handed the wheel to Portago who was happy to have a chance to drive the D-50 again, though this time it was chassis 0006. The Maseratis had regained the upper hand, with Castellotti hanging on to third. When Collins came in again on lap 69, von Trips got his chance to drive as well. When Castellotti stopped with a broken drive shaft, Portago moved up a place, but Maseratis were in the first four spots: Fangio, Behra, Menditeguy, Schell and then Portago. That was how it ended with Portago driving the first surviving Ferrari which he had shared with Gonzales, followed by von Trips in the other 'shared' Collins/Perdisa car. It would be Portago's last Grand Prix.

Gonzales, in the car that Portago would take over, leads a spinning Ferrari.
(Credit - V.Alvarez/Whitefly)

The Grand Prix drivers remained in Buenos Aires, to be joined by something of a mixed bag of sports car drivers. To be fair, there were some good drivers and cars for the Buenos Aires 1000 Kilometers to be run over the Costanero circuit in the eastern area of Buenos Aires. Racing had taken place here before the Autodromo had been built, and the 6.3-mile road circuit was fast and challenging. The main straight was in fact two straights, as the cars would fly up one side of the fast bit of road and return down the other side. At 150 mph, that was a closing speed of 300 mph! The circuit was fairly rough, and when Fangio set a 114-mph lap in first practice, it was decided to re-install a chicane halfway down the straight to slow the cars down. Six hours pounding around this track in what were likely to be very high temperatures looked a daunting prospect. The changes brought the average down by 8 mph, and that was in the fastest car. Maserati had been developing the sensational 450S since it made its debut in Sweden, and it looked to have been improved. This was for Fangio and Moss.

The drivers before the Buenos Aires 1000 Kilometers, with Portago in his typical position, grinning from the side. *(Credit - Autosport)*

Two nobleman, Portago with Wolfgang von Trips. *(Credit - Epoca)*

The works Ferraris were next behind the Fangio/Moss combination. There has always been some question over exactly who drove what at Buenos Aires. There were four Ferrari works entries: 290 MMs for Gregory/Castellotti/Musso (chassis 0626) though it is also thought that this car had been sold to Temple Buell, and for Portago/Castellotti/Collins/von Trips (chassis 0628); then there were two 290S models for Castellotti/Musso/Hawthorn/von Trips (chassis 0646) and Collins/Hawthorn/Castellotti (chassis 0656). From this one can judge that Ferrari were taking no chances of losing after their defeat the previous week in the Grand Prix. The Portago/von Trips pairing in the 290-MM was third quickest of the Ferrari team, seven seconds behind Moss and Fangio. Ecurie Ecosse had entered two Jaguar D-Types for Ron Flockhart/Roberto Mieres and Ninian Sanderson/Larreta. Flockhart had a big crash in practice, escaping unhurt but severely damaging the car. Mieres then moved into the other car with Sanderson. Mieres talked to the author at Monaco in 2004:
"You know, I had done a lot of races in Europe, but I was very happy to be asked by this famous Scottish team to drive in the 1000 Kilometers in a D-Type Jaguar. This was very exciting for me and I was just happy to be doing the race. When the car crashed in practice I thought I was finished but they were very good, and I got to drive. It was a very hard race. We had been 15 or 20 seconds slower than the fastest car in the practice, but we kept going and going. I liked Ninian Sanderson, a very nice man and I was very happy when we finished fourth. I was surprised, but happy. It was a good race."

Moss opened up a big gap at the outset of the race in the big and brutal looking and sounding 450S. He was followed by Gregory and a surprisingly rapid D-Type, Portago and Behra in a 300S. The Hawthorn/Collins 290S was in trouble immediately, refusing to start and retiring on the second lap. Cabalen's Maserati spun into spectators in the early laps, but fortunately no one was seriously injured. Camano's Maserati also crashed and he was badly hurt. Portago moved the 290-MM up to third at twenty laps. Gregory handed over to Castellotti on lap 33, von Trips having taken over from Castellotti in the other car a lap earlier. Fangio lapped every car except the second place machine by lap 44, and Collins was now driving for Portago. Fangio then signaled to the pits that he was having problems, with the clutch as it turned out, and he retired with the gearbox broken on lap 57, letting Castellotti into the lead. Moss took over Menditeguy's 300S, but that was done too late. He pushed the car up to second, however, in an amazing driving display. Moss set fastest lap in the 300S in a time a tenth of a second quicker than the 450S. The Gregory/Perdisa, Castellotti/Musso car took the win in the 290-MM ahead of Moss/Behra/Menditeguy, with the Portago/Collins/Castellotti 290 MM third, and the D-Type fourth. It had turned out to be a very hard and exciting race.

Portago shared this car at Buenos Aires with von Trips and Collins to finish third. ***(Credit - Kirton)***

Portago at the Buenos Aires race 1957. ***(Credit - V.Alvarez/Whitefly)***

Lancia D-50 Chassis 0006, 0007 and 0009
Portago drove for the Ferrari team in Formula 1 for the first time at the French Grand Prix in 1956. He drove 0007 in the French, British (second with Collins, also sharing 0009 with Castellotti coming 11th), German and Italian Grand Prix races in 1956, and had also practiced the aerodynamic body on chassis 0006 at the French race. He then shared 0006 with 'normal' bodywork with Gonzales in the Argentine GP in 1957, finishing 5th. His second place in the British Grand Prix was his best result.

Ferrari 290 MM Spyder Scaglietti Chassis 0628
Collins and Klemantaski drove this new car in the 1956 Mille Miglia where they finished a brilliant second, and then Portago and Gendebien drove it at the Nurburgring 1000 Kilometers, where the car was disqualified. Herrmann/Gendebien were third in the Targa Florio, and Gendebien was second in the Coppa d'Oro Dolomiti. Portago was back in the car with von Trips at Buenos Aires in 1957 where they were third. Phil Hill and von Trips failed to finish at Sebring. Severi used it as a test car in the Mille Miglia, so it may have been used by Portago there. Later in 1957, Jan de Vroom raced it in the Swedish Grand Prix, and then the body was converted to one with pontoon fenders. George Arendts bought the car in late 1957 and Stirling Moss won the Nassau Memorial race with it, and he shared it with Masten Gregory for another Nassau win that year. Ed Crawford was driving it for E.D. Martin in Cuba in 1958 where he was 8th. Luigi Chinetti had the car later in 1958, and Dan Gurney drove it at Watkins Glen, and Bruce Kessler raced it at Lime Rock. It changed hands several times, and in 1981 was restored for Luigi Chinetti Jr. who did the Mille Miglia retro event and several other historic races. It is now owned by John Shirley.

The Ferrari 290 MM, chassis 0628, as it is today. (Credit - van Nes)

Most of the Grand Prix regulars remained in Argentina for the Buenos Aires Grand Prix, a non-championship race to take place on January 27. One of the exceptions was Portago, who flew back to France and then journeyed on to St. Moritz for the World Bobsled Championships to take place over the weekend of February 17-18.

In the meantime, the drivers got on with another race in the busy 1957 calendar. This one at Buenos Aires was to be run in two heats and the results would be taken on aggregate. The conditions for this race were, if anything, worse than the previous two, and there were many drivers both in practice and in the race who had to be revived, suffering from heat and exhaustion. Stirling Moss was one of these, and he retired in the first heat, and recovered enough to share the Maserati with Menditeguy in the second. Fangio, Behra and Castellotti took the first three places in heat one and Musso/Collins won the second from Behra and Fangio, so Fangio and Behra were first and second on aggregate with Musso/Collins third. They were all very happy when it was over. Another one of those odd photos featuring Portago appeared in Autosport on Feb.1, taken before the start of the Buenos Aires 1000 Kilometers. Wilkie Wilkinson, von Trips, Hawthorn and Collins were in the front, with Masten Gregory putting up two fingers behind Collins' head, with Sanderson to the side of Collins and Portago peeking in from the side with a grin on his face.

By the time this photo appeared, Portago himself was in Switzerland, and the following week's Autosport carried a small news item saying that he had crashed his bobsled at 55 mph after the finishing line in a trial run on Sunday February 11. It was reported that this occurred in the four-man bob, which may or may not be correct, as the only existing records document his runs in the two-man bob with Luis Munoz. Portago had injured his shoulder and ribs and it was thought he might not be fit for the Cuban Grand Prix a few weeks hence. That turned out not to be the case as Portago continued with his runs, more or less as if nothing had happened.

When the finals of the competition took place the following weekend, the Swiss had taken the four-man bob, with Italy's Monti and his team in second, and the Americans led by Art Tyler in third. The two-man event was a very hard fought contest and in the final runs, the first five were covered by only a few hundredths of a second. The great Eugenio Monti and Renzo Alvera managed to pull out just enough margin for the gold, the Americans Tyler and Charles Butler got the silver, and finally, with great fanfare, the Spaniards had won a World Championship medal, Portago and Munoz getting the bronze for third place. The detractors who felt Portago's previous attempts were just lucky were truly silenced, and Monti himself paid tribute to Portago for being brave enough to continue on his quest to win glory on the bobsled. It was true tilting at windmills, but this Don Quixote managed to achieve substantial acknowledgement for what he had done. As the King of Spain had been his godfather, it was not surprising that he was showered with royal congratulations.

The Linda Christian autobiography describes being at St. Moritz over Christmas and New Year 1956 when Portago set the Cresta record. She then goes on to describe a number of parties and social events during that period and comes to a point when she says that Portago started talking to her about having to leave for Cuba the following day. The Cuban race was on February 24 so this would have been in mid-February, not in December/January. If indeed she was at St. Moritz in February for the World Bobsled Championships, then there must have been added complications, as Portago's wife Carroll was there as well, though no mention is made of her. Christian describes Portago as enjoying the party scene and reveling in the attention he was getting, and she was very much inclined to see him as something of " a little lost boy". She was also moved at the way he treated Kim. The author's view is that these comments relate to the Christmas period, rather than to Portago's presence in St. Moritz in February. There did seem, however, to be a conversation which must have taken place in Paris in mid-February, during which Portago tried to convince her to accompany him to Cuba:

"In all our weeks together I had known that Fon and I would part when he traveled to Cuba, and I had felt that this separation would be the end; it was in that belief that I had accepted the relationship. At moments lately the feeling had troubled me, and I had pushed away all thoughts of the inevitable day." (Christian, 1962, p.223.) She states that he 'needed her' to go to Cuba with him, as "it's a Grand Prix race and the more of those I win, the closer I come to being champion of the world".

This statement, which might just be a dramatic retelling of a conversation raises some serious questions about the genuineness of the story. Cuba was neither a Grand Prix, nor did it count towards any World Championship. It is impossible to believe that Portago would have made such a statement, except possibly for effect, and even that seems unlikely. However, Linda Christian did go to Cuba. On the long flight, she implies, he told her the story of how he began racing, and her account has a strong similarity to interviews, which were published in the few years after Portago's death. She tells a tale whereby Portago demanded to know from Enzo Ferrari why he wasn't on the Ferrari team in 1955. Ferrari, she says, answered not with a letter but with a photograph of Portago spinning off the road in a race the previous week. Again, it is unlikely that Portago would have even thought of making such an approach to Enzo Ferrari. Portago admitted he was in awe of some of these people, and he would have known that such a 'demand' would not have gotten him a drive. Sadly, Linda Christian, for all the notoriety that resulted from her last months with Portago, didn't seem able to convey a portrait of Portago in any depth. She recognised some of the complexity and humanity, but one has to conclude that this relationship probably remained fairly superficial.

The poster announcing the 1957 Gran Premio de Cuba for sports cars.

The motoring journals were enthusiastic about the race in Cuba, called the Cuba Grand Prix, though it was a race for sports cars, not Formula 1. Moss, Gendebien, Schell, Hill, Simon, da Silva Ramos, Portago, and Hans Herrmann were all reported to be going. The first rumours were that Moss would be driving Franco Cornacchia's private 300S, and that Fangio might just be going. Portago's attendance was said to depend on his recovery from his bobsled crash, which of course he had ignored. By the following week Fangio had been confirmed and Masten Gregory and Eugenio Castellotti were also going.

When the drivers got to Cuba, they immediately began to wonder whether they had made the right decision. It was clear that the organisation of this first race in Cuba was not up to the task, and that poor communications with the shippers and failure to spot a dockers' strike in New York nearly ended it before it began. Fourteen cars had arrived in the USA from Italy aboard the freight vessel Independence, and the strike prevented the unloading of the seven Maseratis, five Ferraris and two Gordinis. The race was then going to be postponed for twenty-four hours while a frantic attempt was made to fly in more cars from the USA. And indeed the race would take place on February 25th, not 24th as a result. When the program came out at the last minute, there was a reasonable amount of confusion about who was in what. Stirling Moss was entered to drive a Scuderia Madunina Maserati 300S but ended up with Chimori's 2-litre Maserati. Castellotti had what was referred to as Portago's 'spare 3.5-litre Ferrari, though this would have been the first time Portago would have had a spare car. The programme had it entered by Luigi Chinetti. Harry Schell took over the Brazilian Pinhero Pines' Maserati 300S, and Schell wasn't in the programme at all. Hans Herrmann, Andre Pilette and Andre Simon all seemed to have been left without a drive. Peter Collins took over American Howard Hively's Ferrari and Carini was in another so-called spare Ferrari, this time a 4.9. Carroll Shelby was driving a 4.9 Ferrari, entered by Chinetti but owned by John Edgar. He was listed as the entrant of the other 4.9 for Carini, though the programme described him as 'Carl Schelby'!

Portago was down in the entry in a car entered by himself, listed as a Ferrari 3.5-litre. This turned out to be the 857S Monza Spyder (chassis 0578M/0584) which he had driven some seven times before. The practice sessions would now be on Saturday and Sunday and the race on Monday. The race was a 500 kilometer or 315 mile event, 90 laps of a circuit just over three miles long. There would be two classes, for under and over two litres. The circuit was an interesting one, somewhat similar to the Costanera circuit in Buenos Aires. A large section was run over the Malecon Highway, which is the seafront road, where occasionally wind would whip up waves, which would come over the wall. The Malecon Highway is a dual carriageway with a wide strip down the middle. The cars would run past each other on both sides of this stretch of road, as in Buenos Aires. This wasn't exactly straight, more curved straights in parallel. One of these ended in an esse bend, the other in a sharp left followed by a short straight and another 90-degree left. It was a bumpy circuit, which had a considerable impact on the big cars, tending to toss them about the road at high speeds.

Conditions varied over the weekend, but Saturday practice was in the dry and Fangio in a Maserati 300S set a not too surprising fastest time at 2 minutes 4.04 seconds but Portago was on excellent form, and he brought his Ferrari around the tough circuit only a half second slower, with Phil Hill in another 3.5-litre Ferrari only two tenths slower. Shelby, Moss, Collins, and Castellotti were all well behind these times, though Stirling Moss in a 2-litre car was a full fifteen seconds ahead of anyone else in the class. Towards the end of the day, rumours were circulating that a kidnap attempt had been made on a driver, and the notables were thus supplied with armed bodyguards. These were the days when Fidel Castro's revolutionary forces were operating from rural and mountain headquarters and making strikes on government and military sites. The then dictator President Fulgencio Batista was seen on both the practice and race days, surrounded by troops but also accompanied by a number of international celebrities. There were reports of the usual Batista heavy-handed tactics, but it has to be said that the President gave no hint that his days were numbered. When the author visited Havana in 1961 and walked around the Malecon circuit, the President was Fidel Castro. Eugenio Castellotti said that he thought the bodyguards were actually there to keep the Cuban women away from the drivers!

Sunday was wet and all the practice times were thus slower. Proceedings were delayed when a pedestrian bridge collapsed and many people were injured, as happened in 1974 in Angola. Both times revolutionary forces had the finger pointed at them, though poor workmanship was much more evident than political trickery. Times were some thirty seconds slower than Saturday at first, but as the road dried, times came tumbling down. A last minute decision was made to take the total of each driver's fastest time on both days and that put Fangio on pole from Portago, Hill and Schell. Rain sprinkled down shortly before the race start on Monday but stopped. The starter hesitated with the flag and the drivers took the decision to go. Phil Hill, in George Tilp's Ferrari, couldn't get his car started and his crew gave him a push, for which he was immediately disqualified.

Alfonso de Portago thundered past the pits in the lead at the end of the first lap, ahead of Stirling Moss who had sneaked through several rows of cars towards the front. Castellotti and Schell were next with Juan Fangio back in seventh and looking cautious and relaxed, prepared to wait in a race that would take over three hours. Portago stretched his lead to some 150 yards over Moss, but Fangio was now making his way though the others, and on lap 15 he passed Moss into second place. Moss had an oil leak in his Maserati and was in the pits two laps later, retiring after a further exploratory lap. Carroll Shelby moved his Ferrari into third. Portago was driving superbly, out-braking Fangio and catching him up at the rate of a second or two a lap. Then came the fuel stops and a few driver changes.

Portago drove possibly his best ever race in Cuba 1957.
(Credit - Car and Driver)

Portago was in on lap 54, with Phil Hill standing by to take over. However, Portago stayed in the car. Schell came in and Moss took over the bigger Maserati, trying to catch Carroll Shelby. When Fangio rushed in for fuel, Portago was out in front and the race looked like it would be his. Then Castellotti came in with a broken valve, and there was Portago right behind him. A fuel line had broken and fuel was pouring out. Fangio had set a fast lap at 2 minutes 2.1 seconds and Portago had responded with a stunning 2 minutes 2 seconds. Portago lost nearly two laps as the car was worked on, and he roared out in a desperate but futile attempt to catch the leaders. He passed car after car as he made his way back up the leader board. On lap 80 he set the race's quickest time of 2 minutes 1.4 seconds, but he could not catch Shelby in second or the wily Fangio, who won by over a minute. Portago had gotten up to third, with Peter Collins in fourth, winning the two-litre class.

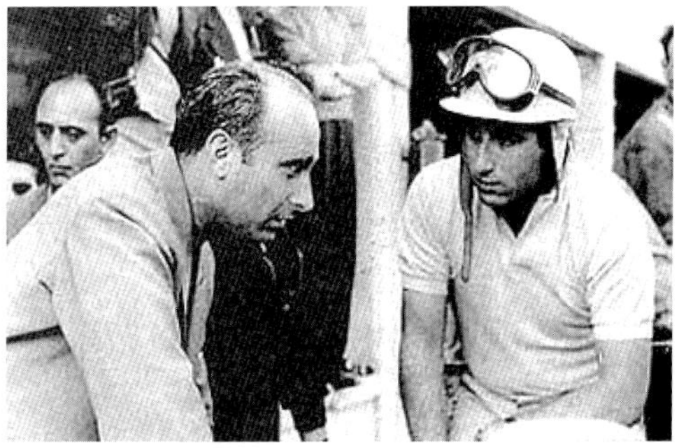
Fangio was effusive with his praise for Portago who nearly beat him in Cuba. ***(Credit - Autopresse)***

As the cars took the flag and headed into the pit lane, Portago was out of the car and was mobbed by the spectators, who followed him up and down the pit-lane for several minutes. When the trophies and prizes were presented, Fangio stepped forward and said that the real winner had been Fon Portago. This was a source of immense pride to Portago. "On the night of the prize distribution, the great Fangio stood up and said, for all to hear, 'I was lucky to win,' leading the tremendous ovation as Fon ran up the stairs to join him on the platform. Portago's performance in Cuba was just another indication of his seriousness...victory had been snatched away from him by the failure of a small tube to the petrol gauge. His reaction to this setback was typical of him. 'Luck is unusually important', he said. 'There's no predicting when a silly little thing will stop a driver just as surely as a major breakdown.' " (Tanner in Motor Racing, June 1957, p.147) This article had already been written and sent to print when the Mille Miglia crash took place.

It was clear then, and it is clear now, that Cuba was Portago's best race. He had had a few races when he showed he could run with Fangio and Moss in equal cars, and in Cuba he demonstrated that he could beat them. Fangio was the first to acknowledge this in public.

In the 1950s and 1960s, when people would buy records with motor racing sounds on them, Riverside Records, the producer of many great jazz albums, came up with the idea of recording not only the sounds of cars, but interviews with and about various drivers of the period, and thus it is possible to have a spoken archive of Phil Hill, Fangio, Moss, Carroll Shelby and Portago. Amongst the people interviewed by Barratt Clark and Bill Grauer was Luigi Chinetti who was asked about Portago's performance in Cuba. Chinetti said that he saw Portago as a possible future World Champion, not only because he had led that race and driven as well as he had, but when the car came in, it was still in virtually perfect condition. The clutch looked like it was new, and this struck Chinetti as fairly amazing. It would also surprise those drivers who had been said to be very worried about Portago's aggressive style in his early races. Chinetti felt that Portago had progressed a great deal through 1955 and 1956 and had improved in the way he managed a car, and by this time he was quite capable of racing with Fangio and Moss. Chinetti remarked on how impressed Fangio was by Portago's progress.

Juan Fangio was also asked about Portago and the Cuban race at Havana, but the recording team had to get Portago himself to conduct the interview in Spanish and then translate Fangio's words: "Fangio says that the circuit is very dangerous and if it rains it is going to be absolute murder. It is completely different from Monte Carlo, which is a slow circuit, and this is a fast circuit. He very kindly and most diplomatically says that I am his most dangerous rival, but I am sure he is exaggerating."

Peter Collins was also brought in to make a contribution about Portago: " He is a man who is devoted to sport whether it is skiing, bobsleighing, water skiing, swimming, fishing, hunting, whatever it might be, but as far as motor racing is concerned, he has got a tremendous enthusiasm, a great deal of ability, and as soon as he learns how to moderate his ability...he knows how to drive well and fast...but he does tend to go off the road, and my own opinion, and he obviously won't agree with me on this, but he does tend to fly off the road and you can't go off the road and win motor races. I think once he can arrive at a decision which can only be with himself that he will drive slower than he wants to drive and he knows that he can, and stay on the road and become reliable, then he will be one of the best drivers there are in the world. I hope he continues to drive like he did today because, in my opinion, on his form today, if he goes on driving like that in sports cars and in Grand Prix cars, he will be up among the world champions tomorrow."

Wolfgang von Trips supported Collin's opinion about his fellow nobleman: "Fon Portago is very bold and he is going for things where you must dare very much, so he started horseback riding, and then he went out for bobsleighs and then he started racing. He started by just sitting in the car and going just as fast as possible, and even if he turned over he wouldn't mind. At first everyone said he is not good because he is rough, and he harms the car and he will turn over, and things like that. Even the factory put him as a second driver because they were afraid. But slowly and in the last year, we all discovered that he is a great, talented driver, and he was working on himself to push his wild emotions down to get to be a real good driver, and I think he is now just about one of the world's best drivers." (Riverside Records, 1957)

Linda Christian also described her own experience of the Cuban race:

"The drivers who had converged on Havana were a fraternity, and spent most of their time together. Harry Schell, Peter Collins, and Wolfgang von Trips were there. Eugenio Castellotti exuded confidence. Mike Hawthorn, the English driver whom Fon had first met in Buenos Aires and who had become his closest friend, was as ever and nonchalant. And the Argentinian Juan Manual Fangio, several times world champion, was quiet and unassuming and reflected enormous strength and assurance. Gary Cooper had arrived in Havana with his wife Rocky, especially for the race. They were both old friends from Hollywood, and I was a fan of his, adoring his sweet and charming personality. That warm quality one saw and felt on the screen was actually the essence of the man. Rocky was talking to Fon, fascinated with the stories he was recounting." (Christian, 1962,p.226-227)

She told the story of the post-race celebrations, remarking that Portago didn't drink at all. She said that at the 1956 Le Mans race, Portago carried a thermos of water in the car, while his co-driver had a thermos of champagne and brandy. She says: "At the height of a practice lap, doing about 160 miles per hour, Fon took several sips of the potent concoction. He choked, lost control, and crashed into two cars directly ahead on the track, putting all three vehicles out of the race". (Christian, op. cit. p.227)

This never happened. There is no record of Duncan Hamilton, despite his reputation as a serious drinker, ever mentioning such a habit. Drivers rarely took a drinks bottle with them in a practice session, and certainly would not have been taking a drink at 160 mph. There was no such incident in practice involving Portago. There is an obvious confusion with the actual race incident, which put Portago out of the Le Mans race. Where this story came from is uncertain, perhaps from Portago's own large repository of 'outrageous stories' which Robert Daley said Portago loved to tell. However, her account of the race in Cuba is quite accurate.

Ferrari 857S Monza Spyder Scaglietti Chassis 0578M

This car has always caused a great deal of consternation amongst Ferrari historians. 0578M started life in 1955 and Gendebien/Gregory drove the car at the Tourist Trophy in October 1955. Then it was supposedly hired by Portago from Ferrari for Nassau in December 1955, and it won the Governor's Trophy and Ascari Trophy races there, and was second in the Nassau Trophy. Hill/Gendebien were second at Buenos Aires in January 1956. Trintignant won races at Agadir and Senegal in February and March 1956 and then Portago/Kimberly retired it at Sebring. In April, Collins/Klemantaski won the Giro di Sicilia, and then Portago/Hill were 5th in the Paris 1000 Kilometers. Portago then raced it at Bari, Caracas and in Cuba in February 1957. It is thought that the car went to America in 1957 and was crashed and the remains scrapped by Luigi Chinetti, and some parts were later salvaged and a totally new car built. There is also the possibility that this car and chassis 0584M had their identities swapped possibly after Hill/Gendebien raced 0584M at the Argentine 1000 Kilometers in January 1956. A car with this chassis number survived, passed through many hands and still survives, while the chassis purporting to be 0578M also has the number 0203M stamped on its chassis.

This is chassis 0584, which may have been the car driven by Portago when it was numbered 0578. *(Credit - Schmidt)*

The Ferrari 857, chassis 0578, as it is today. *(Credit - van Nes)*

The motoring press started carrying previews of the Sebring 12 Hours, which would take place on March 23, early in March, reporting that Fangio would not be driving against the man he had teamed up with in 1956, Castellotti, and that he would be sharing a Maserati with Stirling Moss, while Castellotti would co-drive with Portago. A later report amended this to say that Perdisa would be sharing with Castellotti. All this was academic as Castellotti was killed at Modena in testing for the Sebring race in the car he was to drive in Florida with Perdisa. His car had overturned and the Italian had massive injuries from which he died shortly after. He had won the Mille Miglia in 1956, but success had so far eluded him in Formula 1. He and Luigi Musso were the top Italian drivers at the time and his death was a severe blow to the Ferrari team. Perdisa was so shocked by the crash that he decided he would retire from racing, so another competent journeyman driver was also lost to the Italian strength. Castellotti was 27 years old.

Ferrari announced that Castellotti and Perdisa's car would now be driven by Maurice Trintignant and Phil Hill at Sebring. The rest of the team would consist of Portago, Collins, Gendebien, Gregory, Musso and von Trips.

In the few days before Sebring, Robert Daley, who had spent considerable time with Portago early the previous year at Cortina, met up with him again. This was Daley's first direct contact with motorsport, but it would inspire his lifelong fascination with motor racing. He summed up his connection with Portago recently for the author:

"At Cortina, I spent a fair amount of time with Portago and the bobsledders in general. It meant being up at practically dawn because that is when they practiced. Carroll was always there even at that hour of the morning…I remember that. It was January and it was dark until about 8 o'clock. There was a special atmosphere around the bobsledding partly because of being out that early in the day. It was also special because I could have these conversations with this very interesting guy, and see the bobsleds, which were so exciting. What I felt about Portago was that he was an extremely competent fellow. He knew exactly what he was doing. When I saw him later at Sebring in 1957, he finished wherever he finished, 7th I think. He came in and he was soaking wet with sweat, he had done a great deal of the driving, he wasn't putting on any show at the end of that race. He was very serious. I saw him the two times…at Cortina and at Sebring. At Cortina, I talked to him every morning because I liked talking to him. My story about him ran before the weekend when the two-man bobsled final was taking place. So I then talked to him the following week too when he wasn't in it anymore. I remember this because I was still working hard to get stories for the paper. The first four stories ran with my byline but when I got back, I discovered that the Sports Editor, Raymond Kelly, had pulled my byline after the first four and reduced my fee to $25.00. I was furious but then Kelly got 'deposed' and his replacement was James Roach, who in many respects was responsible for anything I have done since. Roach got the money back for me as well!"

"He (Portago) played a kind of role with me. He may have been putting it on but I wasn't old enough to recognise it if he was. Later at Sebring, there was a guy called Marshall Smith who was the sports editor of Life magazine. I remember Portago going up to Marshall and telling him something. I was standing there at a distance and I remember thinking 'oh, he's on a first-name basis with this famous journalist'. I was young enough to think that and Marshall no doubt took tons of notes and Marshall was going to write something important. I guess that would have had Portago up for a good interview. That was of course later, in 1957. Ken Purdy was there and was going to do something for Esquire and Esquire rejected it, and Marshall was going to do something big for Life. There were others there hanging around by that time too so I knew that Fon had arrived."

"I had had no interest in motor racing before Cortina. After I came back after the Olympics, I started watching all of the race reports looking for Portago's name. Then I was going to get my 'star' as a journalist by writing a profile of de Portago. That is in The Cruel Sport. Later, I went to Sebring to see him. He was awfully nice and polite. I later learned that most athletes, including most racing drivers, are totally self-centered and rude, somebody like Mike Hawthorn. Mike Hawthorn was a very rude man, and Peter Collins was barely polite. Later, somebody like Phil Hill was a 'darling' even though he could be difficult and hard to work with on some days. He was still a really good person. The outcome of meeting Portago at Cortina was that I got involved with motor racing and sport, which became a staple for me at the New York Times, but also it touched something deep, very deep inside me because I then wrote three books about motor racing. That's a lot for somebody with a career like mine. The Fast One takes something from the characters of Portago and Phil Hill. They are not intended to be facts, they are distortions, and you are talking, in the case of Portago, about a legend."

"In many cases legends are more interesting than the real people. As I have said, I wasn't old enough at the time to be able to distinguish between the reality of Portago's stories and the stuff that was part of what you might call the 'legend'. On the other hand, looking back, I don't think the guy was making things up, this was just the way he was. In spite of the stories and way he spoke, he wasn't the one who talked about flying under bridges. Other people talked about those things. I don't know if he actually did what the story says he did at age 17 or not. There is no evidence that he did that, but I wouldn't be surprised if it was true. If he had had a chance to do that, he would do it. He was someone who really liked living far out, in the sense of doing it all, of doing what challenged him. It doesn't seem to matter in some ways whether this happened or not. He has become a legend and people are still talking about it 49 years later! We don't talk about the other guys who got killed that young, do we? There was something there that made him what we now call a legend, whatever some of the facts are. Think of the monument to Portago at Guidazzola. It's huge, and most motor racing drivers don't get a monument like that."

"All of my interest in motor racing since the 1950s came from Portago. I was really focussed on the guy. It all goes back to Cortina. I didn't do what you would call proper interviews. They were conversations…conversations in the snow. They were conversations every morning and were interrupted when it was his turn to go downhill. When he would go, I would talk to Gurner and I would talk to Carroll. I was really focussed on the guy and I don't know why. He had this physical presence. Maybe I was imagining things, imagining things then and still am. But he was the guy you looked at. I had never heard of him before but if he was around, you looked at him. He was a nobleman. He was Spanish. He was seen as good looking by women. He wasn't good looking but he was striking looking, always with the cigarette in the corner of his mouth almost as if he needed that. It was interesting to talk to Phil Hill about Portago…he said 'he was dirty'…in that way that showed how distasteful it was to Phil. Phil said 'he always bragged he was reading books but he never said a word about what was in them!' Phil was immune to legends but I wasn't."

"That meeting in Cortina started something. For my purposes, I saw enough of him to make a career. I wrote 150 pieces a year for the New York Times for six years, but many of them were about this…what came from meeting Portago, the racing and what it meant. All these young men getting killed really touched my soul in some way. It was about people getting killed and coming to terms with death. At one point then I counted up 18 guys who got killed out of a very small number, not even 40, so for me it was a stunning introduction to life, especially as a writer. Even when I went away from the sport of motor racing it was there and made me morbid…it really touched me. I guess it's sort of why I got interested in the bobsledding. There was this very sensual noise, all going on at 7.30 in the morning. Then along came Portago as part of it. I wasn't absolutely sure how he started but I thought it was on the cresta run during the many times that he was a St. Moritz where his family would go regularly. He got interested when he saw that there was bobsledding at the Olympics and that he could represent Spain which had nobody else, so he got his cousins, got some bobsleds, and I don't think there was much more to it than that. In one of his first practice runs he got slung out, and you can see how fast they are coming down the hill. It was a terrific spectacle, and then there was this spectacular guy, and furthermore, I was going to get $50.00 writing about it. That's what was so great about him. It was clear that he had a couple of runs down the cresta and he decided he was going to be a bobsledder. The sleds cost about a thousand dollars at the time, which was a lot of money. At that time, sleds were just beginning to be wind tunnel tested and you couldn't do anything without a high-class sled. But he just did it…because it was spectacular. When you hear of some of the other sports that he was supposed to have done, I have my doubts. I have doubts about Jai Alai which was a 'peasant sport' and unlikely for him to have been involved in and not his type of thing. Car racing was his type of thing. I was always astonished about the gentleman jockey stories because he was so big. Jockeys were supposed to be 135 pounds. I could never understand those stories…but they were part of the legend…and they could be true."

Robert Daley's fascination was mirrored by the attention Portago received from several other journalists, as Daley mentions. At Sebring, he was virtually besieged by people who wanted to interview, record or film him. He had clearly arrived as a celebrity.

Bill Grauer and Barratt Clark of the Riverside Records team, who had spoken to drivers about Portago, also caught up with him in Havana and at Sebring. In many ways, their recordings cast a different light on Portago's words, which in print looked stern and proscriptive, even a bit pedantic, but when heard are much more light-hearted, and a degree of irony and a self-effacing quality are present. There is an element of exaggeration, but it often seems that the very serious American interviewers were hanging on every word and asking to be led on. The important thing about these interviews is that Portago, whatever else he was, was open and revealing:

"To me, cars are not the interesting part of automobile racing. The interesting part about automobile racing is to be able to go faster than somebody else. I believe that riding horses helps one in many sports because it gives you sensitivity that otherwise you might not acquire. I know Stirling Moss has ridden a lot, that Peter Collins has ridden a lot and automobile racing in my opinion is purely a matter of sensitivity. Every curve has a theoretical maximum speed and the ambition of a racing driver is to go around that curve as close to the maximum speed as he can without going over it. That is a matter of sensitivity. You know the second a car is out of control, you're all too aware of it. Some cars won't give you a lot of warning when it is going to break loose, but a Ferrari gives you a lot of warning, you know when something is going to happen and often you can correct it…most things that go wrong are due to the driver over-doing it. It is rare for the same mechanical failure to occur twice. But all you need is a couple of drops of water on a corner and you can have ten accidents in ten seconds and it's nobody's fault."

"I think a good driver is a man who can adapt himself to any car, at least I hope so. If a man is going to become a good driver, he can drive a Ferrari at the start, maybe not a 5-litre but he can certainly drive a 2-litre at the start. All you must have is respect for the car. I have enormous respect for the Grand Prix Ferrari, and I realise if I treat it badly it can very easily kill me, so I have a lot of respect for it. You have to get to the point, which I haven't gotten to in Grand Prix cars but have in sports cars where I feel I am part of the car. I feel that if I am in a corner and I swing the car around the corner, the car is part of me. I don't have that feeling yet with a Grand Prix car and I hope that I get it very soon." (Riverside Records, 1957)

Sebring looked like it would be a straight fight between Ferrari and Maserati, and Ferrari had some reason to feel confident. They brought four cars: a 290 MM (chassis 0628) for Hill and von Trips, and two cars listed by Wimpffen as 315S models, chassis 0674 for Collins and Trintignant and chassis 0646 for Portago and Luigi Musso. 0646 had been

Peter Collins with his new wife and Portago in New York, March 1957.
(Credit - Autopresse)

listed as a 290S, the car driven by Castellotti and von Trips at Buenos Aires which did not finish. For Sebring the engine had been upgraded to 315S specifications, the same as 0674 which was a new car built for Sebring. There was also an 857S which was a practice car only presumably chassis 0578/0584, which was used by all the Scuderia's drivers in practice. There was George Tilp's private 290S for Masten Gregory/Lou Brero (chassis 0656), and Howard Hively's 500 TRC for himself and Richie Ginther, as well as four other private Ferraris. Maserati, on the other hand, had a complete change of approach to this race. They brought the new and so far unreliable 450S for Fangio/Behra, a single 300S for Moss/Schell, and yet another different model, a 250S, for Salvadori/Shelby. This combination had a lot of people shaking their heads, as it seemed fairly evident that the strategy would be to use the big 180 mph 450S to draw the Ferraris into a car-wrecking fight at the front while Moss and the reliable 300S picked up the glory. The 250S would then be a good back up, and privateer Lance Reventlow had his 200S to share with Bill Pollack.

Portago and his wife Carroll at Sebring 1957.
(Credit - Mangeot)

Fangio had set fastest practice time of 3 minutes 25.8 seconds and Behra in the same car was not much slower. One of the highlights of practice was the presence of a team of Corvettes. Again, official Chevrolet involvement was denied but of course it was there. A test car had been brought along to assist in getting the racecars properly prepared for what they thought would be a good result. The Corvette drivers found the cars fast but hard to drive on the demanding Sebring airfield circuit. John Fitch was down as the entrant for Dick Thompson/Gaston Andrey, and Lindsay Hopkins entered Kilborn/Jeffords/Duncan, O'Shea/Lovely and Fitch/Taruffi. Hopkins also entered the test car for Taruffi, Fitch and its designer Zora Arkus Duntov! The regular drivers set a reasonable time in the car, and then Moss and Fangio were asked if they would like to try it. Moss set a good time, quicker than the other drivers, but Fangio went out, came back in with a big grin on his face, having gone only two seconds slower than his fastest lap in the Maserati, some 10 seconds quicker than the regulars, and feeling he could have gotten another two seconds off the time. The maestro was always the maestro…no fuss, he just got on with it, and Portago had told several people about his reverence for Fangio in interviews at Sebring.

Castellotti watches Portago go out to practice at Sebring. ***(Credit - Bernard Cahier)***

If a hard fight between Ferrari and Maserati was the bait, Peter Collins in the V-12 Ferrari fell for it and blasted away from the Le Mans start well ahead of Behra who was first driver in the 450S. Moss was next and Portago was not far behind in the 315S Ferrari. Behra had restrained himself on the first lap but eased past Portago, and then Moss to follow Collins. Then on lap four, Bob Goldich rolled his Arnolt-Bristol, a car with seat belts and no rollover bar, and he was pinned under it and died on the way to the hospital. The rest of the team was withdrawn. On lap 10, Bill Lloyd's D-Type also quit with a gearbox failure. Mike Hawthorn, in a works D-Type with Ivor Bueb, was also taking it easy, recognising that Sebring is very hard on brakes and gearboxes. Behra went into the lead on lap 25 and eased out a gap, taking it easy and driving well within the big Maserati's limits. Fangio took over and continued this easy pace while Moss waited a bit further back for the 'inevitable' failure of the big car. Collin's car started to lose some ground and Portago moved in to keep on the tail of Stirling Moss, and this was thus another of those races which Moss would tell the author that indicated Portago's competence.

There was relatively little drama in the first half of the race, though the quick Maserati of Salvadori/Shelby was disqualified on the 68th lap for refueling early, having not waited the minimum 20 laps between stops. Four of the D-Types were out by this point, and Reventlow retired on lap 88. After six hours, Fangio/Behra still led from the private Ferrari of Gregory/Brero, Hawthorn/Bueb, Portago/Musso and Collins/Trintignant. Moss and Schell had dropped back with a number of small problems, but were working their way back through the field. The Hill/von Trips works Ferrari had departed on lap 106 with transmission failure. Portago and Musso then established themselves as the main threat to Fangio and Behra and remained near the front for many hours. After the halfway stage, though, they began to stop to try to sort out a persistent brake problem…there weren't any! Moss and Schell were almost in trouble with the officials as they too had refueled before time. However, they realised what had happened and that fuel was pumped back out. Journalist/photographer Bernard Cahier had been out at Sebring's hairpin corner taking photos when Moss came round this rather tight and slow bend. He signaled to Bernard that he needed a drink and next lap he slowed and was handed a Coke. He drank it on the move, and duly returned the empty bottle, which landed at Cahier's feet!

Portago at Sebring 1957.
(Credit - Ferrari)

The Ferrari in practice at Sebring 1957.
(Credit - Author's Collection)

The Fitch/Taruffi Corvette retired with many problems, though overheating was given as the official reason. Chevrolet claimed satisfaction with the potential of the Corvette SS. While all the drivers in the top four or five waited for the Fangio/Behra Maserati to retire, Moss, having dropped to 8th by hour six, pulled back to 3rd in the 7th hour and 2nd the next hour. Portago and Musso displaced Moss in hour nine until more stops were required and the Ferrari dropped to ninth but eventually finished 7th. Moss held 2nd in the last three hours, all of those waiting for Fangio to stop had to wait until the end, and the 450S confounded everyone by winning easily. The Hawthorn/Bueb D-Type was an unspectacular 3rd, the private Gregory/Brero Ferrari 4th and the first works Ferrari was the Collins/Trintignant in 6th.

Portago shared the Ferrari at Sebring with Luigi Musso, but they were only 7th after various problems.
(Credit - BRSCC Archive)

A typical view of Portago at work, looking quite relaxed. ***(Credit - Ferrari)***

MOTOR RACING

JUNE 1957 and MOTOR RALLY MONTHLY 2/-

Spanish sportsman, The Marquis de Portago, who has made the Driver's World Championship his target in motor racing, is here driving a Ferrari.

PORTAGO—SPANISH ADVENTURER

READ HIS FABULOUS LIFE STORY THIS MONTH

Motor Racing was so impressed with this photo they put it on the cover.

Portago made a stop in New York before heading back to Paris, as he was entered for the Coupe de Vitesse meeting at Montlhery on April 7. This was the opening of the French racing year, with the day consisting of races for sports cars, touring and grand touring cars. While a number of the Americans who were at Sebring went west to Palm Springs in California for a Sports Car Club of America event, the Europeans were in the damp, gray climate of the Paris suburbs. Portago was running his Tour de France-winning Ferrari 250 GT long wheelbase car again (chassis 0557GT). The main race, the Coupe de USA for sports cars, was only an eleven lap, 70-kilometer race, but Portago was up against a number of nimble sports cars in his heavier GT Ferrari.

Paul Hemard's Panhard Monopole took the first touring car race from a bunch of other French machines, and Jean-Claude George's Alfa Romeo Super Sprint won the GT event from several Alfa Giulietta Veloces. Portago's main protagonists were Louis Cornet's 1.5-litre Maserati and old friend and co-driver David Piper in an 1100 cc. Lotus. French journalist Jabby Crombac was in a similar Lotus. Portago was taking the minor race quite seriously and broke the existing lap record several times. He went out in front from the beginning and it was clear no one was going to stay with him and he won with ease. Cornet, Hamilton, Peron (Ferrari), Dutoit (Porsche), Crombac, Clement (Maserati) and the rest of the mixed field followed. Dominique Pascal's fine history of Montlhery contains an interesting photo of Portago chatting to a young and attractive French girl, remarking that Linda Christian was also present!

Despite getting the race out of sequence in her autobiography, Linda Christian was there and described it in some detail:

"He was wearing khaki trousers and black leather jacket, and a white helmet was on the floor of the car when he picked me up. 'You're off to your first race," he said briefly. The track was outside Paris, he explained on the road, and it was not a very important race he had entered it to keep in practice…'I could do this one blind-folded', he commented as we pulled into the area where hundreds of cars had converged and crowds were milling around in a carnival spirit. Important or not, this world he was showing me was different from any I had ever known. We drove onto the track itself, to stop before a dugout where several men dressed in oil-spattered overalls were arguing among themselves. When Fon pulled up, they broke off and surrounded the car, moving quickly for the race was about to get under way. This was the pit, the life-center of every track. It was my first taste of the oil and dirt in my mouth, and the stinging sensation of gas fumes as you breathed them in; the odor was acrid."

"A mood of intense excitement reigned, augmented by reporters dashing through for a fast photograph or a question. I watched Fon pull on his helmet, his face set in a smile that had a tautness underneath, for all his confidence that his was the best car and that he could win…Fon was increasing his lead now with every turn, and when the final checkered flag descended, he had won with ease. His mechanics clapped him on the back as he drove alongside the pit. He nodded graciously, put me in the car beside him, and moments later we had left. 'Aren't you even waiting for your prize?' I asked. He shook his head they would send it along. 'But how did you like it?' he asked. 'So this is your world' I answered. 'If for no other reason, for the smell and noise alone, I'm not too fond of it.' He brushed my comment aside. 'Don't worry, you'll get used to it.' There was complete confidence that I would yield; certainly he had no intention of changing. Racing was his life.' " (Christian, 1962,p.218-219) Christian's memoirs then include a number of 'premonitions' about the up-coming Mille Miglia, and anxiety that he would not survive it.

Ferrari 250 GT Long Wheelbase Berlinetta Scaglietti Tour de France Chassis 0557GT
This Tour de France version of the long wheelbase 250 GT was completed in early September 1956, having been ordered from the works by Portago. He took delivery of it just in time to compete in the Tour de France from September 17 to 23rd. He and co-driver Gurner Nelson won the event, then he won at Montlhery in October, Castelfusano later that month and then again at Montlhery in April 1957. It was sold to Ferrari expert and historian Hans Tanner shortly after Portago's death, and then to bobsled competitor and friend Keith Schellenberg who had it for some 26 years. It went to Paul Palumbo in the UK, and in November 1992 was sold to Lorenzo Zambrano in Mexico. It appeared regularly at the Pebble Beach Concours from 1994 to 2004. There have always been arguments about the original colour of this car, and the best evidence indicates that it started out grey and at some point was painted French racing blue which it has remained.

Portago's successful 250 GT, chassis 0557, as it appears today.

Linda Christian wrote that following Montlhery "we still had a month's holiday". This is not possible as Portago would have been in Italy preparing for the Mille Miglia at the beginning of May, and in fact Dorian Leigh confirms that Portago came to visit her in Paris on her birthday, April 23, and to see Kim. Nevertheless, Portago and Linda Christian did go to London briefly and then to the Netherlands to see her father who was living in The Hague. They had a day in the old town of Volendam where the residents wear traditional Dutch clothing, and Portago gave in to pressure to dress up in the same apparel, looking a bit sheepish with a long clay pipe. Then they spent some days in Madrid, where she says there were a number of discussions about his retiring from racing and her 'premonitions' about the Mille Miglia. There is no verification for these conversations of course.

Portago then flew to Milan, and according to Linda Christian she flew the next day to Rome and he drove down from Milan to meet her, and then he arranged to see her on the practice runs as they came through Rome, though this in fact didn't happen.

Linda Christian took Portago to see her father in Holland in April 1957. ***(Courtesy of Linda Christian)***

While Linda Christian makes it clear that Portago was virtually never out of her sight for the month of April, Dorian Leigh's book casts a very different light on what happened during the month of April. She says that he came to visit her on her birthday, April 23. According to Dorian, Portago said he was going to win the Mille Miglia and that would provide them with enough income for a considerable time. She states that he said the divorce from Carroll would come through on May 9, the day after the race. Of course, the race was to be on May 12, not may 8, but that is a fairly minor error. She quotes him as saying that the three of them would live together, and when asked about Linda, he replied she was only "after me for the publicity". According to Dorian's autobiography, she relented, they made love, and he left for the Mille Miglia.

So, two women closely involved with Portago claim to have been on the verge of a new life with him, at the same time. It isn't possible to confirm or dismiss either of these stories, and they conflict with what Portago's wife Carroll has said consistently, especially about the imminent divorce. Were these just two publicity seeking women who constructed a story to portray them in a certain light after the facts? Was a very busy racing driver managing to move from race to race at short intervals and carry on such a spectacular love life at the same time? He certainly would have found it difficult to be in two places at the same time. Perhaps the answers to these questions are not so important, and in fact,

It was no surprise Linda Christian got a lot of media attention. (Credit - Author's Collection)

the 'mystery' is just part of the legend. However, it would diminish the man and the legend to get stuck on what was going on in Portago's relationships. The Mille Miglia was about to get under way and Portago saw this as an important race of which he had no experience.

Linda Christian and Portago at Malpensa Airport on the way to the Mille Miglia. ***(Courtesy of Linda Christian)***

Portago's wife said he couldn't resist a beautiful woman...this is Linda Christian in a publicity photo. ***(Credit - Author's Collection)***

Discussion of the 1957 Mille Miglia can probably be divided into three areas, all of which have had many thousands of words written about them: the event, the speculation about what happened to Portago and Nelson, and the consequences.

Sportscar Graphic used this photo of Portago and Nelson for its coverage of the Mille Miglia.

By early May, over 100 entries had been received for this 24th edition of the famed and terrifying 1000 mile open road race, though the complete route was in fact 992.3 miles. While it is often said that the Portago crash in the 1957 race ended the Mille Miglia, there were already many concerns about the safety of this event, and perhaps even more concerns about the cost of policing 1000 miles of public road, closing these roads, interfering with business and a number of other issues, never mind the politics of who gained from it or controlled it. The 1957 entry would cause more concern, as some of the cars were capable of running at 180 mph, a long way from what the cars could attain in the pre-war days. Autosport's pre-race editorial of May 10 said anything could happen in the Mille Miglia...not knowing how accurate that was. Early reports had Maseratis for Taruffi, Behra and Scarlatti, and Ferraris would be sent for Musso, Collins, von Trips, Portago, Gendebien and Gregory. This would change somewhat when the teams started practice.

Enzo Ferrari talks with Portago at practice for the Mille Miglia. ***(Credit - Ferrari)***

A rare photo of Portago shown giving an autograph. (Credit - Autopresse)

The official Maserati entry featured a rather special version of the 450S, which had won at Sebring. This car had a unique two-speed arrangement on the five-speed box, which actually gave ten gears. The pedal to activate the two-speed mechanism, according to some reports, was on the co-driver's side of the car, so Denis Jenkinson would be in charge of that. However, Jenk's own report of the race mentions his surprise shortly after the start when he noticed Moss using this overdrive, effectively engaging 6th gear! This was considered to be the fastest car ever to run in the event. Jean Behra had a more conventional 450S but he crashed in practice near Modena and wrote the car off, breaking his wrist and putting him out of the event. Maserati took a 300S chassis and put a 3.8-litre V-12 engine from the 350S into it, and this was to be driven by Hans Herrmann.

Piero Taruffi's inclusion in the Maserati team didn't happen as he had been invited to join Ferrari and was thus driving solo in a 315S (chassis 0684), and Wolfgang von Trips was also solo in a 335S (chassis 0674). Peter Collins was teamed with photographer Louis Klemantaski in a 335S (chassis 0700) and Portago and Ed Nelson were in the final 335S, which was chassis 0646, the Sebring car which had been upgraded from 315S to 335S specifications for this event. This car had a 4.1-litre engine while the others had 3.8-litres. One of the areas of speculation concerns how Portago was driving a 335S when it appears that he had intended to enter his 250 GT (chassis 0557GT) on the basis that Gendebien had done so well in 1956, winning the Grand Touring class and coming 5th overall in chassis 0503GT. Gendebien was driving another 250 GT long wheelbase in this race (chassis 0677GT) and this was a works entry. Hans Tanner reported that Portago's car was chassis 0676 but that is inaccurate. (Tanner,1989,p.531) While some later reports had Portago switched from his 250 GT at the last minute by Enzo Ferrari, there was in fact no entry for Portago's 250 GT, and Tanner confirms that Portago was in the car originally intended for Luigi Musso who was ill.

Von trips, Portago and Peter Collins before the Mille Miglia. *(Credit Autopresse)*

Brock Yates later wrote in his book about Ferrari that Gendebien had revealed something that went on just before the race: "Gendebien recalls an incident prior to the race that is revealing in terms of how Ferrari tried to manipulate his drivers and to play one off against the other. Gendebien wanted the Musso car. He felt he deserved one of the sports cars, having proved his worth in the Grand Touring class for two consecutive years. He had a meeting with Ferrari to plead his case. Ferrari would not budge; he would drive the 250GT and that was the end of it. Gendebien stalked out into the factory courtyard as Portago entered the office. A few minutes later Portago came out. He walked over to Gendebien and lit a cigarette. 'Ferrari says you want my sports car, but the son of a bitch says it doesn't matter. He said you'll beat me anyway, no matter what I drive.'" (Yates, 1992, p.297)

Practice in road cars, test hacks and actual road cars had been going on for over a week, with parts of some of the roads closed briefly in some locations. For the most part, however, the roads remained open as hundreds of drivers of varying skill sped around Italy. No reports of deaths seemed to make their way into the press, but of course there were many accidents, Behra's eliminating one of the important cars.

The cars line up for the start and Collins looks concerned. *(Credit - Publifoto)*

The car recorded as the first to start according to Wimpffen was number 2343, which had departed from the Brescia start at seventeen minutes before midnight. This was the Adria/Maran Fiat 1100 which set out on a hoped for journey of 1597 kilometers. The cars left Brescia and headed towards the Adriatic, passing through Verona, Vicenza, Padua, and Ferrara on the way to Ravenna. The route follows along the Adriatic coast from Rimini down to Pesaro, Pescara and Aquila. It then climbs the Carrese Pass and heads to Rome, before turning back north over the mountain sections. After Viterbo comes the classic sections of the Radicofani Pass to Siena, and then Firenze to the Futa Pass, the Raticosa, and then Bologna. This is followed by the faster sections to Modena, Parma, Piacenza, Cremona and Mantua, before the final swing north to Brescia and the finish. Adria and Maran in their Fiat didn't make it that far dropping out after seven and half-hours.

The start of the Mille Miglia with Portago and Nelson taking the flag.
(Credit - Archive Fodisch)

Stirling Moss and Denis Jenkinson were the last of the 301 cars to be sent off by the starter, number 537 as it was 5.37am. This must have been one of very few motor races in which Stirling Moss did not pass a single car. He and Jenks got twelve kilometers down the road, just past Pericolo when Moss used the brake pedal. It snapped and he was fortunate to be able to bring the car to a halt from about 130 mph without a major accident. They had become the first retirement and the Maserati hopes had taken a big blow. But as if that wasn't bad enough, Hans Herrmann in the special 350S Maserati became the next car to stop, just making it to Ferrara before the engine blew.

At the front Ferrari was already in command. Von Trips was leading as the cars reached Ravenna, with Peter Collins 36 seconds behind, Taruffi third, Portago fourth and Gendebien fifth. At this early stage it was all Ferrari, which might mean there would be some serious in-team rivalry. As the cars approached Forli, Collins pace had brought him past von Trips, and there was a hard fight going on between Ron Flockhart and American Ak Miller in his El Caballo 'hot rod' which was Chrysler-powered. On the open sections along the coast, Flockhart was flying and moving up the field to latch onto the Ferraris. At Padua Collins was averaging 121 mph, an incredible speed, and he had opened a gap to von Trips and Taruffi, with Portago fourth and Flockhart now fifth. By Pescara Taruffi had gone past von Trips but Collins still had a good lead, and Gendebien was leading the GT class with no difficulty.

There are intense looks on the faces of Portago and Nelson as they leave a control point. (Credit - Archive Fodisch)

Though the roads were much tougher over the mountains to Rome, Collins extended his lead over Taruffi, and was under Stirling Moss' 1955 time. He now had a five minute cushion, but of course everyone started to repeat the old phrase 'he who leads at Rome never wins the Mille Miglia' which of course was not true, though it would in fact turn out to be true for Collins! It was interesting that only nine cars had retired by Rome, but they now included the Jaguar of Flockhart and Ak Miller's machine as well.

Linda Christian had stayed in Rome, waiting for Portago to come by in the practice runs, but he never did. She says that he phoned her on the Saturday evening to say that he had hit a wall in his racecar and didn't make it to Rome, and that a new car was being sent. This is inaccurate, as the car Portago and Nelson were using in practice was Portago's 250 GT (chassis 0557GT). MotorSport confirmed that "Portago's Gran Turismo was considerably more battered than when it left." (MotorSport, July 1957, p.203) However, she adds that Portago was being given a 'new' car for the race and this was 'experimental'. If indeed it was chassis 0646, then it was not a new car, though it would have been upgraded. Hans Tanner says the 335S had what was technically an experimental engine, though not experimental in the sense that Linda Christian seemed to interpret it. This of course led her to panic somewhat, especially when Portago said his starting number was 531, which she contended added up to nine which was very unlucky in numerology, supposedly signifying major change or ending. The phone conversation ended with Portago saying he would meet her in Milan where they would have dinner with von Trips! There is some evidence that even though Portago allegedly told Linda that he had not made another lap, it seems that he probably did and she just did not know about it. MotorSport adds another dimension to this as their report implies that Portago might have been thinking he was going to race his 250 GT, though again, this car was never in the entry.

She made the decision to try to be at the checkpoint just outside the centre of Rome when Portago came through the 'Eternal City'. The chances of managing to do this and make contact would have seemed impossible, and if it weren't for the number of photographers who captured the moment, no one would believe it. She described the events: "Hurriedly I dressed to get to the check point. There was not too long to wait. From the officials I learned that Fon was in fourth place, moving up fast; he would be here in minutes. Suddenly, I thought to write him a note, to tell him of his position; I would run to the car and give it to him and see that he was all right. Quickly I borrowed a pencil and found a piece of paper and began to scribble. At the bottom I pencilled in Spanish: 'Te quiero mucho: I love you deeply. Then abruptly his red sports car was shooting toward the control point so fast that he was unable to brake to a stop until more than fifty yards beyond. I began to run and the two buttons on my white shoes popped off. Instants later I was standing beside Fon. He hadn't expected to see me there, and his face showed his surprise. Around us officials were clustering and photographers were shooting their pictures. All was confusion."

" 'Fon?' It was suddenly all I could say, and I gave him the note. 'I don't want to waste minutes, they're important.' "

" 'That's all right, darling, what do you want to say?' "

" 'It's on the piece of paper.' "

"He grinned and reached upwards to kiss me. ' I'll see you tonight in Milan'. "

The kiss...at the Rome check point. Linda Christian made sure the photographers were there. *(Credit - International News)*

"I had to lean to touch him, and I had a strange sensation with that kiss; it was cold. And it caused me to look for the first time at Gurner Nelson seated beside him. He seemed to be like a mummy, gray, ashen, as if mesmerized. He had the eyes of someone who had suffered an enormous shock. The big red car shot forward, its exhaust thundering into the distance, and I stood there transfixed, feeling as if all emotion had been drained from me. As Fon disappeared, a sense of horrible futility swept my body. Elga (Anderson) was tugging gently at my sleeve. There was nothing more to hold us here. He had come and gone." (Christian, 1962, p.238-239)

Linda Christian wrote "and then he was gone".
(Credit - International News)

Piero Taruffi had a long service at Rome at that same checkpoint on the Via Aurelia to repair problems with the rear axle or suspension. By the time the cars had gotten to Firenze, Collins had opened up a lead over Taruffi of over eight minutes. A Dutch TR3 driver crashed and was killed around this time. At the city of Bologna, Collins had opened this up to eight and a half minutes, von Trips two minutes behind Taruffi. Gendebien was now in fourth, some eleven minutes behind von Trips, and Portago had dropped to fifth, 20 seconds further back. Scarlatti was a long way behind in 6th, and Maglioli's Porsche was 7th from three Ferraris. Then it all changed as Collins pulled over at Parma, halfway between Modena and Piacenza, with a broken drive shaft and seriously damaged differential. He had actually driven on one half-shaft for seven kilometers but the car would go no further. Enzo Ferrari was at the Bologna service area himself, and he, Collins and Klemantaski all groaned as Collins pulled away, as clearly the differential was breaking up. When Portago had fueled at Bologna, his differential was noisy and it looked like his Ferrari might end like Collin's. Taruffi's car was also very noisy at the back end and would not have gone much further than it eventually did. Some of the Ferraris had also been suffering when hitting the larger bumps on the Italian roads. Both von Trips and Collins were nearly hurled from their cars and Collins at one point had to grab passenger Klemantaski and haul him back into his seat after hitting one of these bumps.

Public protection was minimal on the Mille Miglia.
(Credit - C.Casale)

The Ferrari 335S speeds north towards Bologna.
(Credit - C.Casale)

So, Collin's retirement had moved the other cars up a spot, with Gendebien in third but five minutes behind von Trips and Portago still 20 seconds back in fourth. One of the great speculations about the Mille Miglia concerns what Enzo Ferrari said or was 'thought' to have said to his drivers. Taruffi later made it clear that he wanted to retire at Bologna when he heard how bad the differential sounded. He said that Enzo Ferrari encouraged him to carry on, and as he had been running at an easier pace than Collins, he felt that was not too unreasonable. He was only using top gear, running no more than 150 mph and he had not seen Collins parked on the side of the road at Parma. There were some stories that when Portago came in to the service area Ferrari told him that he was second, and thus encouraged him to go for the lead. While this might seem a possible tactic, it also was clear that throughout the race Portago and Nelson were kept well informed about their position, and they would have been informed in the usual way at Bologna. This becomes a contentious issue, however, on two counts. There were reports that Portago had hit a kerb and bent a wheel, but he rushed out of the pits without taking time to change the wheel, which he might well have done if Ferrari himself was urging him on. According to Yates, a mechanic saw a bent lower control arm on the front left side, but when an attempt was made to change the wheel, Portago waved the mechanics off. (Yates in Car and Driver May 1986, p.175) The other issue concerns the ailing differential, and the pressure on him to ignore this would have been considerable. There was also a special award for the fastest time between Mantua and Brescia, the Gran Premio Nuvolari. Brock Yates, in his book on Ferrari, adds more to the intrigue, which didn't appear in his magazine article. Yates says that Ferrari told Portago that Gendebien was beating him just as he had predicted, and a few minutes earlier, he had told Gendebien that Portago was catching him. This is supposedly when the mechanic spotted the bent control arm and the body rubbing on the tyre. Portago set off after Gendebien. According to Yates, from that point on Gendebien's wife referred to Enzo Ferrari as 'the assassin'. (Yates 1992, p.300) Ferrari himself said in another book that after he had spoken to Portago, Portago spoke to a reporter who mistakenly told him he could speed up and make up a place. (Ferrari, 1998,p.191)

This is the Bologna check point where Portago spoke with Enzo Ferrari and then rushed off, allegedly refusing to change a wheel, though this stop looks leisurely enough to have done that job if required. *(Credit - Autopresse)*

Leaving the Bologna check point. *(Credit - Ferrari)*

The Ferrari is shown within one hundred miles of the finish. *(Credit - Publifoto)*

The Portago/Nelson Ferrari is now in fourth place, heading for the finish. (Credit - Publifoto)

Whatever did happen at Bologna, MotorSport reported the outcome: "Victory celebrations were quickly muted when word came in from Guidizzolo, about 18 miles from the finish, that Portago had crashed when in fourth place. On the straight, at about 180-mph, a tyre burst for reasons which are still not clear. The car veered off the road, uprooted a massive granite marker stone, then flew through the air, snapping off a telegraph pole, and cutting to pieces spectators at the roadside who were pressing forward, regardless of danger, to see the cars pass. Annihilating its crew as it went, it bounded into one ditch, then hurtled across the road into the ditch on the opposite side. The Marquis de Portago, his passenger, Ed Nelson, and nine spectators, of whom five were children, died and several injured." (MotorSport July 1957, p.206) About a kilometer south of Guidizzolo, a small road crosses the highway. This is where a number of local people gathered, near a farmhouse. Some reports from survivors of this group said that the car had veered left in the distance and hit the marker stone, and some thought it had hit the stone first.

An artist's drawing of the Portago crash at Guidizzolo.

The car as it ended up in the water filled ditch. (Credit - Archive Fodisch)

Both driver and passenger were thrown from the car before it went into the ditch and were killed instantly. ***(Credit - Archive Fodisch)***

Enzo Ferrari would write in 1985: "The race was drawing to a close. I was in the pit in Bologna, the first stop before the final leg to Brescia (which was nearly a straight stretch across the plain and so wasn't particularly suspenseful). The difficult parts were over, the game was played. We had four cars leading the race, and I'd already spoken to the racers: Taruffi would be an easy win with von Trips on hand as a back up; De Portago would come in third, invulnerable, no problem. And Gendebien would be careful since it was very important to bring the debuting "250 Gran Turismo to the finish line. On a wide curve between Goito and Guidizzolo di Mantova, De Portago's left front tyre blew out, and the outcome was catastrophic. The press, TV, radio and newspapers, all picked up the battle cry. My cars were confiscated and I was subjected to public moral outrage; then I was charged, or as we now say, I received a summons." (Ferrari, 1985,p.230-231)

This matter was investigated over a period of four years, the charge being that Ferrari had used Engelbert tyres which were not suitable for the high speeds reached by the cars. The fact that no tyres on the other cars 'burst' was not taken into consideration, but the whole affair was eventually dropped and no charges were leveled at either Ferrari or Engelbert. Ferrari's explanation of what happened was that "De Portago's tire was punctured when he skidded over the metal reflectors on the dividing line of the road on that curve, thus causing the blowout. It was only as a result of this tragic incident that those 'innovative' lights were abolished on every road and highway." (Ferrari, op. cit. p.235)

Many people would not agree with the proposition that somehow Ferrari should gain some credit for abolishing unsafe road markers through this disaster. He makes no mention of the failing differential, the possible bent wheel or any other factors. Wimpffen's report has the cause of the crash as axle failure. Phil Hill said that Portago had ignored a plea to change a wheel, and that a blowout was the likely cause of the accident. Hans Tanner also said that it was a tyre blowout, and though that is quite possible, some of these people were likely to have gotten their information from Ferrari, where no comment had been made about the failure of the differentials on the other cars. Tanner, oddly, said in an article in an Australian magazine that a wheel had fallen off, though this was not reported elsewhere. (Tanner, in Modern Motor September 1957.) Brock Yates gave some support to the theory favoured by Enzo Ferrari, when he says that Portago himself admitted that he had bent the suspension on the reflectors in the road on the Volta Mantovana section of the route. This admission was supposedly made at Bologna, though the source isn't given and this notion may well have come from Ferrari. In the 1960s, the American journal Automobile Quarterly published an article about Portago, and was very harsh in its judgement that Portago was solely responsible for the crash and the deaths of the spectators. In their Summer 1969 edition, they published an interesting retraction, saying that the staff had been to Italy and investigated the crash, and now came to the conclusion that all who were killed or injured had some responsibility in the event. By this, they were also accusing the crowd of recklessness. It was an interesting and unusual stance for such a journal to take.

The Ferrari victory was largely overshadowed by the crash and resulting deaths and injuries so near the end of the race. Taruffi had won the Mille Miglia after many attempts, but immediately promised his wife that he would not race again. Part of this was awareness of just how narrowly he had avoided disaster. Von Trips finished second, and Gendebien was third, winning the GT class. In the confusion after the crash, it wasn't clear how many people had been killed, and some of the figures released counted the spectators but not Portago and Nelson. The final figure was probably ten, but it is thought that some of the injured died sometime later. Both Portago and Nelson had been killed instantly, suffering huge injuries, Portago having his torso severed by the car's bonnet when it became detached.

Piero Taruffi won the Mille Miglia and promptly retired. ***(Credit - Il Campione)***

Journalist/photographer/friend Bernard Cahier went to the accident scene, which he said was "terrible". *(Credit - Bernard Cahier)*

Gregor Grant, who had driven his Lotus 11 very competently in the race, wrote a serious analysis of the consequences of the Portago crash, finding the race very dangerous, and recognising that it would be hard to argue when a number of children had been among the fatalities. However, he did point out that the death toll on an ordinary weekend when the roads were open was always higher than the number killed in the crash. He also paid a substantial tribute to Portago: "The death of marquis Alfonso de Portago has robbed the world of one of the greatest all-rounders ever known. His deeds in every branch of sport were a byword. Crack swordsman, horse-rider, boxer, wrestler, skier, bobsleigh rider, tennis player, aircraft pilot, racing driver, 'Fon' was all of these. I knew him well and found him to be a brilliant scholar with a bent towards European history which caused him to study the two world wars from a purely technical angle, with a view to writing a book on the 'Futility of War'. His motor racing career was highly spectacular, and, in a very short time, he jumped in among the really top-line men, earning a place in the Scuderia Ferrari team. Just to prove he could rally as well as race, 'Fon' took his Ferrari coupe in the 1956 Tour de France, and won it outright. Yes, de Portago will be sadly missed. He was one of the genuine personalities in the game, and although considered slightly eccentric, he was admired by all he came in contact with." (Autosport May 17, 1957,p.618)

Ferrari 290S Chassis 0646

This car was a new 290S which Castellotti/Musso/Trintignant shared at the Buenos Aires 1000 Kilometers in January 1957. The engine was then upgraded to 315S specifications for Sebring for Portago and Musso where it was called a 315S. The engine was either enlarged or changed and ran in 4.1-litre configuration at the Mille Miglia for Portago and Nelson, where it was listed as a 335S. The car was destroyed in their fatal crash, but the engine, number 0744, was later used in a single-seater, and then found its way into the 412MI, the single-seater which Musso would drive in the Race of the Two World on the banked Monza circuit, where American Indy cars came to Italy to challenge a rather small field of Europeans.

The Ferrari 335S, chassis 0646. This is a model of the car by French model maker Badot.

Dorian Leigh wrote that she heard of Fon's death from his mother, Olga, who phoned her with the news. This led to further conversations and the revelation that Portago had established a trust fund to pay $500 per month for Kim's support. Dorian later met Olga and Portago's sister Soledad and they maintained some degree of contact. She does not say what effect Portago's death had on her. Dorian Leigh went through more difficult relationships and marriages, had another abortion, another child, and a difficult time with Kim. Kim became addicted to cocaine and heroin and jumped to his death from his apartment in New York in 1977. Dorian Leigh eventually returned to live in Paris.

A 1977 photo of Dorian Leigh and her son Kim, who bears a marked resemblance to Fon Portago. Kim died in 1977. ***(Credit - Leigh)***

Linda Christian described the events following Portago's death in considerable detail. She had flown to Milan from Rome after seeing Portago at the checkpoint, and when the plane landed she was informed of what had happened. She insisted on being driven to the site of the accident and then to the morgue to see the body, which was refused. She describes her horror when she was told of the extent of his injuries. She telephoned Portago's mother and they were already making arrangements to fly to Milan, and she met them at the airport. She quotes Portago's mother as saying "We've removed some seats for Fon's casket. But there's a place for you Linda, you're coming back with us. You made his last months happy. I thank you for that." (Christian, 1962,p.243) She reported that the step-father, Isidro Martin-Montis was the only person allowed to view the body and do the official identification, and he emerged from the experience "pale and shaken and could talk to no one." The death certificates listed Cavriana as the place of death.

Up to this point, neither Dorian Leigh nor Linda Christian had even mentioned Portago's wife Carroll and her possible role in the arrangements for his funeral, or whether she even knew about the crash. Neither of these 'other' women had allowed themselves to believe fully that Portago had been continuously dishonest with them about his intentions towards them. They had ruled Carroll Portago out of his life, which was of course not what had happened. But Carroll was now on her way to Europe with her children, Antonio, three, and Andrea , six.

Carroll Portago, Andrea and Anthony arrive at the Milan airport on the way to the funeral. ***(Credit - Archive Fodisch)***

Soledad had to inform Linda Christian that Carroll was arriving in Paris from New York and was proceeding to Milan. Then she would accompany the family to Madrid, so it would not be appropriate for Linda to be on the same plane. Linda says that she was offered help with travel by Aly Khan, Stavros Niarchos and Gianni Agnelli, and left on Agnelli's plane to Madrid. She went to the funeral service and to the cemetery, and then flew back to Paris. There were some reports that there was a 'fuss' at the funeral over her presence, but that may had been related to the press being there and taking photos. Back in Paris, she came across the handwritten notes, which Portago was using to write an article about the Mille Miglia. The final lines of this article said: It is wonderful to be alive, even more so when I know tomorrow I may be dead, but all things considered, I wouldn't miss the Mille Miglia for anything in the world. " (Christian, op. cit.,p.245) The author was unable to find a record of these notes being published.

Linda Christian was soon back in the news in a volatile relationship with socialite 'Baby' Pignatari , and in 1962, she married her former actor lover Edmund Purdom, they were divorced in 1963, and she now lives in California. Her daughter Romina Power told the author that her mother always considered Portago the "love of her life".

Linda Christian in later years.
(Credit - Author's Collection)

Portago was buried in the family tomb of the Linares, which was the family of his step-father Isidro Martin-Montis in San Isidoro in Madrid, and his ashes were not spread in the way he had been said to have requested, and this is not surprising as Catholics did not agree with cremation in the 1950s. Portago's mother Olga, stepfather Isidro Martin-Montis and sister Soledad, his wife Carroll and two children Antonio and Andrea were all together. Juan Fangio was one of the pallbearers, and a number of other drivers went to Madrid for the funeral, which was attended by thousands of mourning Spaniards, who had truly lost their legendary hero. There was a great out-pouring of bereavement, even though Portago spent little time as a resident of Spain. His achievements in the Olympics guaranteed a huge funeral.

Portago's mother Olga and Carroll Portago with veil at the funeral.
(Credit - Paris Match)

Left to right: Soledad, Carroll Portago and Olga. (Credit - Archive Fodisch)

The Linares family tomb where Portago was buried.

In Italy, at the same time as Portago's funeral was taking place, the spectators who had been killed in the crash were also being laid to rest. These included: Anita Boscaini, 10, Silvestro Franzini, 27, Virginia Rigon, 9, Valentino Rigon, 7, Giovanni Consato, 8, Romeo Stancari, 50, Angelo Dobelli, 48, Carmen Tarchini, 10, Pietro Grandelli, 52. There were others, and more of the injured died later.

Some of the motoring journals predicted the likelihood of a ban on the Mille Miglia, though emphasizing the dangers of ordinary road travel. Autosport reminded its readers that a 'mechanical breakage' was the cause of the accident, though this was still at the speculative stage, and this journal also said eight adults and five children had died in the crash including Portago and Nelson. The implications of the crash were a main agenda item on the RAC 's next Competitions Committee meeting. Within a week all of Ferrari's Mille Miglia cars had been impounded by the Italian police while an investigation was carried out. At the Monaco Grand Prix on the weekend of May 19/20, there was a special meeting of race organisers to discuss the cancellation of races. The Belgian and German Grands Prix looked in doubt because of a disagreement over the scale of starting fees. In addition, it was announced that the Italian declaration of a ban on road racing the previous week because of the Portago crash meant the cancellation of the Targa Florio, the Messina 10 Hours, the Dolomite Cup race and the Circuits of Calabria and Umbria. It was thought the Pescara race might also be cancelled. The Belgian Grand Prix did not take place, and the Dutch race had already been cancelled, but the others did take place. The Ferrari team missed the first practice session at Monaco because a technical panel was examining the team's Lancia D-50s after the Mille Miglia crash, even though these were totally different cars, and it by now being recognised that the breaking differentials in the Mille Miglia was a result of them being asked to handle too much power from the 3.8 and 4.1-litre engines.

Gordon Wilkins reflected on the longer-term consequences of the Portago accident. Wilkins saw motor racing as facing a state of crisis, not only in relation to safety but also because of the cost of racing and the need for driver training. After the 1955 Le Mans disaster, this latest event made road racing organisers look like 'irresponsible speed maniacs', at least according to some sections of the press. Dr. Biscaretti, president of the Italian vehicle manufacturers' federation said the Mille Miglia no longer 'had any practical value or interest for the industry'. This was not an altogether surprising view from an organisation that represented essentially non-racing manufacturers. Ferrari, Stanguellini and Maserati had met at Modena and made their own declaration that road racing had indeed contributed a great deal to improvements in motor cars. Perhaps Count Maggi did not necessarily help himself by declaring that as soon as the ban was lifted, he would go ahead with planning for the 1958 Mille Miglia. Many proposals were being put forward to continue the race, either by allowing only Grand Touring cars, or having it at a circuit such as Monza, or at a series of circuits. There were also proposals to limit the capacity of engines, something which was already known to have limited impact. Wilkins implied that the desire to sell cars to the American market had an influence on the production of bigger and faster engines. (Wilkins, G. in Motor Racing, July 1957) In fact, the Mille Miglia did return in 1958 as a regularity event for Grand Touring and Touring cars. There was a fatality, and the event come to an end, though it was revived as an historic regularity meeting in the 1980s.

Robert Daley, who had been the first journalist to interview Portago seriously, reflected in his book Cars At Speed, published in 1961, after the Mille Miglia had been ended, that he did not believe that the Portago crash would end road racing permanently, though clearly it had made a serious dent in it: "For the conviction is inescapable that the Mille Miglia was stopped not because Portago's car killed eleven persons, but because it killed a figure as glamorous as Portago. He had been a romantic in an age which had no time for romance. He had been a sort of conquistador, and much of the world watched breathlessly the fantastic things he tried and got away with. Other races have killed more people (Le Mans, Argentina, Monza) but were raced again the next year. For no driver as renowned as Portago was killed, and the headlines had died out in a day or two. It was, to my mind, the Portago publicity which stopped the Mille Miglia, the grisly funerals at Guidizzolo, and then again at Madrid; the impassioned declarations of the movie actress he had been living with; the photos of his wife, his children, and the former mistress who had borne him an illegitimate son; his fantastic wealth; the pronouncement of the grief-stricken Fangio, Portago's friend, that the Mille Miglia, first raced in 1927, must not be run again." (Daley, 1961, p.26-27)

There was one thing, however, that Robert Daley said which was wrong, and that was that the monument at Guidizzolo was a monument to Portago. It wasn't. It was a memorial to the people who had been killed there.

LA DOMENICA DEL CORRIERE

Supplemento settimanale illustrato del nuovo CORRIERE DELLA SERA - Abbonamenti: Italia, anno L. 1870, semestre L. 1000 - Estero, anno L. 2805, semestre L. 1470

Anno 59 — N. 21 | 26 Maggio 1957 | L. 40.—

Tragica "Mille Miglia". Una delle più terrificanti sciagure che la storia dell'automobilismo ricordi ha funestato la XXIV edizione della gara; mentre, lanciata a oltre 280 chilometri all'ora, correva sul rettilineo, appena fuori di Guidizzolo (Mantova), la macchina guidata dallo spagnolo Alfonso De Portago, per lo scoppio di un pneumatico, usciva di strada e finiva, con un pauroso volo, in mezzo a un gruppo di persone. Nella catastrofe hanno perso la vita lo stesso De Portago, il suo secondo pilota, il giornalista americano Eddy Nelson, e nove spettatori, tra cui cinque bambini.

(Disegno di Walter Molino)

The horror of the crash was portrayed by Domenica del Corrieri.

The Guidizzolo memorial. (Credit - Quillen)

EPILOGUE

Very little was written about Alfonso de Portago in his lifetime and over the years after his death in 1957, many articles appeared in the motoring and occasionally the general press. As has been said earlier, a great deal of this material was based on the few items actually published while Portago was still alive, such as Robert Daley's reports in the New York Times, or on an interview by Ken Purdy done in 1957, or one with Hans Tanner. A very small number of journalists ever interviewed Portago, and only a few of those recognised that he was likely to be very extravagant in describing what had happened to him, and most of those rehashed what the other three had already written, and in some cases added to it. It was clear to Robert Daley that Portago enjoyed telling outrageous stories. For Daley this was an essential part of the legend of Portago. For others, who took the quotes literally, the legend was created from a mixture of truths, exaggerations, and downright fiction. Thus the legend has to include all of these elements, with no means of distinguishing whether some of them contained any truth at all. Did Alfonso de Portago ever fly a plane under a bridge for a bet? He was a keen photographer himself and no photo exists of him in or with what might have been the airplane he flew. Again, as Robert Daley said, 'does it matter?' His contention was that it is the legend that matters and the facts are just part of the legend.

What was clear, however, was that Portago had the capacity to make an impression on people, an impression which was powerful and lasted. Brock Yates spoke to a well-known clothing designer who knew Portago, almost 30 thirty years after the Mille Miglia crash: "Actually, Fon was an unconscionable snob. He could be wonderfully charming as long as he wasn't around those he considered his inferiors. Yet he might behave marvelously around racing mechanics, commoners, but insufferably with those he considered to be bourgeois. I can recall introducing him to a prosperous Spaniard who was a friend of mine. Fon merely stared him down and walked away. Despite all that was written about him, he was hardly a witty man. In fact, I'd have to call him boring, basically only interested in cars, horses, and sex." (Yates, in Car and Driver, May 1986, p. 169) It is interesting that Yates was one of the writers who recognised that much of the truth about Portago had been embellished, and he was one of the people who did that!

Alfonso Portago.
(Credit - Author's Collection)

Carroll Shelby's first impression of the Spaniard, when they met and raced against each other at Nassau, was typically forthright: "We banged fenders all around the course. He was aggressive as hell, but you never knew quite where he was going to go." (Car and Driver, May 1986, p.170) Shelby was also alleged to have said that Portago was trying to gain enough status and notoriety in sports to give Juan Carlos a contest for the throne of Spain when Franco finally died! Yates also quoted another unnamed 'friend' appraising the impression Portago made on the swish social set at Nassau in 1955: "Fon was dressed in a filthy black leather jacket, and his Ferrari was painted a dull black to match. He painted his number thirteen on the doors by hand, intentionally making it look like a schoolboy's script. He was unshaven, and his hair hung over his ears. Worse yet, he was like most Spaniards of the day: he didn't bathe much, and he reeked of onions. He did it, I think, purely for the shock value. Fon liked the idea of being outrageous."

The various moods of Fon Portago as drawn by racing driver Nick Faure. *(Credit - N.Faure)*

Louise Collins King, the widow of Portago's fellow Ferrari driver remembered Fon mainly by the sight of his black leather jacket, a sight she got used to seeing as Portago was dragging some woman off. She recalled him as very high-spirited and almost omnipresent. To her he seemed to have the capacity to be everywhere. She also found him to be 'rather rough'. While she recognised that Portago was attractive to women, and that they found him exciting, Louise said that she didn't personally see the attraction. In retrospect, it is clear that many of Portago's relationships that had some impact on him began not on the basis of mutual knowledge of each other, but rather as a result of impulsive behaviour. His relationships with the three key women mentioned in this book all started as joking, flirting conversations in nightclubs, where Portago's first evident aim was to pick these women up. Louise Collins King was one of the few women to ever get the chance to say she didn't find this approach particularly attractive.

The late sports car and Grand Prix driver, Cliff Allison, perhaps the driver with the most acute sense of humour from the '50s and '60s, remembered meeting Portago at a number of races: "I would see him and chat to him at drivers' briefings and meetings at first. He was 'up there' and I was 'down here'...he was in the big classes, not the upper classes, and I was in the small class...not lower! He was driving Ferraris when I first met him, and I was in a 500 cc. Cooper. I remember him as a serious driver, and I believe he was looked upon as a regal sort, given some deference for his position. I thought he was interesting and a very good driver. I even went out to watch him in his race at Oulton Park. He was straight in at the deep end of racing and I thought doing a good job with it."

1961 World Champion Phil Hill had close contact with Portago. They were in the same team, Ferrari. They co-drove the same car on occasion, and stayed in the same places, and traveled together. When Robert Daley wrote his fictional account of motor racing, he used Hill and Portago as the models for the two main characters, Jack Blakemore and Prince Alessandro Cavelli. He drew on aspects of their characters and also on some of the things that they may have said about each other, especially Hill about Portago. In 1997, Nigel Roebuck was at Spa for the Belgian Grand Prix, and he spoke with Hill about current and past drivers: "When I first met 'Fon' de Portago in early 1954, he knew absolutely nothing about race cars. Nothing. He was also ahead of his time, in that he was the first guy I ever met who deliberately...dressed down, let's say. He wore this scruffy leather jacket, shaved about every four days, looked like he had nothing. Then I saw his card one day, with his address on Avenue Foch in Paris, and that's when I realised you could be fooled by appearances. Anyway, he was a natural athlete , and he learned to drive, and he got into Formula 1 before I did! Ferrari was working on a shoestring in those days, so if you had something other than driving ability to offer, it could serve you well." (Autosport, August 28, 1997,p.31) Phil Hill took exception to things he had heard about Portago being an avid reader, quipping that he'd bet he didn't understand what he was reading. Hill's irritation was probably provoked by what Ken Purdy had written, quoting Carroll Portago as saying: "During most of the eight years I was married to Fon I think he read a book a day. He read history and biography, and little else. I don't believe I ever saw him reading a novel, a modern novel, although he did like Robert Graves. He thought most novels a terrible waste of time. One day, coming back from a race in Nassau I read Peyton Place on the plane. Fon muttered about it all the way home. He said it was idiotic to waste time on such books." (Purdy, K. 1972, p.65)

Perhaps the most considered view of Portago was that of Robert Daley, who, as Brock Yates had said, virtually discovered him. Daley was surprised by that remark when he discussed it with the author, but he did admit that Portago had made a lasting impression on him: "His life was intense and, at twenty-eight, complete. There are those who wrote afterwards that he was in love with death but they did not know him and this statement is absurd. Alfonso de Portago was in love with life. 'Perhaps we appreciate life more', he wrote of racing drivers, 'because we live closer to death.' He seemed to me the

Fon Portago by Porsche driver Nick Faure.
(Credit - N.Faure)

most alive man I had ever known. He was sensitive, restless, curiously gentle, and it is impossible to describe that impression of straining vitality which he communicated, not to do justice to the overwhelming disbelief his friends felt when news of his death arrived. It seemed he had everything a man could need with which to challenge life: charm, looks, wealth and courage. If he failed, his friends thought, what chance has anyone? The answer was obvious: none. Portago was not merely killed. In the wreck the hood of the car lashed back and cut him in two." (Daley, R. 1961, p.33)

Journalist and photographer Bernard Cahier met Portago on many occasions, and photographed him regularly. He sat down with the author at Monaco 2006 to recount his memories:

"He was a grandee of Spain, but always very casually dressed, usually with a leather jacket, not always shaved…I remember his appearance very well…smoking a lot, and having a full time with many girls although he was actually married to a very lovely lady who lived in New York. They had a daughter who was living sometime in Biarritz and in the USA. I know Portago's friend Nano da Silva Ramos, and he still lives near Biarritz. I especially remember being with Portago at Sebring. It has great memories because there was a great group with Fon, Harry Schell and Rubirosa. It was the playboy club. Rubirosa was a wonderful guy, the best gigolo in the business, certainly the busiest. The night before the Mille Miglia I had dinner with Fon because we were very good friends, and with his co-driver Nelson, and we had a nice dinner. I remember he went to bed pretty early because he had to leave at five in the morning. So I went upstairs to say au revoir and bon chance, and Nelson was there on the bed resting. Fon was in the bathroom, and he heard me and he said 'oh Bernard, I am sorry, I am having a shit'. So I said I would see him tomorrow at the finish, but that was the last time I talked with him…and he was laughing. Then I went to the place of the accident and it was terrible, because it was not long after it had happened. It was terrible. So, it was a great loss. He was very talented, actually more than people thought. He could drive very well, even though you might call him an amateur, a gentleman driver. He was a part of that very interesting group of gentlemen drivers which has disappeared, like Harry Schell, and Rubirosa. Peter Collins was also a part of this group, and Portago was a good friend with Fangio. Fangio had great respect for him, and that was helped because they spoke the same language. It was a great loss. He was a person of the '50s, really. I remember one time he was going to New York, and he was dressed in his leather jacket. I was with him and we went to passport control, and they looked at him, and then he gives them his passport, a diplomatic passport. The guy couldn't believe it. He was truly a man from another epoch, an epoch which we all enjoyed because we had relationships with each other, lots of camaraderie, no stories, no money involved, no public relations people, no motorhomes. We stayed together in the same hotel often, and had meals together…it is a good souvenir, a good memory."

Portago left behind his family, his wife Carroll who some years later remarried Milton Petrie. Andrea Portago lives in California, and her brother Antonio sadly died in New York in 1990 at the age of only 35, having been active in the music business. Carroll Petrie and her husband established very substantial charitable foundations in New York in his memory. Portago's mother Olga died on February 8, 1980 in Lausanne, Switzerland, survived by Isidro Martin-Montis. Alfonso's sister Soledad, married to Forrester Labroucher, has a son A. Forrester Labroucher, who was born in 1951. Soledad lives in Madrid and Biarritz. Portago's son Antonio married very young and had two children Teodora and Carolina.

Over the years, various memorials were established in Portago's name, including an annual important steeplechase at Pau, called the Prix Alfonso de Portago. At St. Moritz, a group of friends and family set up a fund to keep the bobsleigh run in good condition and the Portago Corner is located near the bottom of the course.

****

Who was the Marquis de Portago? Brock Yates asked whether he was on his way to deserved immortality as a racing driver/athlete as Ken Purdy had suggested, or was he 'an aristocratic clown who drove too fast'. When Yates asked that question, it was rhetorical, and he didn't attempt to go any further in answering it. He said that the search for Portago continues. (Yates, Car and Driver May 1986, p.177) Even after this book, the search may continue as always happens with someone who has attained legendary stature, deserved or otherwise. It is the observer who has to judge the evidence and decide according to their own subjective criteria whether Portago deserves to be considered a legend. The author has to admit that he never cared whether Portago could or should be considered as such, but was looking for the reality of the man, and particularly the man as competent racing driver. It is an interesting contrast that today's top racing drivers are celebrities only in that they are top racing drivers. Today's Grand Prix stars don't seem to have a life in any other sphere, especially while they remain under contract to an F1 team. Therefore they are almost entirely 'judged' on their performance in that one arena. Portago lived and died in an era, the 1950s, when fame and celebrity was mixed with class, notoriety and achievement.

In many ways, Portago symbolized the difference between the drivers of the 1950s and those of today and the last twenty years. He saw himself as an individual and a driver, not a team member. He was generally unguarded in what he said, he spoke about injury and death and about his fellow drivers. He used the platform of interviews as a stage for himself. He never had a thought for public relations, and acted accordingly, he was extravagant. And the times were different. No one talks about death and injury today, because cars and racing have changed so much, it is not such a big issue, and it wouldn't suit the 'pr' team! When he was being interviewed by Grauer and Clark, Portago enjoyed the drama of talking about danger:

"I think there are certain requirements to become an automobile driver, a racing driver. A lack of fear is a requirement, and I think the man who wants to become a driver has to have at least a spirit of adventure because there is very little security in it. He doesn't know if he is going to live, if he is going to be a success, if he is going to lose an arm or leg. Nobody has any sympathy for the driver who goes off the road, you expect it but you don't get it, everybody thinks he is an idiot. You have far more disappointments in racing than you have triumphs. It is a difficult life. In Europe you can make a decent living just from the starting money you get. Some drivers who are not the quickest have earned reasonable money. Rosier who died recently made a lot of money racing but he wasn't the fastest. Still, I would have never won the Tour de France without his help when I just followed him for several days. I had been driving his car at the race where he got killed. We discuss death constantly. If a driver gets killed on Sunday and he is a close friend of yours, well you think what a stupid sport this is and maybe you will give it up. On Monday you might think he was just unlucky and I shouldn't give it up yet, maybe I'll give it up next year. Then on Tuesday you think there's a race next Sunday and maybe I'll go, and on Wednesday you go to the race. There was a plane which crashed at the Farnborough Air Show and 57 people were killed. Is that reason to stop all air shows? It was just an extremely unfortunate occurrence."

"If you think about death and this is going to happen to you, then there is no point in racing, but usually the first time you know of an accident, you see the ambulance or the crashed car itself and you know who is in the car because of his number or the colour, and the pit gives you a signal that he is alright, or they just don't say anything. As soon as the race is over you go and find out what happened. But I have a rule, I will never go and see anybody who has been killed. I went with the wife of Musy who was a Spanish girl and it was terrible…I won't even go and see someone who is in the hospital. Every driver believes it can't happen to him, and I *know* it won't happen to me. All drivers feel that way. The thing that troubles us is when somebody gets killed because the steering arm broke or a wheel came off. That worries us a lot, because if it happened on that car and I have to drive the same type of car, it may very well happen to me…I never worry that the car is going to break down. If it breaks down, it breaks down and I can't do anything about it. The only thing I am careful about is not to over-rev the engine, and I try to change gear as smoothly as possible."

"I race because I want to be the champion of the world. Life to me is a wonderful thing and even if I lived to be 100 I ,still won't be able to do a twentieth of all the things I want to do, or read all the books I want to read. But I still want to get the most out of it, and I have no time to lose. I certainly wouldn't race if I didn't think I could accomplish what I want to accomplish. I will do racing for so many years of my life and then I will stop completely and never race again. If I became champion once, I would give up racing. A racing driver can go on until 45 but there are a lot of other things I want to do…racing drivers are a very happy lot of people because they appreciate life more than the average man does." (Riverside Records, 1957)

Portago was an ideal subject of speculation, gossip and guessing. All of this made evaluating his achievements in any one area difficult. His determination to win, to do his best, to out-drive and out-maneuver tended to get lost in the myths that surrounded him. Some of these myths remain there, still to be confirmed or dispelled, but most of them are unimportant. Many of those who have written about Portago, even in admiration, both added to the legend but obscured the reality. The reports of Portago as boxer, as Olympic swimmer, as champion Jai Alai player were all inaccurate, and created further layers that need to be removed to find the substance of the person. Portago was a vulnerable boy who grew into a vulnerable man, vulnerability he covered with bravado and over-compensation. The vulnerability prevented him from establishing many…any…deep and lasting relationships. There was depth to him that only occasionally broke through the protective and sometimes offensive covering layer. And he was a product of his position in an era that forced a certain kind of behaviour. His rebelliousness, at least in retrospect, was probably very predictable. He behaved, as his wife said, as if he was 'titled and therefore entitled'. If only we could now ask him how he would respond to the people who remember him, like Stirling Moss does, as 'a nice man'. He would, I guess, just laugh.

While Riverside Records made it possible for Portago's words to remain accessible for perpetuity, they also perpetrated something of an injustice in 1969, when they recorded an album of folk songs about sports cars…Sing A Song of Sports Cars The singer/song-writer was none other than Paul O'Shea, a very accomplished SCCA driver who won two national championships in Mercedes Benz 300SLs. Sadly, he wasn't that great as a singer. One of the tracks is the Ballad of Fon Portago and here are the first and last verses:

Something lives in Fon Portago
Something wild and free
Something we have lost in living
In this century…..

Fon Portago, Fon Portago
Brave and strong and true
When he died at Mille Miglia
Part of me died too.

It is a pretty awful testimonial…but the last line got to the author!

The quintessential gentleman driver, Marquis Alfonso de Portago. ***(Credit - G.Simpson)***

APPENDIX - LIST OF RACES

Year	Date	Race	Car	Co-driver	Position	Number
1953	23/7	Midget races at Reims	Quarter midget		1st	
	19-23/11	Carrera Panamericana	Ferrari 340MM	L.Chinetti	DNF	45
1954	24/1	Buenos Aires 1000 Kms	Ferrari 250MM	H.Schell	2nd	30
	7/3	Sebring 12 Hours	Ferrari 250MM	H.Schell	DNF	22
	29/5	Aintree International	Maserati A6GCS		DNA	
	13/6	Le Mans 24 Hours	Maserati A6GCS	C.Tomasi	DNF	28
	27/6	Metz Sports Car Race	Maserati A6GCS		1st	
	4/7	Reims 12 Hours	Maserati A6GCS	L. Chiron	DNF	
	1/8	Rhineland Cup	OSCA MT4		DNF	51
	3-12/9	Tour de France	OSCA MT4	E.G.Nelson	DNF	228
	19-23/11	Carrera Panamericana	Ferrari 750 Monza		DNF	2
	11/12	Nassau 5 lap race	Ferrari 750 Monza		2oa, 1cl.	13
	11/12	Bahamas Auto. Cup	Ferrari 750 Monza		1oa, 1cl.	13
	12/12	Nassau Trophy	Ferrari 750 Monza		2oa, 1cl.	13
1955	13/3	Sebring 12 Hour	Ferrari 750 Monza	U.Maglioli	DNF	26
	27/3	Valentino GP Turin	Ferrari 625		DNF	10
	11/4	Pau GP	Ferrari 625		8th	30
	17/4	Coupe de Paris,Montlhery	Ferrari 375S		4th	
	24/4	Bordeaux GP	Ferrari 625		DNF	24
	7/5	Int. Trophy, Silverstone	Ferrari 625		DNS	24
	20/8	Goodwood Nine Hours	Ferrari 750 Monza	M.Hawthorn	DNF	6
	3/9	Aintree	Ferrari 750 Monza		DNF	
	24/9	Oulton Park Gold Cup	Ferrari 625		DNF	3
	6/11	Venezuela GP	Ferrari 750 Monza		2nd	10
	9/12	Nassau 5-lap Production	Ferrari 250 GT Europe		4oa, 4cl.	23
	9/12	Governor's Trophy	Ferrari 750 Monza		1oa, 1cl.	13
	10/12	Albert Ascari Trophy	Ferrari 750 Monza		1oa, 1cl.	13
	11/12	Nassau Trophy	Ferrari 750 Monza		2oa, 1cl.	13
1956	24/3	Sebring 12 Hours	Ferrari 857S	J.Kimberly	DNF	19
	27/5	Nurburgring 1000 Kms	Ferrari 290 MM	Hill/Gendebien	DSQ & 3rd	4 & 2
	17/6	Oporto GP	Ferrari 857S		1st	
	24/6	Supercortemaggiore GP	Ferrari 500TR	O.Gendebien	4th	65
	1/7	Reims GP de ACF	Lancia D-50		DNF	16
	8/7	Rouen GP	Ferrari 290MM		9th	4
	14/7	British GP	Lancia D-50	Collins/Castellotti	2nd & 11th	4 & 3
	22/7	Bari GP	Ferrari 860 Monza		DNF	44
	29/7	Le Mans 24 Hours	Ferrari 625LM	D.Hamilton	DNF	11
	5/8	German GP	Lancia D-50	P.Collins	DNF	5
	12/8	Swedish GP	Ferrari 860 Monza	Hawthorn/Hamilton/Collins	3rd	2
	26/8	Cannonloppet, Karlskoga	Ferrari		2nd	1
	2/9	Italian GP	Lancia D-50		DNF	30
	17-23/9	Tour de France	Ferrari 250GT	E.G.Nelson	1st	73
	7/10	Coupe de Salon,Montlhery	Ferrari 250GT		1st	33
	21/10	Rome GP, Castelfusano	Ferrari 250GT		1st	24
	4/11	Venezuela GP	Ferrari 860 Monza		DNF	4

Year	Date	Race	Car	Co-driver	Position	Number
	7/12	Nassau Gov.Tr.heat	Ferrari 860 Monza		7th	13
	7/12	Governor's Trophy	Ferrari 860 Monza		2oa, 2cl.	13
	8/12	Ferrari race	Ferrari 857S		2oa	13
	9/12	Nassau Trophy	Ferrari 860 Monza		3oa, 1cl.	13
1957	13/1	Argentine GP	Lancia D-50	F.Gonzales	5th	20
	20/1	Buenos Aires 1000 Kms	Ferrari 315S	Collins/von Trips	3rd	8
	25/2	Cuba GP	Ferrari 857		3rd	12
	23/3	Sebring 12 Hours	Ferrari 315S	L.Musso	7th	12
	7/4	Coupe de USA	Ferrari 250GT		1st	14
	12/5	Mille Miglia	Ferrari 335S	E.G.Nelson	DNF	531

BIBLIOGRAPHY

Books and articles

Bollee, M. Les 1000 Kilometres de Paris Bollee Paris 2000
Breslauer, K. Sebring-The Official History of America's Great Sports Car Race David Bull Publishing Cambridge, Mass. USA 1995
Christian, L. Linda Crown Publishers New York 1962
Clark, B. and B. Grauer The Marquis de Portago Riverside Records USA 1957
Daley, R. Cars At Speed Collier Books New York 1961
Daley, R. The Cruel Sport Motorbooks International Minnesota USA 2005
Daley, R. The Fast One Crown Publishers New York 1978
Della Carri, L. Gli Indisciplinati Fucina Milan Italy 2001
Ferrari, E. Ferrari-Piloti Che Gente… Conti Editore Bologna Italy 1985
Ferrari, E. Una Vita Per L'Automobile Conti Editore Bologna Italy 1998
Hamilton, D. Touch Wood! Barrie and Rockliff London 1960
Leigh, D. with L.Hobe The Girl Who Had Everything Doubleday and Co. New York 1980
Moity, C. The Le Mans 24-Hour Race 1949 - 1973 Patrick Stephens Cambridge UK 1974
Moretti, V. La Scomessa Di Gianni Lancia Edizioni di Autocritica Rome 1986
Nolan, W.F. Phil Hill: Yankee Champion Brown Fox Books California 1996
Nye, D. 'Fon' Classic and Sports Car May 1985
O'Neil. T. The Bahamas Speed Weeks Veloce Publishing Dorset UK 2006
Orsini, L. and F.Zagari OSCA:La Rivincita Dei Maserati Georgio Nada Editore Milan 1989
Pascal, D. Les Grandes Heures de Montlhery E.T.A.I. Paris France 2004
Purdy, K. "Portago" Car and Driver August 1957
Purdy, K. Ken Purdy's Book of Automobiles Playboy Press Chicago Illinois 1972
Roebuck, N. "De Portago-Conquistador" Autosport March 4, 1976
Salvadori, R. with A. Pritchard Roy Salvadori Racing Driver Patrick Stephens Wellingborough UK 1985
Sheldon, P. and D.Rabgaliati Record of Grand Prix and Voiturette Racing-Vol.6 St. Leonards Press Bradford UK 1987
Smith, A.R. Fifties Motor Racing-The GP Scene Haynes Publishing Somerset UK 1990
Tanner, H. with D. Nye Ferrari Haynes Publishing Somerset UK 1989
Tanner, H. Great Racing Drivers of the World Sports Car Press New York 1958
Tanner, H. "Spanish Adventurer" Motor Racing June 1957
Wimpffen, J. Time and Two Seats Motor Racing Research Group Washington USA 1999
Yates, B. Enzo Ferrari-The Man and the Machine Bantam Books London 1992
Yates, B. "The Search for the Marquis Alfonso de Portago" Car and Driver May 1986

Journals/magazines

Automobile Historique
Automobile Quarterly
Auto Motor und Sport
Autosport
Car and Driver
Classic and Sports Car
Competition Car
Il Campione
Life
Modern Motor
Motor Racing
Motorspeed
Motor Sport
Oldtimer-Markt
Paris Match
Road and Track
Speed Age
Sports Illustrated

INDEX